# The Challenge to Spanish Nobility in the Fourteenth Century

# THE CHALLENGE TO SPANISH NOBILITY IN THE FOURTEENTH CENTURY

The Struggle for Power in Don Juan Manuel's *Conde Lucanor*, 1335

James A. Grabowska

The Edwin Mellen Press
Lewiston•Queenston•Lampeter

**Library of Congress Cataloging-in-Publication Data**

Grabowska, James A.
   The challenge to Spanish nobility in the fourteenth century : the struggle for power in don Juan Manuel's Conde Lucanor, 1335 / James A. Grabowska.
     p. cm.
   Includes bibliographical references and index.
   ISBN 0-7734-5913-8
   1. Juan Manuel, Infante of Castile, 1282-1347. Conde Lucanor. 2. Social classes in literature. 3. Nobility in literature. I. Title.

PQ6401.A1C635 2006
963'.1--dc22

2005056156

*hors série.*

A CIP catalog record for this book is available from the British Library.

Front cover: Photo of the portrait of Don Juan Manuel from the "retalbo" or altarpiece in Escalona.

Copyright © 2006 James A. Grabowska

All rights reserved. For information contact

     The Edwin Mellen Press       The Edwin Mellen Press
           Box 450                              Box 67
      Lewiston, New York            Queenston, Ontario
       USA 14092-0450               CANADA L0S 1L0

The Edwin Mellen Press, Ltd.
Lampeter, Ceredigion, Wales
UNITED KINGDOM SA48 8LT

Printed in the United States of America

## Dedication

To my mother and father who never imagined that it would be this way.

## Table of Contents

**Preface**     i
Anthony N. Zahareas

**Acknowledgements**     x

**Introduction**     1

**Chapter 1**     5
Introduction to the Problems of Rhetoric and Power
in the *Conde Lucanor*

**Chapter 2**     17
Socio-political History and Literary Production
in Fourteenth-century Castile
    Penchants of Juan Manuel Criticism     26
    Strategies Toward a New Model of Criticism     29
    The Vernacular and Didactic Purpose     38
    The Social Right to Write: Building *Auctoritas*     43
    Within the Oral, Medieval Literary Tradition
    (Exempla and Proverbs)     46
    The Power of Scripting Experience     52

**Chapter 3**     61
Organizational Keys to the *Conde Lucanor*
    Aristotelian Causae and the Prologue to the *Conde Lucanor*     62
    The efficient cause     63
    The material cause     66
    The final cause     67
    The formal cause     69
    The Question of Order in the *Conde Lucanor*     70
    The Function of Memory     72
    The Three Levels of Hermeneutic Dialogue     73
    Memoria ad res     76
    Illumination as Memorial Mnemonic     77
    Brevitas     78
    Virtue and the *De regimine principum* of Giles of Rome     80

|  |  |
|---|---|
| The Function of Prudence | 82 |
| Advice and Action as They Relate to Prudence | 82 |
| Prognostication and memory as components of Prudence | 86 |
| The Qualities of a Nobleman | 91 |

## Chapter 4 — 103
### The Moral of the Story: Politics and Morality in the Exemplary Tales

|  |  |
|---|---|
| Empowering Deceptions: Ends and Means in Tale 1 | 106 |
| Nothing is Nothing: Foresight is Power in Tale XXXII | 113 |
| The Measure of Nobility: Giving Truth to the Lie in Tale XXII | 116 |
| The Power of Knowing Thyself: Shame in Tale L | 121 |

## Chapter 5 — 133
### From Storytelling to Proverbial Lore

|  |  |
|---|---|
| The Function of Obscurity and Rhetorical Construction | 133 |
| *Sentenciae* and Experience in Book One | 141 |
| *Sentenciae* and Experience in the Succeeding Books | 146 |
| Proverbial Texture and Its Function | 147 |
| The Proverb as Text | 151 |
| The Proverbs and Their Context | 152 |

## Chapter 6 — 159
### Juan Manuel's Rhetoric of Power: the Fifth Book

|  |  |
|---|---|
| Rewards and the Rhetoric of Power | 161 |
| Good, Bad, and the Function of Contraries | 162 |
| Doing Good Works: The Sacramental Nature of Nobility | 167 |

## Chapter 7 — 181
### Conclusion

|  |  |
|---|---|
| A Model for Future Studies | 187 |

## Bibliography — 193

## Index — 205

# Preface

Within this volume, Dr. James Grabowska builds bridges between two different concerns: the ideological foundations of power and, in particular, a reexamination of medieval rhetoric in the works of don Juan Manuel (1282-1349?). The 50-51 tales, several proverbs and treatises that comprise the "five" books of *El Conde Lucanor* (1335) have as a necessary feature (200 years before Machiavelli) the "ends-means" controversy. The intriguing historical problem about the uses and abuses of power is examined from the limited angle of medieval fiction: the imaginary dilemmas by which the fictional Count Lucanor experiences dangers to his inherited privileges blend meaningfully with diverse exemplary tales which his counselor, the fictional Patronio, analyzes the source of trouble, explains the dangers to his estate and provides, rhetorically, urgent solutions to the immediate problems. Grabowska shows how Juan Manuel's rhetorical strategy was to create, <u>always with exemplary precision</u>, the correspondences between the fictional situations of traditional tales and the historical function of them--<u>advice</u> about power and the <u>consent</u> to use it.

Both traditional tales and proverbs usually had the status of universal truths. Medieval authors like Juan Manuel used them to confirm propositions or refute arguments. Just as Patronio shows rhetorically how his exemplary storytelling is relevant to the analysis of concrete events, so Dr Grabowska provides a framework within which we can examine how modern concerns with the "rhetoric of power" were functioning as early as 1335 in the *Conde Lucanor*. It's not an easy task. Among the many controversial issues in *Lucanor*, one of the most controversial--and most notorious-- is that, in order to defend his vested interests, Lucanor not only must use his legitimate powers but at the same time do so as moral justification of his noble ends. Where the "end" is just, the "means" are just. The objectives of nobility should be to "conserve" what are traditionally conceived to be inherited and hence legitimate estates and privileges. Rhetoric in *Lucanor* is that verbal quality by which Patronio, as speaker, seeks to persuade his master, and Juan Manuel, as writer, seeks to persuade readers of the validity of Patronio's discourses.

Grabowska's study provides an analysis of the rhetoric of power in *Conde Lucanor* and, on that empirical basis, offers a historical interpretation of the "ends/means" controversy: under special conditions what is morally incompatible can be--or at least appear--compatible. The purpose is twofold: first, to argue that two centuries before Renaissance treatises about the modern state, Don Juan Manuel (following the generic tradition of the "Regiment of Princes") elaborated an ideology of hegemony and power as they were invariably manifested in the nobility of feudal Spain; and, next, to suggest that such an ideology anticipated not only a Machiavellian type of thinking but also prefigured the evolution of a rhetoric of power from ancient times to our day. The tales and proverbs organized by Juan Manuel into a Collection illustrate relentlessly, in one exemplary situation after another, how and why those with legitimate power (a subtle reference to the noble class of the author himself and that of his protagonist) must, in a clearly articulated conservative vein, "stay the course."

Now, the means used to preserve privileges in feudal Spain and the spiritual ends of Christian doctrine were considered moral opposites: the one urges individuals to use power towards material self-interests, the other justifies such use of power as acts of Christian charity. In the *Lucanor,* however, Christian ends of salvation and secular means to socio-political power are presented as necessary and complementary to each other, even though they may be opposites. The contradictions within the "ends/means" controversy are of significance because they dramatize the controversial problems involved in using power in the name of religion which, it is true, are not resolved but which are revealed in the contradictions themselves.

The result is a double perspective: the imaginary representation of a noble's Christian ideals as a justification of his material interests (based on inherited privileges), was parallel to feudal justifications of inheritance, privilege, honor and power which also existed outside Juan Manuel's fiction. His rhetorical strategy in representing for readers (outside the text of *Lucanor*) a series of fictional paradigms (inside the text), relies on the construction of an angle from which two opposites--the <u>fictional</u> solutions of a noble's problems and their potential references to <u>history</u>--generate and depend upon each other.

And here is the rub: outside the *Lucanor*, in the social reality of XIVth century Spain to which the nobleman's problems correspond (a Spain dominated more and more by the religious fervor of the reconquest) can there be a real unity and compatibility of real opposites? It's a hard sell, but that is what happens. When, in order, Patronio advises what's to be done, Lucanor consents to follow that advice and Juan Manuel approves the example for inclusion in his Collection, what takes place--among other things--is a series of meaningful and even deliberate discrepancies. So far removed from each other are the two planes of consciousness on which advice and consent are perceived in the *Lucanor*--the plane of Lucanor's secular reality and the Christian image of itself--that the result is the perception of the coexistence of two wholly different realities. The way the medieval author works out the moral problem structurally in the 50-51 frames of the Collection may be the way both to the ideology that lurks behind the *Conde Lucanor* and to the historical function of Juan Manuel's art of storytelling.

It is hard to discuss meaningfully a medieval collection like *Conde Lucanor*, because the tales are unfamiliar to modern readers. Consider, as only one of the examples, Juan Manuel's exemplary version [much before Cervantes and H.C. Anderson] about the notorious "emperor's clothes." According to the story pattern, "clothes" acquire a social meaning only because they automatically refer to the king's "nakedness"--nakedness as a socio-political reality and as a metaphor of gullibility. In Patronio's adaptation, the king who, as the head of state had duties and responsibilities, ends up in the public domain, literally, wearing nothing: insecurity leads to fear which in turn induces credulity to the point that, once duped, he cannot "see" that he "sees" nothing. The point Patronio is driving into Lucanor is that the socially induced insecurity regarding nothing less than a king's own identity as the legitimate ruler, is what covers his nudity with non-existing clothing; common sense, on the other hand, is meant to help him foresee that nothing is indeed nothing. The danger is not only the art of deception but, internally, the weakness of the nobles themselves.

The major structural and exemplary problems of the *Conde Lucanor* are fully present in this as well as in all the other tales. Each one of the 50 titles refers only to the tale but the exemplary framework involves a series of carefully narrated steps: the noble tells his troubles to the private tutor who responds with a tale full of correspondences (between, say, the naked king of fiction and the potentially vulnerable noble of history); Lucanor agrees to do what Patronio's tale suggests--metaphorically, he'll not be caught with his pants down because, unlike the king of the tale, he'll not be taken in by appearances; and, finally, for the sake of readers outside the tale, the author enters the framework of the tale to announce why the tale is worth including in his book.

Rather than an anthological scrap-heap of stories and proverbs (a common practice in medieval collections) the tales adapted by Juan Manuel, although various in time, depth and subject, have been collected only because they receive an underlying unity from the rhetoric of power practiced by the writer -- a conservative ideology of power, Grabowska points out, which is best illustrated by the very variety of the elaborated stories. Each story is intended to be self-contained, but each sheds light on the others. In that way, the diversity of stories highlights the variety of dilemmas while the repeated format of "advice and consent" emphasizes the strong conservative message of staying the course. Every story assumes that, no matter how fictional, a sense of reality is to be conveyed to the troubled listener. That is, each tale is adapted and then made to fit the problem confronted by the nobleman.

In this sense, the author of *Lucanor* is perhaps the least confused of medieval minds that have come to us. In each of the 50-51 tales, Juan Manuel <u>wrote</u> down what was discussed <u>orally</u> and hence privately between feudal lord and adviser. As the storyteller who interprets the message of the tale, Patronio deals subtly but firmly with the ends-means controversy; his practical recommendations to be self-seeking and, if need be, calculating are absorbed subtly by the simultaneous rhetoric of Christian virtue. The language of practical warnings ("they will deceive you," "don't take risks," "praises are false," "do not trust," "dissimulate," "look to your own interest") is often integrated to the spiritual language of Christian morality ("good works," "do good," "God's grace," "serve God," "soul," "salvation," "charity," "with God's help"). Of course the need for "divine grace" in order to gain "worldly goods" and other advantages is, at least rhetorically, a corruption of the discourse of practical ends by a discourse of religious means.

The connections between means-and-ends are so compelling that the secular and thus practical aspects of the message become evident. The perspective throughout the collection is performative: to be a feudal lord or a wise counselor is to play a role which arouses certain expectations and to which a set of duties are related. The tale recreated for the benefit of Lucanor by Patronio presents problems that are make-believe and thus rehearsed; presumably, the problems bothering Lucanor are real and not rehearsed. There are two audiences: the author and the readers constitute the third party to the narrative interaction of Lucanor and Patronio--an interaction that if the story-like situation were historically real, author and audience would not be there. The ways in which impressions are controlled and guided, and the kinds of things Patronio and Lucanor may or may not say while meditating the importance of power is related to the nature and functions of rhetoric.

Grabowska reexamines the *Conde Lucanor* in terms of the history of the concept of power. He suggests that author and work occupy a place of singular importance in history because the encounters of noble-and-mentor [as in the "Regiment" of Princes genre] are witness to a time of feudal crisis and historical transition. Juan Manuel's total contribution to the understanding of power at a time of crisis and the role of rhetoric in propagating such power (i.e., "the rhetoric of power") has, for Grabowska, anticipated the tradition of greatness established later by political thinkers -- Machiavelli in the *Prince*, Guicciardini in *Ricordi* or Gracian in *El héroe* and *Oráculo Manual*. Like these, Juan Manuel's primary concern (at least in *Conde Lucanor*) was with what we might modernly call rhetorical solutions to the historical problems of power. It is a salutary reminder: the *Conde Lucanor* may be one of the most mediated of "fictions" in its relation to the ideological base of hegemony and power.

If Grabowska is correct in questioning such omissions on the part of many critics, then the very grounds of Juan Manuel criticism may be--at least potentially--shifting. Rather than add to the number of studies, he has confined his study to those problems of power and rhetoric about which it is possible to say something historically constructive. His purpose is to exhibit the *Lucanor* as an integral part of the author's social and political life. This purpose demands that in order to analyze the various stories and proverbs the rhetoric of power must be developed through several levels of political theory until it is ultimately able to grasp the complexities of each case of advice and consent. The *Lucanor* is intended to present, one after another, clear rhetorical expositions of certain legitimate areas of hegemony with the ultimate purpose of exposing these areas to a thorough critique.

The role of Patronio is obviously crucial. The counselor is an experienced intellectual -- a brain for hire. The tradition of mentors and counselors is a perpetual present: it includes, among many others, the role of Aristotle to Alexander, Machiavelli to princes, Richelieu to the French king and, lately, Henry Kissinger and Carl Rove to American Presidents. What counselors have in common is the rare ability to organize rhetorically the problems confronting their superiors and thus persuade them about the role that power must play in their career. Traditional nobles or modern rulers already possess power which is theirs by right, by inheritance or by law. The challenge of Patronio in the *Conde Lucanor*, therefore, is to instruct the noble to understand the meaning of his own nobility; that a noble is not a noble unless he uses his inherited powers to exercise control over his own will in the pursuit of goals of action, regardless of resistance or deceptions.

On 50-51 occasions in the *Conde Lucanor* the challenge of the counselor is to discreetly persuade his superior that he must learn to persuade powerfully. Therefore, in the name of a "noble or moral cause" the noble must not hesitate to use force and even violence; no matter how questionable are his means they can be justified by the cause of his ends. This involves rhetoric: the art of persuading how, where and why a noble has to use what he already possesses. Power and rhetoric become inextricably united. In the context of "the rhetoric of power," counselors like Patronio, Aristotle or modern advisors to presidents are "intermediaries", that is, they help clarify within a political system (as, for example, in the feudal middle ages) the differences between the dominant class of nobility and the other subordinate classes.

As an expert in practical solutions, Patronio resolves the contradiction between powerful means (which may be unjust or cruel or arbitrary) as a way to moral ends (which always must appear just, virtuous etc.) If a noble is confronted with serious problems, the counselor has the task of analyzing clearly to him the potential danger to his estate. He must therefore bring into focus, "rhetorically', <u>the components of the problem</u>-- what does the danger or the dilemma really consist of. He chooses as the most efficient way the exemplary, often Aesopic, tale in order to articulate parallel situations. If the tale is to function rhetorically as a viable example, there must be correspondences between the outcome of the tale's plot and the dilemma of the Count, that is, the historical situation of the Count. The fictional components of the story must coalesce in order to correspond to the historical realities of power.

Finally, the conservative basis of power determines the literary structure of Juan Manuel's *Conde Lucanor* as a whole, as well as the rhetoric of its three protagonists -- pupil, teacher, and author. Political, religious, and legal institutions of the feudal middle ages, as well as the ideas, the images, the ideologies by means of which individuals supposedly understood the world in which they lived, their proper place within it, and themselves -- all these in Juan Manuel's collection of tales are reflections of well-known conservative attitudes: an automatic defense of the customs and institutions which have long surrounded people and a rhetorical propagation of the doctrines (religious, moral, or secular) by which an adherence to these attitudes is explained and defended. Grabowska correctly treats the *Lucanor* as a rhetoric insofar as it deals with the producing of effects--within the fictional tales, upon the noble, and, outside the frames of the Collection, upon the reading audience.

His study is intended to provoke inquiries into Juan Manuel's aesthetic solutions to the historical problems of a conservative attitude -- perhaps the most common attitude in human history. The relevance to that history of a close reading of the *Lucanor* should be apparent: certain of the conservative ideas about tradition and legitimacy, values of honor or privilege and the feelings of permanence during changes by which individuals experience their societies at various times, are available to modern readers in Juan Manuel's *Conde Lucanor*. It's noteworthy that throughout Dr. Grabowska has tried to be objective, but he does not claim to be detached. No critic of works like *Lucanor* can or should be, especially when the issues are about the ideology of power. Thus the answer to our modern question, "What is the medieval *Lucanor*?", consciously or unconsciously reflects our own political positions and forms part of broader questions regarding conservative views of power and rhetoric. What

Grabowska's sketch of the rhetoric of power provides is a general framework within which further historical studies of medieval works can be elaborated.

As an attentive critic, Grabowska has extracted the social and political attitudes of Juan Manuel in his moral examples through the formal analysis of the rhetoric of those texts. The rhetoric of *Lucanor* produced a historically identifiable contradiction: within the privacy of Lucanor's visit to Patronio, the tutor's oral message of caution and stability to his master glosses over the contradiction of identifying "worldly" and "spiritual" gains and, with various clever means of rhetorical concealment, transcends the contradiction by not revealing the apparent or potential "opposition" between means/ends; simultaneously, however, within Juan Manuel's structured discourse of the framed visit and oral message, the author hides nothing and, on the contrary, allows readers to read everything that might be contradictory in what the tutor tells and the nobleman listens.

The narrated frames of the elaborated tales are presented to all readers or listeners, subtly, as if they were the resolved cases of a contradictory advice. Because, ironically, what might appear contradictory in morality during Juan Manuel's age is harmonious in his fiction. This is why modern readers can learn to see in *Conde Lucanor* what rhetoric of power the author has rhetorically learned to cover up. It is encouraging to see, upon a close inspection of the new study, that the historical questions broached through medieval fiction are so vast, so important and so fascinating.

Anthony N. Zahareas
Professor Emeritus
University of Minnesota, Twin Cities

## Acknowledgments

I want to thank my wife, Kimberly Contag, who so wholeheartedly and unselfishly provided emotional and moral support from the beginning of this endeavor to its end. It could not have been done without her. I'd also like to thank Professors Anthony Zahareas and Ron Martínez whose thoughtful, probing questions, insight, and careful reading of the text in its initial phases were invaluable to this project. Financial support for this project included grants from the College of St. Theresa Alumni Foundation, Winona Minnesota, and the University of Minnesota, Twin Cities. Thanks to Silvia Roca-Martínez in the preparation of the English translations of lengthier citations. Some material from Chapter 4 appeared in South Central Review 11 (1994): 45-61. It is used with permission.

# Introduction

Power is the ability to act or to cause to act. It may be irreverent or arrogant; it is however, at times, very subtle. Power is a commodity that can be won or lost, grow or diminish, be latent or active; it is inherently paranoid. Rhetoric is a mode of discourse that seeks to move an auditor to adopt a particular point of view. It is inherently emotional in nature relying on the structure of the discourse and the words employed to gain good will, to move to dislike, hate, love, to empathize, sympathize, feel one way or another; it too may be subtle. In the case of the *Conde Lucanor*, Juan Manuel uses his text to communicate rhetorically and subtly a conservative ideology of power, how to keep it, use it, make it grow, so as to preserve it. The rhetoric of power is impassioned, intense, because power is addictive. Proof of the addictive nature of power and its hold on Juan Manuel lie not only in the historically verifiable acts of war, assassination and political intrigue in which the nobleman was involved, its greatest manifestation lies in his choice to write books about the maintenance of power.

The purpose of this study is to examine the ideological foundations of medieval tales and proverbs by focusing on the rhetoric of power in Don Juan Manuel's exemplary tales and *sententiae* collected in his *El libro del Conde Lucanor*. As understood throughout the Middle Ages (and in the case of this study, by the fourteenth century intellectual noble, Don Juan Manuel) the art of putting indispensable thoughts over in a particular relevant and profitable manner was a demanding task not to be avoided: it required not only learning but also a command of a number of artfully different manners of expression and persuasion. In this sense the rhetoric of power is a double-edged weapon: it is concerned with teaching those who hold responsible positions the means of exercising authoritative control, and at the same time, in its very act, rhetoric becomes itself a weapon that wields power. Few writers have been as aware of the interplay between rhetoric and power as Don Juan Manuel. His *Conde Lucanor* is a testimony to a long tradition.

*El Conde Lucanor* was written during the first third of the fourteenth century and according to the text itself, was finished in 1335. It exists in five different manuscripts, none of which dates from the fourteenth century. Modern problems of editing the texts are inevitable. The entire collection is comprised of an ante-prologue, the Prologue to the contents, the first Book which contains fifty or fifty-one exemplary tales, the second, third and fourth Books which contain collections of proverbs (100, 50 and 30 respectively, according to the narrator), and the fifth Book which is a treatise on the performance of good works and the avoidance of bad works. In all five Books the fourteenth-century nobleman Don Juan Manuel communicates specific ideas and notions about governing and maintaining social prestige. The author assumes that readers were concerned with defining their gubernatorial role in a society that was changing from centralized to loose feudalism. In particular, my project depends on the functional relationship between form and content or narrative structure (narrative scripts, rhetorical devices and fiction), and communicative content (scripts for behavior, historical devices and situations).

An analysis of Juan Manuel's texts illustrates how the fictional representation of cultural, legal, religious, and political situations correspond to the ways the fourteenth century confronted serious social issues. At the same time, it may help illustrate how aristocrats like Don Juan Manuel handled the difficult and frustrating responsibility of teaching others how to govern well, guard their estate, and maintain power. To maintain power in a society where the maintenance of privilege was defined by the accumulation of honor and wealth was in turn vital to the "salvation of the soul." Juan Manuel's texts happen to highlight the important power relationships between nobles and their constituencies.

The exemplary tales and proverbs are Don Juan Manuel's preferred means for transmitting messages of social indoctrination and responsible behavior. The exemplarity of tales as a cultural phenomenon of medieval times has been taken for granted; it is the interpretation of their social implications in texts and the estimate of their historical function that have not only raised difficulties but led to academic debates. The same is true of proverbs. Tales and proverbs have traditionally had an historical impact on populations because their means of transmission is accessible and non-threatening. They teach through the power of persuasion and example. For this reason, the reappraisal of the language of persuasion in the *enxiemplos* and *sententiae* of *El Conde Lucanor*, as much as any other instance, can provide a test case of how, in general, historical power relations can be taught through fiction. The subjects about which Don Juan Manuel wrote include many issues which appear to be highly political and are therefore relevant to the reading, analysis and explanation of the tales or proverbs.

Study of the fourteenth-century rhetoric of power has importance for historians, literary, and cultural scholars of the period. This importance also holds for scholars today since politicians and administrators still grapple with many of the same problems of persuasion that challenged Don Juan Manuel. An investigation of rhetoric in the diverse tales and proverbs in the *Conde Lucanor* raises theoretical problems about the nature of power, as well as about the function of fictional representation of politically potent social relations. In this study the specific art of using words effectively is the subject of analysis. The discussion of the rhetoric of power in the *Conde Lucanor* has to be made concrete through analysis; it includes an examination of the formal strategy whereby characters, deeds, tales and ideas are used to teach the unsuspecting and hence vulnerable administrator and nobleman how to behave in typical dangerous social situations. The study covers the powerful rhetorical structure of the fifty or fifty-one enxiemplos, found in Book One, the 200 odd proverbs divided into three successive books, and the fifth Book which synthesizes the rhetorical tropes and figures used in the previous books. Together they make up a powerful rhetorical whole.

I quote from Don Juan Manuel's *Obras Completas*, edited by José Manuel Blecua (1983) unless otherwise noted. This choice was made for the reasons highlighted by the editor himself: in the case of the *Conde Lucanor* the chosen manuscript, of the five available, is most free of errors, without perceptible additions or modernizations of language. Except for the *Crónica abreuiada*, all the remaining works of Don Juan Manuel exist in one single manuscript. Translations or paraphrase from texts are mine unless otherwise noted. Citations concern the issues of the study; there are many bonafide issues concerning Juan Manuel's works (hence the continuous addition of scholarly criticism). Rather than interrupt the reading of the following chapters with these legitimate concerns, I highlight passages (use of italics), and interpret them to emphasize the problems with which this particular study is concerned.

# Chapter 1: Introduction to the problems of rhetoric and power in the *Conde Lucanor*

A.J. Minnis and A.B. Scott in their introduction to the teachings of Arnulf of Orleans observe: "...for the historians of the Middle Ages (and beyond) their subject was at its best not a mere record of facts but a repository of illustrative stories (or *exempla*) which showed the reader what actions should be done and what should be shunned; not objectivity but a deliberate moral bias was what was valued" (Minnis 115). The medieval view of past history as guardian or safekeeper of exemplary lessons for the present, that is, the didactic function of history, is a typical starting point for historiographies of the Middle Ages. Judson Allen, for example, in describing the poetics of the Middle Ages concurs with Minnis and Scott that poetry and ethics converge in the later Middle Ages. The problem of modern scholarship has been how to examine old exempla or stories and, in the case of Juan Manuel's *Conde Lucanor*, proverbs as well, in the light of medieval poetics which presumably stressed the moral message over its form of communication. The challenge has been to determine the political and moral bents contained within the tales and pithy sayings. The fusion of political power and morality is especially important since storytelling was often acted out. The so-called "act" of tales and proverbs, when placed within their historic context, can reveal much about power relations, as well as the structure of the tales and language employed to put those relations into practice. Hence the close relation between power and rhetoric.

Juan Manuel's collection of exempla and *sentenciae* in the *Conde Lucanor* serve as an excellent test case for a study of the rhetoric of power. Power in the later Middle Ages was generally conceived as a combination of force and aptitude. The privileges or rights of the nobility to exercise control over others was, in view of economic, social, and political changes, indispensable in preserving traditional authority. By the fourteenth century it was often not enough to have power; it was important to know how to use vested powers effectively. Thus a comprehensive historical understanding of the rhetoric of power through the *Conde Lucanor* must take into account the significant, if not central role rhetoric played in the perception of the older medieval kingdoms. In this sense, the art of effectively communicating the urgent need for nobles to "stay the course" became a part of a larger historical problem which for decades has aimed to evaluate the ideas, values and concerns by which all the classes (*oradores, defensores, labradores*) experienced the social transitions of the time.

Almost all of these noble ideals, moral values, and practical concerns are available to us today in Don Juan Manuel's literary collection of fifty or fifty-one stories, 180 proverbs or maxims, and a rhetoric of good works. All of them, simply or in clusters, contain the dilemmas the invented noble named Count Lucanor had to face and solve.[1] To understand how the rhetoric of power functions in the framed tales, proverbs and rhetoric of the *Conde Lucanor* both individually and collectively is to understand the evolution of the role of power more deeply; in particular, how power relations were maintained, transformed, shifted, used, and abused. A premise of this study is that such understanding can contribute both to social and literary histories of the function of exemplarity.

The Prologue to the *Conde Lucanor* sums up neatly the medieval view of history-as-example. Juan Manuel did what Minnis and Scott describe to be the test of medieval historians: to teach people how to behave in social circumstances. To date scholars have followed a variety of directions: socio-historical evidence is used to provide the underpinnings for modern readings of the medieval text (Lida de Malkiel, DeVoto, Blecua); medieval thematics and their literary elaboration to evaluate the art of the collection (MacPherson, Dunn, Ayerbe-Chaux), almost exclusively concentrated on the tales of the first book; determine the social context within which the various texts were produced

(De Stefano, Maravall, Valdeon, Martin); and most recently the application of contemporary literary techniques of theory to diverse parts of the collection (Diz, Biglieri, de Looze). Scholars have not dealt in depth with the rhetorical strategies that Don Juan Manuel employed. By integrating the strategies mentioned above to a close, detailed analysis of the tales and proverbs it can be shown how the tales and proverbs succeed in articulating a cohesive rhetoric of power in fourteenth-century Castile.

This study concerns medieval notions of the rhetorical aspects of power and, in particular, their applicability to a thorough re-examination of Juan Manuel's collection of stories and maxims. Although the subjects of power and rhetoric often include abstract theoretical models of their nature and use, they are ultimately relevant to the concrete analysis of medieval stories, proverbs, maxims, and exemplary discourse in general. This analysis of the rhetoric of power requires a survey of literary theory in the Middle Ages to see what Juan Manuel may have been exposed to (and to whom), a survey of the period to discover the socio-political climate in which he lived and wrote, analysis of both the overall structure of Juan Manuel's book and the structure of each tale, proverb, book, and rhetorical/historical analysis of the tales and proverbs in the light of historical conditions under which the rhetoric of power functioned. In other words, this study, as part of the subject of power, offers simultaneously a reappraisal and recombination of existing scholarship. It highlights the oft-ignored (in terms of Spanish medieval studies in general, and Juan Manuel in particular) corpus of medieval literary theory (John of Salisbury, Matthew of Vendôme, Geoffrey of Vinsauf, Augustine, Aquinas, Brunetto Latini, Hugh of St. Victor, for example), and contemporary exegetical scholarship (Judson Allen, Mary Carruthers, Alastair Minnis, Larry Scanlon, Jacques Le Goff, J.J. Murphy, Glending Olson, Georges Duby). The aim is to illuminate Juan Manuel's art of rhetorical discourse and show how it functioned in fourteenth-century Castile.

The fifty tales make up the bulk of the *Conde Lucanor*. Nevertheless, this collection of tales is followed by four pertinent books full of proverbs, maxims and explanations. Together all the popular tales and traditional comments form a collection with a well-worked out frame of its own. Significantly the over-all structure was called *libro*. Yet individually the parts need not be like each other. This *libro* is rarely read, studied, or even understood as a collection. To begin, the first book is studied much more extensively than the four books that follow. So much so that in modern times the *Conde Lucanor* automatically--and erroneously-- refers only to the popular tales that the noble hears in private from his mentor Patronio. The rest is disturbingly ignored, especially by students. What is there about the stories that make them what they are? How can they be re-examined without sacrificing the other neglected parts of Don Juan Manuel's *libro*? Juan Manuel had reasons for writing the book, not limited to the tales but, deliberately as a five part collection. These reasons, as we shall see, are inscribed in the book itself. He incorporated his own comments about the book by way of prologues, references and summary interpretations at the end of each tale. Don Juan Manuel is, in fact, a unique medieval author for refusing to release his work to readers even after it is out in manuscript form. He goes out of his way to warn readers about what is or is not authentically his own in all they are reading. As a minimum then, a mentor called Patronio acts out fifty stories in the first book, each of them an exemplary story exemplarily told; he declaims 180 proverbs of greater exemplary value than the stories, and articulates an epideictic and demonstrative rhetoric on the value of good works. The entire *libro* written purposely in Castilian prose--*romance*--is to be narrated under specific rules within a rigid framework as an advice to the teller's master, a powerful noble, Count Lucanor. Here traditional materials are structured and stories framed into a consistent pattern of "advice" and "consent." A typical process of medieval times was that a moral order always goes with the story pattern as if this is the way things are to be done and these are the consequences if not so performed.

In the first book Patronio selects stories from the past (among innumerable ones) in the light of his master's present predicament. Behind the choice of each one lies a series of criteria for the selection. The criteria always have to do with exemplarity: how to avoid danger in order to do the right thing. Patronio tells a past story only in the context of his master's present situation. The traditional elements of the story pattern therefore undergo subtle changes due to the reciprocal relations of a "past example" and its "present use." This reciprocal action between "teller" and "listener" involves and even dramatizes a key historical reciprocity between present and past: Patronio addresses the present situation of Lucanor while the exemplary details of the story belong to a traditional past. The art of Don Juan Manuel therefore, is to make the past examples of the story and the present delivery of it necessary to one another. The story chosen by Patronio without Lucanor's predicament would be rootless and futile, while the noble's exemplary dilemma without the storyteller Patronio would be irrelevant and meaningless. What are the collections of tales and proverbs in Don Juan's *libro* all about? They are a repeated, continuous process of interaction between present predicaments and past exemplary solutions.

The process of solving historical problems through fiction continues through the second, third, and fourth books. All three are collections of proverbs with a higher degree of exemplarity than that found in the tales. The attribution of authority to figures of the past endows proverbs with a sense of truth that is absent from the exemplary tales. It is only through the context of seeking advice that the tales are made to mean whereas each proverb already carries by itself a meaningful example. The second book is comprised of 100 proverbs, the third, 50, and the fourth, 30. Patronio thus presents 180 proverbs or maxims whose statements are much pithier than the exemplary tales. Although each proverb has a precise meaning, its "general nature" is integrated to the interchange between Patronio and Lucanor. They progress in difficulty from being merely obscure in the second book to most obscure in the fourth. Absent from the three collections are the specific socio-economic predicaments in Book One faced by Count Lucanor and which trigger Patronio's storytelling. Instead, the nobleman requests that Patronio teach him more because of the need to know: "el saber es tan buena cosa, tengo que non me deuedes culpar por querer ende aver yo la mayor parte que pudiere" (454). Lucanor names the three necessities of man: the first is knowledge, the second honor, and the third is enough food to live. Because knowledge is the most important, Lucanor wants to feed his brain and learn more. What Patronio narrates for his lord then are maxims whose truth have stood the test of time, and are therefore worthy bits of knowledge. In fact, they are indispensable for the nobleman who wishes to exercise power properly. Like the exemplary tales, these past popular sayings, as exemplars of truth metamorphose through use and gain a specific relevance in the context of a noble's needs and a counselor's advice. The second through fourth books thus continue the process of interaction between past and present established in Book One.

Book Five is a rhetorical exposé on the rewards that accompany "good works" as opposed to the damnation that comes when doing evil. Patronio is again the vehicle to narrate the final, polished articulation of Juan Manuel's rhetoric of power. Unlike the first four books, the pretext this time is not a petition from Patronio's lord, Count Lucanor. In a hybrid manner, the counselor combines exempla (like those in the first book), and proverbs (like those in the succeeding three books) in an epideictic and demonstrative rhetorical presentation: it is a *summa* on the issue of power and its proper use. The exempla and proverbs, available in myriad compilations in the later Middle Ages and separated by divisions called "books" in the first four parts of the *Conde Lucanor*, are neatly combined in Juan Manuel's final book as proofs and confirmations of the truths that Patronio has been pronouncing all along. Hence the integral composition of the five parts into a "whole": with the fifth book, both Juan Manuel's *libro* and his rhetoric of power converge to become one complete entity. It has been misleading to divorce one part from the other. The text as a whole employs traditional, historical material, and through the three protagonists (author, narrator and the noble listener), uses this material in new, historically meaningful ways so as to make each tale, proverb and rhetoric refer exemplarily to specific cases of the present. Juan Manuel's rhetoric of power, divided into five parts, is ultimately joined together to form the *libro, El Conde Lucanor*. To give an account of this important work without examining the interplay of all the factors that have shaped it as a whole has led to inadequate criticism.

The study concerns itself on the one hand with Juan Manuel's elaboration of rhetorical strategies in the *Conde Lucanor* in terms of medieval literary theory, and on the other, the internal and overall structure of the nobleman's text in the light of the historical conditions during which his rhetoric was articulated. These rhetorical strategies are recognized as both a process and particular concern of the author, and are available both literally and symbolically in his text. An understanding of Juan Manuel's puzzling *Conde Lucanor* in terms of medieval social history needs to develop a model for understanding the evolution of the concept of power from medieval to modern societies.

What was, for example, the position of this collection of exemplary tales and maxims within the cultural process of the early fourteenth century? Obviously, Juan Manuel depended upon many recognizable techniques of story telling and exemplarity in writing the *Conde Lucanor*: the ways of narrating past action included syntactical problems like the alternative states of preterit and imperfect; the modes of inserting short dialogues into the narrative involved stylization of portraits, especially in fixing social "types"; the modes of preaching entailed strategic pauses for irony, humorous techniques, the formulas of beginning or ending stories, the manners of retelling or paraphrasing anecdotes, the acting out of problems, among many others. These techniques were part of the rhetorical arts of the time, arts which Juan Manuel studied and implemented carefully. He had not only a clear awareness of their useful function but also of the danger of misuse. Since biographical facts are sketchy, the final shape or structure of the collection provides the only authentic set of relations between Don Juan Manuel and his readers from then to now. The question is whether there is anything new either in the messages of the *Conde Lucanor* or in the modes of their communication. It is to be expected that the messages are conservative in that they urge awareness of "new" dangers to the established nobility of fourteenth-century Castile. Awareness leads to alertness. To communicate the conservative message of alertness in the face of social changes, the writer Juan Manuel reconstructed rhetorically the traditional storytelling form at his disposal.

Don Juan Manuel produced the *Conde Lucanor* under historical conditions, that is, the structure of the contents were determined by the particular situation under a feudal system in transition and hence in crisis. The work deals with relations between the nobility represented by the Count Lucanor and his counselor Patronio. The fictive relations of the two are represented with other members of medieval society: kings, nobles, peasants, hustlers, philosophers, servants, manipulators, merchants, advisers, beguines, priests, saints, cardinals, blind men, thieves, seneschals, Moors, emperors, and the like. In these very correspondences enter ideas, values, and feelings by way of which people expressed beliefs about the world and society. The exchange between master and mentor provides a framework within which both the noble and the readers understand and participate in the society of their time. These ideas make up a vision of the world, and this vision corresponds to the dominant ideologies of contemporary society. The challenge is to see whether this correspondence is in accord or in conflict. Almost everything borrowed or adapted in the book is rewritten, including the pattern and expression: modes of narrative, dialogue, typification, advice in accord with the ideals of nobility, in short, maintenance of the status quo.

To what degree does the cultural background of story, proverb or rhetoric fit or is made to fit the needs of Count Lucanor, and in general, the views and values of the high nobility? An evaluation of Don Juan Manuel's writing lies in how he structured or shaped the cultural, collective material he borrowed and adapted. The position taken by this study in dealing with these materials is that *El conde Lucanor* is a unified totality with a clearly discerned vein of organistic thinking which, of course, determines much of medieval exemplarity. Within this exemplary totality there are also many things that are not said; there are perceived gaps, silences, the fact above all that what is necessarily practical in the decisions and acts of a noble may not always be morally Christian, even though all practical steps are to be taken in the name of Christian morality. To what degree can what is secular be at the same time Christian is one of the tasks of Don Juan Manuel's rhetoric. The contradiction needs to be explained, both in the texts and their age. The study attempts to re-examine the totality of this historically important book but to do so in terms also of the exemplary gaps and silences within it.

The fact that collections of exempla and proverbs embody cultural phenomena of medieval times is a given; nevertheless it is the analysis of the social implications of exemplary discourse as manifested in texts and the interpretation of the historical function of exempla and proverbs that have raised difficulties among modern scholars. This is why a reappraisal of the language of persuasion and its presentation in the *enxiemplos* and *sentenciae* of the *Conde Lucanor,* as much as any other instance, might provide some insight for a general notion of the rhetoric of power and its application in the literature of the later Middle Ages.

The following second chapter of the study reappraises and even questions the key aspects of modern interpretations of the *Conde Lucanor* by Don Juan Manuel scholars in terms of what Juan Manuel himself had to say in the Prologue to his collection. The purpose is to determine how the nobleman himself authoritatively articulated for readers medieval notions of literary, and hence rhetorical construction. The implications of existing scholarship and analysis of the components of the Prologue together are means to illustrate Juan Manuel's conception of the text as a whole within which each part has a key role to play. The chapter also includes an analysis of Juan Manuel's specific use of the traditional *enxiemplo*. It includes the exemplary frame provided for each adaptation; a re-elaboration of each popular tale's physical structure; the stereotyped and therefore predictable conduct of characters (most notably Count Lucanor, Patronio and Don Iohan); and the choice of order in the general structure of the collection of exemplary tales. Finally, this chapter deals with Juan Manuel's intended reader(s), his de-emphasis or secularization of religious language and the new "pragmatization" of old moral examples. It is important to see how the nobleman as author circumvented authorial incursions by the Church in the sphere of politics, as well as his appropriation of the authority of kingship to establish the *auctoritas* of his own text.

Chapter Three provides a detailed analysis of the various Prologues to the different parts of the text. Together, the author's introductory observations help clarify the function of Juan Manuel's chosen structure especially if seen in the light of contemporary notions of the role memory played in the learning process. This is important because, first, it highlights the role of oral culture in didactic literature and helps explain the consistent patterns of the art of Don Juan Manuel's diverse adaptations in the *Conde Lucanor*. There is also an exposition of the organizational features of Giles of Rome's *De Regimine Principum* as an example of the well-known genre of the "regiment of princes." The ways that these features were articulated in the *De Regimine* may have been appropriated by Juan Manuel as the organizational keys both of each story and the collection. In this sense, the prologues to the book are really epilogues and represent the author's interpretation of what is read and his expectations of how it should be read.

Chapters Four, Five, and Six of the study follow the first three logically as illustrations: close analyses of the collections of exemplary tales, the proverbs, and the problematic fifth book in the light of the general information contained in Chapters Two and Three. Here we can examine the degrees to which this practice fits or does not fit Juan Manuel's theory of power and his rhetorical means of propagating it to his class. In each chapter, structure and discourse are considered to show how Juan Manuel's rhetoric of power prevails. It is considered that as a contribution to a rereading of the medieval canon this movement from "cause" to "effect" emphasizes that, in order to understand more thoroughly concrete works of the Middle Ages, the doctrine of the exemplary mode of persuasion (as well as the basis of prudence, and of the rhetorical strategies that go with it), must be developed through several levels of discussion until exemplarity is ultimately able to grasp the complexities of concrete cases.

These three chapters are followed by a short conclusion in which, after pulling together the general, theoretical arguments with the results of the empirical analyses, it is argued that if the findings about Don Juan Manuel's *Conde Lucanor* are valid then there is a need to open up new ways of examining textually and analytically the historical functions of the arts of the rhetoric of power in the Middle Ages.

## Notes

[1] The number of exempla and proverbs have been a subject of debate (Keller, Alvar, Blecua, Ayerbe-Chaux). This study relies on Juan Manuel's assertion that there are fifty tales and 180 proverbs. The tale that comprises the "fifty-first" *Lo que contesçio a vn rey christiano que era muy poderoso et muy soberbioso* is un-numbered in Manuscript S as well as the subject of debate with regard to authorship (England). The proverbs add up to different totals depending on the editor of the text and the divisions or combinations of lines chosen to represent a "complete" proverb. The number of tales and proverbs is important in its relation to the function of memory and the structure of the text. The fact that Juan Manuel emphasizes that there are fifty tales in three different places (the end of tale L, the introduction to the third Book, and the introduction to the fourth Book) in the text is significant (he recounts the numbers of proverbs in the *Escusacion* of the third book, the *Razonamiento* of the fourth Book, and again in the introduction to the fifth), and this study analyzes the text in the light of Juan Manuel's enumeration.

## Chapter 2: Socio-political history and literary production in fourteenth-century Castile

The literature of the late Middle Ages is filled with stories, legends, fables, tales and anecdotes that serve to illustrate various points of view about social, political, ethical, moral, and economic issues. For modern exegetes, these stories have become the means to illuminate all manner of perceptions of the Middle Ages, especially the reason for the didactic roles played by all types of medieval letters.[1] Juan Manuel's *Conde Lucanor* fits within that purview. This chapter elucidates how the text fits didactically within its historical milieu; the purpose is to demonstrate the practical underpinnings upon which a medieval text relies, how well those underpinnings imparted meaning to a medieval reader, and how their elucidation in turn illuminates Juan Manuel's medieval rhetoric of power to a twentieth-century reader.[2] This chapter also includes a review of textual and historical criticism with regard to the author and his literary corpus, specifically the *Conde Lucanor*. The review is a background to my approach and methodology based on close textual re-reading of the problems. Informed by medieval concepts of art as well as contemporary literary criticism, I examine how Juan Manuel's rhetoric of power functioned socially and obtained historically.

The first problem in discussing the conception, articulation and varied practices of political power in the Spanish Middle Ages is that the problem itself is historically immense yet it is here treated through the more or less limited angle of one literary collection of purely fictional stories. The other problem is that the stories themselves, in the hands of modern Hispanic studies, have been subject to sweeping verdicts and contradictory or simplistic interpretations. One cannot take the necessary historical and cultural background for granted. In this case, therefore, I start by sketching the medieval context of the *Conde Lucanor*, the shift from oral to written works, and the subsequent fixed nature of codes which in turn affected the crisis of the nobility during the last part of the reconquest. To what degree nobles were cognizant of the crisis is central to the concept of power and its rhetoric in the *Conde Lucanor*.

It is assumed that all literary genres were often integrated into performance. The historical function of these genres shaped the composition of texts since they explained their condition as well as determined their conscious function in practice. The *Conde Lucanor* is a witness to the shifts from oral to written tales. The benefits of an oral tradition are flexibility and the penchant for performance of written materials before others. A singer or jongleur could, within certain parameters, change or modify myths and legends according to the perceived needs of his audience. It has been argued that literacy caused social change through complaint and rebellion rather than "through silent evolution and selective remembering" associated with the oral tradition (Coleman 160). The emergence of literacy led to more fixed modes of discourse, which in turn fixed traditions during the Middle Ages. The flexibility of orality fades and is replaced by the more rigid allegoresis. The change from open performance to closed reading led to a reinterpretation of most fixed cultural traditions. Allegoresis is the concession of literal to other figural meaning; it is to this day the dominant method of literary figural interpretation. It serves to explain problems or highlight inconsistencies that become apparent in a written text and in turn leads to further investigation of the original problem and its proposed solution.[3] In other words, the growth of the written word effectively fixed traditions in texts and encouraged complaints against perceived inconsistencies between ideal conduct (usually expressed in a text) and the actual practice (usually expressed in a variety of discourses).

The codified Spanish law, for example, as articulated in the *Siete Partidas*, composed under the direction of Alfonso X, was the subject of such complaint. It can help advance the argument about oral versus written codes, especially since the written law deals with the powers of nobility as articulated by Don Juan Manuel. In it, Alfonso explicitly places administrative power in the hands of the monarch at the expense of the nobility.

> Et naturalmente dixieron los sabios que el rey es cabeza del regno; ca asi como de la cabeza nacen los sentidos por que se mandan todos los miembros del cuerpo, bien asi por el mandamiento que nace del rey, que es señor et cabeza de todos los del regno, se deben mandar, et guiar et haber un acuerdo con él para obedescerle, et amparar, et guardar et endereszar el regno onde él es alma et cabeza, et ellos los miembros. (*Partidas* II, 1, 5)

Using the familiar concept of the body politic, explained later in more detail, Alfonso emphasizes the king as the head and soul of the kingdom: "like the senses which originate in the head, and by which all the members of the body are directed, *so too ought all to be directed and guided by the commandment originating with the king*, who is lord and head of all the people of the realm. The king's subjects should offer and initiate an agreement with the king to obey, aid, protect and support the kingdom of which he is the soul and the head, and they are the members." By placing the power to direct and guide all others, which includes nobles, through his own command, Alfonso explicitly places the nobility in a subservient and therefore weakened position.[4] In the feudal sense of reciprocity, the king gave land, titles and wealth to those who aided him. For our purposes, Alfonso's *franqueza* affected Don Juan Manuel and is reflected in the *Conde Lucanor*.

Alfonso X was very generous to soldiers and lower nobility, as befitted a good king, especially with those who helped him during the reconquest of the Iberian Peninsula.[5] His so-called "generosity" created an ever-growing number of landed gentry, many of whom became the *hidalgos* (*fijos de algo*) so often ridiculed later in Golden Age texts. It also created the problems that he sought to curb through the attempted promulgation of the *Partidas*. Those very noblemen who were enriched by the Reconquest argued vehemently against the promulgation of the *Partidas* because the law code tipped the balance of power between nobleman and sovereign in the direction of the king, ceding rights and privileges to the king that had traditionally belonged to the nobleman. The reconquest of the Iberian Peninsula opened up huge tracts of land that had to be maintained and repopulated. This activity fell to the nobility who found themselves in control of a series of smaller rural holdings sometimes scattered over a wide area which, over time and through incorporation, became large properties (*señoríos*). The lord of the *señorío* gained considerable socio-economic control over his holdings and these lords fought any attempt by the monarchy to abridge their control.[6] This was intensified by Alfonso's political aspirations to the throne of the Holy Roman Empire which led him to exact heavy taxes on his subjects. He constantly struggled to control a restless nobility. In fact, the struggle between monarchy and nobility characterizes much of Spanish medieval history up to and beyond the Catholic Kings.

Members of this restless nobility included Alfonso's own wife, brothers, and children. Alfonso had his brother Fadrique drowned after finding him guilty of encouraging doña Violante, Alfonso's wife and the mother of Sancho IV, to flee Castile during the fight for succession between Alfonso's grandson Alfonso de la Cerda and Sancho. Primogeniture versus the custom of direct inheritance of the throne by the next surviving child was the issue. Alfonso decided, Solomon-like, to divide the kingdom between his son and his grandson. Neither one was happy with the division, nor was the Castilian nobility. Alfonso's younger brother and confidant, Manuel, the father of Juan Manuel, sided against Alfonso in the struggle to name a successor, as did Violante, Alfonso X's wife, Alfonso's sons Pedro and Juan, and a majority of the Castilian nobility. In the ensuing contest of power, Sancho won the battle, but lost the war.

Sancho IV, due in part to his inauspicious ascension to the throne, as well as the promises made but never kept to win noble support for his pretensions to the throne, also faced opposition by the nobility. Almost immediately upon his ascension, throughout his reign and the reign of Alphonse XI, Castile suffered various attempts by nobility to gain more and more control of the realm and to increase their wealth and power by practically any means possible. The analogy of king as head of the body politic was not questioned in theory, but in practice was fought tooth and nail. Juan Manuel's texts were all written during these turbulent times of transition from practically independent fiefdoms to a more centralized state government. Juan Manuel's texts overtly denounce the Castilian monarchical line, and exalt the nobility. The most complete articulation of Juan Manuel's political position and denunciation of the royal line is found in the *Libro de las armas* in which the nobleman recounts the deathbed "confession" of Sancho IV. Sancho, according to Juan Manuel, and in his own words, dies a damned king...damned by his parents and by his sins. On the other hand, in receiving the blessing denied Alfonso X from Fernando, Alfonso's father and Juan Manuel's grandfather, and Fernando's sword *Lobera*, the noble line of the Manuels is exalted. The sword symbolizes virtuous deeds.[7] By referring to the virtuous sword and the royal blessing, Juan Manuel effectively damns Alfonso XI and his line, and exalts his own. This is not to imply that Don Juan Manuel espoused an alternative or that he had any or all noblemen in mind other than himself and his family line; simply, Juan Manuel chose to represent himself as an exemplary nobleman, in effect, saw himself without peer as a high nobleman. It is this clear awareness of the coherent conflict between the high nobility and monarchy that emerges in his work. His texts privilege and emphasize noble codes of behavior as well as reiterating the feudal belief in the "static" organization of civil society based upon the celestial and monarchical order. It is important to re-examine this organization.

Analogous to the perceived heavenly social order, civil society was divided into three social strata: *oradores, defensores,* and *labradores,* that is, the clergy, the nobility and all those who performed the remaining tasks of society.

Each one of these groups was assigned a specific set of rights and duties that served to identify it as a "group" and, at the same time, integrated each class with the other. The Castilian glossator of Giles of Rome's *De regimine principum*, Fray Juan García de Castrojeriz, was a contemporary of Don Juan Manuel. His gloss of the treatise on governing provides another illustration of this carefully constructed relationship called the body politic.

> E por ende Plutarco, en el libro que fizo para informar a Trajano, puso muy buena comparación del rey a los sus súbditos, e dice que toda la república o la comunidad es así como un *cuerpo*, cuya *cabeza* es el rey e cuyos *ojos* son los sabios e cuyas *orejas* son las alcaldes e jueces. E cualesquier propósitos que resciben las leyes e los mandamientos del Sennor e los ponen en ejecución, cuya *lengua* e cuya *boca* son los abogados, cuyas *manos* son los caballeros, cuyos *pies* son los labradores.    (*Glosa* 28, my italics)

*Therefore Plutarch, in a book he wrote to educate Trajan, used a very good comparison of the king to his subjects. He claimed that the republic or community could be compared to a human body. The head represents the king, the eyes represent the wise men, the ears are the mayors and judges, the tongue and the mouth are the lawyers, the hands are the knights, and the feet are the peasants. Any purpose the Lord intends his laws and commandments to have, the body receives and executes.*

The figures of speech connecting a human or mystical body to the members of the ruling class is used to function as a point of comparison with the *oradores* and kings or emperors as the head or heart and the *defensores* and the *labradores* as the arms and legs/feet. No part can function completely by itself without the aid of all the other parts. The metaphor was meant to correspond to the historical reality; like a fixed code, it was not to be questioned. John of Salisbury's description in the *Policraticus* two centuries earlier is much more detailed in its description, and provides for earthly subjugation to the Pope, something noticeably lacking in Alfonso (13th century), Juan Manuel (14th century), and Castrojeriz' gloss. It is worth quoting extensively in order to highlight Juan Manuel's parallel concerns.

The position of the head in the republic is occupied, however, by a prince subject only to God and to those what act in His place on earth, inasmuch as in the human body the head is stimulated and ruled by the soul. The place of the heart is occupied by the senate, from which proceeds the beginning of good and bad works. The duties of the ears, eyes and mouth are claimed by the judges and governors of provinces. The hands coincide with officials and soldiers. Those who always assist the prince are comparable to the flanks. Treasurers and record keepers...resemble the shape of the stomach and intestines; these, if they accumulate with great avidity and tenaciously preserve their accumulation, engender innumerable and incurable diseases so that their infection threatens to ruin the whole body. Furthermore, the feet coincide with peasants perpetually bound to the soil, for whom it is all the more necessary that the head take precautions, in that they more often meet with accidents while they walk on the earth in bodily subservience; and those who erect, sustain and move forward the mass of the whole body are justly owed shelter and support. Remove from the fittest body the aid of the feet; it does not proceed under its own power, but either crawls shamefully, uselessly and offensively on its hands or else is moved with the assistance of brute animals. (*Policraticus* 67)

The metaphor had different historical ramifications and consequences during the three centuries mentioned. In fourteenth-century Castile, the nobility, to whom the defense of the community was relegated, at the same time ruled local communities, even entire territories, and extracted funds in the form of rent, taxation and even extortion from these communities and territories for the purpose of maintaining their estates and the way of life commensurate with their rank. This penchant for power and wealth was considered a "right" even though often at the expense of the community they were deigned to protect and serve, and caused a backlash of sorts. The backlash developed generally on two levels. One was through the formation of *hermandades*, brotherhoods that served to protect municipalities from the marauding nobility. The other was through legal complaints voiced at the *Cortes*, a legal proceeding called by the king to hear cases and dispense justice. Two complaints articulated in the *Cortes* of 1329 held in Madrid, for example, claimed that the audacity of the noblemen knew no limits: they had taken foodstuffs from royal holdings, and the advisers to the nobility were guilty of causing violent acts that led to the depopulation of the kingdom (Valdeón *tensiones sociales* 186).

There are innumerable examples. They all reveal the contradiction of analogies worked out in historical practice. So too with the author of the *Conde Lucanor* who could not be presumed just in his dealings with those he was sworn to defend. Alfonso XI condemned Don Juan Manuel's abuses of power committed in Murcia, land pertaining to the kingdom of Castile, but under the nobleman's control as *adelantado*. In 1328, the Castilian monarch complained of the 'quemas et estragamientos et dannos' that Don Juan Manuel committed (Valdeón *tensiones sociales* 186). Like the rest, Juan Manuel undid in practice what he propagated in theory.[8] The complaints against Juan Manuel and other noblemen of fourteenth-century Castile illuminate a turbulent society in transition from rural fiefdoms to a more centralized way of governing. Centralization affected the independent use of power by the nobility. The need to be aware of change is at the heart of the *Conde Lucanor*.

The constant rebellions and discomforts of burgeoning societies in transition during the Middle Ages of the Reconquest helped give rise to collections of sermon handbooks and collections of exempla in the vernacular as well as in Latin. Clergy and layman alike used these collections to teach citizens how to behave in society in relation to their God, their king and their lords. That is, they provided entertaining examples of the serious contents of treatises. The two orders most influential in the development of vernacular preaching through exemplary tales were the Dominicans and the Franciscans. They compiled collections of exemplary tales such as the *Liber Exemplorum Ad Usum Praedicantium*, *Exempla Communia*, *Exempla Deodati*, *Gesta Romanorum*, *Alphabetum Narrationum*, and the *Dialogus Creaturarum*. What these diverse collections had in common was a penchant for reproof or exhortation of people by way of examples to be found in traditional storytelling.

In Spain similar handbooks abound in secular titles (many of them translations of Arabic or eastern collections), such as the *Bocados de oro, Calila e Dimna*, Pedro Alfonso's *Disciplina clericalis, El libro de los buenos proverbios, Libro de los engaños, Barlaam y Josafat, Sendebar, Libro de los gatos, Exemplos muy notables*. Don Juan Manuel's *Conde Lucanor* falls within this category of manuals of exemplary behavior through traditional storytelling. Moreover, as we shall see, each story was framed as a "live" situation which in turn framed an exemplary message.

The exemplary tales mixed sacred and secular tales that were organized so as to make the material easily accessible to audiences. The *ordinatio* of these collections was generally based on a numerical or alphabetical arrangement which employed key words to which a given exemplary tale could be applied, for example, *Abstinentia*. Typical of this type of organization is the Spanish *Libro de los exenplos por a.b.c.* Not only the content of each exemplum was important but also the physical structure and ordering of the compilation. The didactic structure of any text as much as the tale itself was designed to facilitate understanding and highlight the proper exemplarity.

The universities and scholasticism taught a different form of study from the older monastic tradition of reading as spiritual exercise. Scholastic reading emphasized reasoning and harmonization of authorities that required a more orderly and accessible presentation of the text. New forms of *ordinatio* developed during the thirteenth and fourteenth centuries. Coupled with the rediscovery of Aristotelian logic in the late twelfth century, and the need to structure texts for transmission to the public, there was a need for precision in ordering knowledge for others. Specifically, compilations were divided into books and those into chapters with running titles. A text was also equipped with a table of contents so as to facilitate accessibility. Don Juan Manuel's collection of fifty tales in the *Conde Lucanor* as well as the books of maxims and the fifth Book manifest all of the organizing aspects of *ordinatio*, and, like the other collections, its formulaic form of imparting exemplarity through reading is crucial not only to understanding the text and its rhetorical function, but also to see how the above sketched socio-political order of Castile was represented in exemplary storytelling.

To sum up the sketched background of the *Conde Lucanor*: the Middle Ages were marked by the frequent application of corporeal or anatomical metaphors to the historical realities of organized political rule. The very administrative activities of the head of state were increasingly being cloaked in the analogical rhetoric of the head of the body. The purpose and effect was to show that, like the question of the proverbial chicken and the egg, the monarch, nobility and church were inseparable; they were necessary and complementary to each other, but in historical practice, the vested interests of different groups created oppositions and conflicts. The practical codes fixed one set of relations while historical changes created a continuous process of problematic interactions, first between monarchs and nobles and, next, between nobles and their subjects. Metaphors proposed, but historical realities disposed otherwise, hence the crisis. In the *Conde Lucanor*, Don Juan Manuel, a noble with vested interests in noble power and simultaneously a cultivated writer with a concern to communicate the dangers, inscribed in his tales the full extent of the crisis.

## The Penchants of Juan Manuel Criticism

The corpus of scholarship on Don Juan Manuel has dealt with, to one degree or another, many of the already mentioned areas regarding the function of tales. Daniel Devoto's bibliography of Juan Manuel studies through the early seventies as they relate to the *Conde Lucanor* in particular is a detailed catalog of diverse views that highlights the scholarly popularity and value of Juan Manuel's writings. What is noteworthy is that the preponderance of scholarship has focused on *El Conde Lucanor* and, in particular, on the first Book, the collection of fifty exemplary tales. Most critics have adopted the position that of the five parts, the major one is the first and therefore the one most worthy of study.[9]  Nor has this focus changed in the intervening years. Even recent book-length studies and most essays concentrate on the collection of tales, historically speaking at the expense of Books II, III, IV (the collections of maxims) and V (rhetoric on the benefits of doing good works).[10] Modern scholarship has been "unhistorical" in separating parts of a "libro" whose author conceived it as a whole of five separate parts and each part divided into smaller components.

Within this subset of criticism (that dealing with Book One), the focus includes the study of the sources of the diverse tales as a way of appraising Juan Manuel's artistic elaboration of them (Reinaldo Ayerbe-Chaux, Germán Orduna, Ian Macpherson). These studies are valuable from a variety of perspectives. Chief in importance for the purposes of this study is the perspective that such studies provide with regard to Juan Manuel's manipulation of inherited sources in the service of his rhetoric of power. Ayerbe-Chaux's and other similar studies are exemplary. Arabic and eastern influences on the text are highlighted, and although under-investigated to date, so too are the relationships between the prominence of the nine animal tales in the *Conde Lucanor* and their important role in Arabic literature for the purposes of teaching Islam (notably, the *Qur'an* which contains five chapters named after animals).[11] What these studies do not tackle are the crucial relations between the first book of tales to the four books of proverbs. The "unified" text has a different form than Book I, and taken together, it functioned differently in fourteenth-century Castile.

Daniel DeVoto among others, when discussing the text, highlights the "indicación tectónica importante" associated with Juan Manuel's mention in the Prologue of the Second Part of having completed the book of exemplary tales: "Despues que yo, don Iohan,...ove acabado este libro del conde Lucanor et de Patronio...(439), but ignores the rest of the architectural image: "que fabla de enxienplos" (439), distinguishing between the first book and what is to follow in the second through fifth Parts. In 1335 Don Juan Manuel's contemporary view of his book was a whole of five parts. In the same prologue for example, Juan Manuel asserts: "...yo non quis poner en este libro nada de lo que es puesto en los otros, mas qui de todos fiziere vn libro" (441). That is, all the seemingly separate parts make up the whole. There are various implications of this "authorial" assertion. As virtually all critics agree, MS "S" which contains all five parts is the closest to the original. The omission of the collections of proverbs and the fifth Book either in editions of the *Conde Lucanor* and especially in almost all efforts at textual exegesis is, therefore, a matter of literary artistic appeal or a question of convenience, but not one of textual integrity nor of textual interpretation. The result on all counts is an "incomplete" reading of its form and message. Another implication of the author's clearly stated intentions is that it defies the notion that what Juan Manuel does is reiterate in the succeeding books that which has already been said in Part One (See Diz: Chapter IV, 121). In short, to give an account of the *Conde Lucanor* without examining all the components which shaped Don Juan Manuel's rhetoric of power is inadequate.

Other studies have dealt with the didactic nature of the collection. (Ermanno Caldero, Peter Dunn, Ana Marta Diz, Aníbal Biglieri). Menéndez Pelayo's *Orígenes de la novela* offers, apart from the nationalist-oriented hyperbole, some exceptionally valuable observations regarding the possible influences of Arabic "mirrors for princes." The connections are related to didactic concerns and exemplarity. While the present study argues that Juan Manuel primarily looked west, not east, there is no doubt that *El Conde Lucanor* belongs to the well-known genre about the education or regiment of princes. Pelayo's argument was later taken up and expanded in the 1945 study by Castro y Calvo, *El arte de gobernar en las obras de Juan Manuel*. Castro y Calvo calls attention to Juan Manuel's mention of the importance of Giles of Rome's *De regimine principum*, an exemplary "mirror," although he sees its relationship to Juan Manuel's texts as purely formal. "Citado por Don Juan Manuel, acaso no ofrece tantas semejanzas como pudiera pensarse, sino más bien es una influencia meramente formal" (208). María Rosa Lida de Malkiel's "Tres notas sobre Juan Manuel" highlights the same citation from the nobleman's *Libro Enfenido* in which he names Aegidius Romanus as the author of a particularly useful book, *De regimine principum* (114). Rather than looking for influences on Juan Manuel, Lida de Malkiel illustrates the nobleman's tendency to avoid *auctores*. It is worthy to note that of the errors in attribution that Juan Manuel makes when "citing" the few authors that he actually mentions in his texts according to Lida de Malkiel, the nobleman does not err in his pairing of author and work when referring to Giles of Rome. Juan Manuel and in particular the *Conde Lucanor* are greatly influenced by the work by Giles of Rome. This study hopes to rectify such scholarly omission.

There is no doubt that the history of Hispanic studies has shown a preference for the fifty exemplary tales and it is perhaps natural for scholars to investigate most rigorously that which has endured. The problem for this investigation is that analysis of the exemplary tales at the expense of the remaining four books divorces the text both from itself and its historical context. While providing interesting and valuable insights into the nature of the exemplary tales employed by Juan Manuel, such scholarship is necessarily incomplete to an understanding of the text in light of medieval literary theory, medieval history, and more specifically, the socio-political reality of fourteenth-century Castile.[12]

## Strategies Toward a New Model of Criticism

Juan Manuel's text encompasses and reflects the importance of the cardinal virtues and that of *Prudence* in particular, combined with the function of memory as a structuring agent in the composition of the *Conde Lucanor*. It thus illustrates how the fictional representation of cultural, legal, religious, and political issues can inform modern readers about how fourteenth-century representative characters dealt with serious issues. At the same time, analysis shows modern readers how aristocrats like Don Juan Manuel proposed to handle the difficult and frustrating responsibility of teaching others how to govern well and maintain power concomitant with the maintenance of privilege. In fourteenth-century Castilian society maintenance of privilege meant the accumulation of honor, wealth and the salvation of the soul. Juan Manuel's text highlights important power relationships between noblemen, their peers, and their inferiors. A close examination of the text of *El Conde Lucanor* indicates that through the rhetoric of "pastoral" power, Juan Manuel hoped to maintain royal power on a societal level. By utilizing pastoral power and the implications of self-sacrifice for the salvation of others (a Christian doctrine of spiritual means), Juan Manuel justifies the use of royal power (the ideology of social material ends).[13] Royal power in this instance is used to describe the status quo of the fourteenth-century Castilian social order in which sacrifice is not demanded for the preservation of the throne per se, but rather for the maintenance of the existing social order in general, and noble power at the expense of the throne in particular.

Juan Manuel criticism has gained a position of eminence in medieval studies. Yet there are reasons to subject inconsistencies in emphasis which, taken all at once, make unclear what it is that Juan Manuel did in the *Conde Lucanor*, or for whom, or why. The overall structure of the *Conde Lucanor* requires more careful analysis and articulation of all its components than it has hitherto received. The rhetoric of power can best be understood if examined in terms of all five parts. The burden of my argument involves two dimensions of discourse. First is the contention that the *Conde Lucanor* is an exemplary as well as a formal rhetoric to such an extent that the important issue of the rhetoric of power cannot be properly understood unless the text is also thoroughly evaluated as a whole of five books. The second argument is that while the rhetoric of power has not been attended to enough (especially in terms of the five parts of the *Conde Lucanor*), the very speed and quantity of small, itemized studies of innumerable "findings" make it vital to design some systematic conceptual scheme in which all kinds of studies can be comprehended and evaluated. This study employs Juan Manuel's own prescription as a guide to articulate and define the books that comprise the *Conde Lucanor*, each book's parts to the whole, the relationship of each book to the others, and in the end, his rhetoric of power

As already indicated, the vast majority of studies on Juan Manuel's works deal with the sources of Don Juan Manuel's tales, his literary contribution to the retelling of these tales, the meanings extracted from them, and the insight that manueline writings provide into medieval life. How these tales teach the codes of behavior considered so important in fourteenth-century Castile that Juan Manuel recorded them in written form is one of the purposes of this investigation.[14]

Juan Manuel himself provides clues to the code of behavior in the Prologue to the *Conde Lucanor* by defining the end of exemplary behavior.

> commo quier que los omnes todos sean omnes et todos ayan voluntades et entençiones, que atan poco commo se semejan en las caras, tan poco se semejan en las entençiones et en las voluntades; pero todos se semejan en tanto que todos vsan et quieren et aprenden mejor aquellas cosas de que se mas pagan que las otras.
> (27)

*since men are men and all men have wills and intentions and although their wills and intentions resemble each other as little as their faces resemble one another. Nonetheless, these men are so similar to each other that all of them use, wish and learn better only those things that are most rewarding.*

Juan Manuel outlines difference and similarity among men of all estates. Everyone (*todos*) is bent by his will and his intentions whether it be cleric, nobleman, or laborer. As different as they may be physically, they are also different in their approaches to different situations. These examples of human nature to demonstrate differences and similarities recall Boethius' *Consolation of Philosophy* in which Philosophy tells the narrator that "In all the care with which they toil at countless enterprises, mortal men travel by different paths, though all are striving to reach one and the same goal, namely, happiness, which is a good which once obtained leaves nothing more to be desired" (79). Juan Manuel tells the reader that all men despite their differences learn those things that are most satisfying ("aquellas cosas de que se mas pagan"), that make them happy. Hugh of St. Victor in the *Didascalicon* refers to the acquisition of knowledge in a similar manner: "let these other things be read, for sometimes we are better pleased when entertaining reading is mixed with serious, and rarity makes what is good seem precious" (89). There are many such parallel discourses. Juan Manuel wishes to educate the honorable, honorable at least in medieval Castilian terms, and decides to follow his own rationale: he will provide satisfying examples to those he wishes to teach. More specifically, he suggests that subtlety can confuse readers and that in order to teach effectively not only must the lessons be satisfying, they must also be simple to read and understand.

> Et porque a muchos omnes las cosas sotiles non les caben en los entendimientos, por que non las entienden bien, non toman plazer en leer aquellos libros, nin aprender lo que es escripto en ellos. Et por que non toman plazer en ello, non lo pueden aprender nin saber asi commo a ello cunplia. (28)

*There are many men who fail to conceive difficult concepts because they do not understand them well. They do not take pleasure in reading those books, nor in learning what is written in them. Since they do not take pleasure in it, they can not learn it nor comprehend how it is applied.*

The nobleman puts the issue quite bluntly: readers do not enjoy reading what is not clear. This is a notion that is reiterated in several of the prologues in the *Conde Lucanor* as well as in other texts by Juan Manuel. There is a similarity to Hugh of St. Victor's Preface to the *Didascalicon* in which Hugh posits two types of people poor in their ability to comprehend even simple things.

> There are those who, while they are not unaware of their own dullness, nonetheless struggle after knowledge with all the effort they can put forth and who, by tirelessly keeping up their pursuit, deserve to obtain as a result of their will power what they by no means possess as a result of their work. Others, however, because they know that they are in no way able to compass the highest things, neglect even the least, and, as it were, carelessly at rest in their own sluggishness, they all the more lose the light of truth in the greatest matters for their refusal to learn those smallest of which they are capable. (43)

Juan Manuel takes up this issue directly after the end of the fifty tales when introducing the collections of proverbs in the *Conde Lucanor*. Juan Manuel's view of rhetoric for the common reader stresses that the message should be packaged in such a way as to entertain or cause satisfaction and that the message itself should be easily understood. Simple articulation of important messages was of course a commonplace of medieval rhetorical theory.[15] He places himself within a camp influenced by Aristotelian notions of the function of literature, specifically, literature as ludic. The pleasure that is derived from recreation is not due to its simple entertainment value, but because of the realization that one is participating in virtuous activity (Olson 95). The same notion is mirrored above when Juan Manuel says that the effect of using pleasurable examples leads to learning and understanding, the ends of reading books. Reading is recreation according to Juan Manuel, not in a frivolous, useless sense, but rather as a positive means to a laudatory end. Thus, chain-like, entertainment helps reading which in turn helps understanding which leads to salvation.

Juan Manuel defended writing as opposed to other activities in the *Libro Enfenido*: "...pienso que es mejor pasar el tienpo en fazer libros que en iugar los dados o fazer otras uiles cosas" (*Obras* I 183). Juan Manuel conceives of his efforts at literary composition, by and large the telling of stories and the recitation of proverbs, as a type of meaningful recreation as opposed to another type of wasteful/sinful play, that of dicing.[16] He says that he has been criticized for his indulgence in play and answers his critics "...yo se [que] algunos profaçan de mi por que fago libros, digo vos que por eso non lo dexare" (I 182). Dicing and writing books are both recreational but Juan Manuel privileges book-writing because, on the one hand his books contain good advice and truth and do not do harm; "ay en ellos pro et verdat et non danno." On the other hand, the truly great lords will not only protect estate and honor but will also do good works; "deuedes saber que todas las cosas que los grandes sennores fazen, todas deuen ser guardando primera mente su estado et su onra, mas esto guardado, quanto mas a[n] en si de vondades, tanto son mas conplidos" (I 182). Writing books is a form of recreation, but it is at the same time the performance of good works. So, too, is the reading of these books recreational and the performance of good works.

Through a series of known medical topoi Juan Manuel illustrates what it means to teach through pleasurable example. He elaborates the well-known medieval metaphor of sugarcoating bitter medicine.[17]

> Et esto fiz segund la manera que fazen los fisicos, que quando quieren fazer alguna melizina que aproueche al figado, por razon que naturalmente el figado se paga de las cosas dulçes, mezclan con aquella melezina que quieren melezinar el figado, açucar o miel o alguna cosa dulçe; et por el pagamiento que el figado a de la cosa dulçe, en tirando la para si, lieua con ella la melezina quel a de aprouechar....Et a esta semeiança, con la merçed de Dios, sera fecho este libro... (*Obras* I 28)

*There are many men who fail to conceive difficult concepts because they do not understand them well. They do not take pleasure in reading those books, nor in learning what is written in them. Since they do not take pleasure in it, they can not learn it or comprehend how it is applied.*

Doctors know that the liver is attracted to sweet things, and thus use something sweet as a vector to introduce medicine and cure the ailing organ. Juan Manuel shall do the same: he will sugarcoat his messages, a medieval commonplace. This echoes Lucretius (*De Rerum* Book IV) and Boethius (*Consolation* 49-52) among others. Like the poetic voice in *De Rerum Natura* or the character Philosophy, Juan Manuel is going to reach readers as if tending to the sick. The focus on the medical metaphor cannot be reduced to the role of sweetness in making something palatable, but above all, readers must recognize the existence of illness. "El aprender por ejemplos es una manera de padecer en carne ajena curándose en salud" (Barcia 19). People are attracted to sweet things, and, therefore, sweet words and stories carry and couch the medicinal message to "sick" readers. Juan Manuel plans to teach those who read or hear his stories to such an extent that even those who do not look for a lesson in the sweet stories, those who read only for pleasure or those who are not "sick", will be able to learn from the "cosas aprouechosas."

> ..et aun los que lo tan bien non entendieren, non podrian escusar que, en leyendo el libro, por las palabras falagueras et apuestas que en el fallaran, que non ayan a leer las cosas aprouechosas que son y mezcladas, et avn que ellos non lo deseen, aprouecharse an dellas...
> (*Obras* I 28)

*... and even those who do not understand it well, by reading this book written with nice and flattering words, they are not going to be able to keep themselves from reading the beneficial things written in it and, despite of their reluctance, take advantage of them ...*

According to Juan Manuel, he uses the surest method of successful teaching that brings guaranteed results. Not only will the tales teach those who are capable of understanding the messages contained in them, they will also teach those who may not understand the message through the use of beautiful language and entertaining stories. This summary of the value of the text reflects a statement made earlier in the Prologue in which Juan Manuel delimited the fourteenth-century Castilian status quo: a society divided by three. There are those who serve God, those who serve their lords, and those who work. The first two groups have the ability to understand, but the third does not. In this case, Juan Manuel's textual medicine is to be applied specifically to those "sick" members of the second estate and through them to those of the other two estates.

Much critical and historical discussion has focused on Juan Manuel's emphasis on *onra, fazienda, estado,* and *salvar las almas* and upon the fact that three of the four states that the nobleman as governor wishes to affect are secular; only one is religious. Luciana de Stéfano and José Antonio Maravall among others have shown the importance of the first three states to the attainment of the last in medieval society. The relationship of these three states to the reader of the exemplary tales and proverbs needs to be explored. Everyone pertains to a particular *estado*, but according to contemporary thought in fourteenth-century

Castile, *salvar las almas, onra* and *fazienda* were limited to those who occupied the estates of *orador* (clergy) and *defensor* (nobleman) (de Stéfano *sociedad estamental* 129). Those whom Juan Manuel will teach specifically are the members of the second estate. Evidence to support this argument comes from the narrator who comments on Juan Manuel's purpose in the Prologue to the *Conde Lucanor*: "Et por ende, fizo todos los sus libros en romançe, et esto es sennal çierto que los fizo para los legos et de non muy grand saber commo lo el es (24). *Legos* were those without a certain level of education, namely, *legos* lacked a background in Latin. The clergy were considered preeminent in the social hierarchy since they perpetuated the presence of Christ in Christian society, held sacramental power, were entrusted with the defense of the faith, and had an honor and received special consideration not accorded to members of the other estates (de Stéfano 59-60). In the second book of Juan Manuel's *Libro de los estados* the character Julio, after delimiting the members that comprise the first estate, evaluates their chances of gaining salvation.

> Et, sennor infante, commo desuso vos dicho, todo clerigo missa cantano, desde el papa fasta el mas mesquino capellan que puede seer, pueden caer en este yerro tan grande si non lo guardan commo deuen. Pero asi commo vos digo que pueden caer en estos yerros, asi vos digo que si este santo sacramento fazen commo deuen, an el mejor meresçimiento que puede seer. (I 493)

*And, your highness, as I have already told you, each religious man from the pope down to the simplest chaplain are going to make this same mistake unless they keep themselves from it as they should. The same way I am telling you that these mistakes can be made, I am also telling you that should they comply with this holy sacrament as they must, they would be most rewarded.*

The clergy is able to fall into error and lose their chance at salvation just like those of the second estate (recall Dante's *Divine Comedy* and many of the occupants of *Malebolge*), but the ability to say Mass (requiring a certain proficiency in Latin) is a great boon, and if they complete this sacrament as it should be done they will earn Paradise. Juan Manuel's text is not specifically for the clergy. Neither is the book for those who pertain to the group of laborers, who, while capable of achieving salvation, find the way very dangerous going.

> -En pos [d]el fisico [et] del despensero, ay otros muchos ofiçiales en las casa de los enperadores et de los reys et de los otros sennores asi como coperos...et otros muchos ofiçiales mas menudos, que paresçe mejor en los callar que en los poner en tal libro como este. Todos estos ofiçiales sobre dichos, seruiendo bien et leal mente sus ofiçios et non faziendo enganno al sennor nin a las gentes de su casa nin de la tierra, pueden muy bien saluar sus almas; *mas por que cada vno destos a muy [grant] aparejamiento para errar por cobdiçia o por mala entençion, por ende sus estados son muy peligrosos para saluamiento de las almas.*
> (I 409, my italics)

*Besides the doctor and the pantryman, there are many other servants in the emperors', king's and other noblemen's dwellings such as the cupbearers... and many other servants of a lesser rank. It seems best not to mention the latter in a book like this. All those servants abovementioned may very well save their souls by completing their duties well, loyally and by not fooling their master, the people in the house, and the people of the land. Each one of these servants is in a great risk to act out of greed or bad intentions; therefore, their position puts the salvation of their souls in much jeopardy.*

Juan Manuel lists eight low officials in the service of emperors and kings such as doormen, messengers and cooks and allows for even "lower" positions. All of these are capable of attaining heaven if they live according to their estate, but because they are prone to error, most notably their innate covetousness and evil intentions, they have a difficult time saving their souls. The same is true of rural folk who occupy an even more dangerous situation "por el aparejamiento que an para non fazer todo lo mejor, et por que muchos destos son [tan] menguados de entendimiento, que con torpedat podrian caer en grandes yerros non lo entendiendo" (I 409-410). These people do not understand their dangerous situation; they may be too clumsy and fall. Only the nobility remains, but there are dangers and they need to be forewarned.

## The Vernacular and Didactic Purpose

Juan Manuel, who was a member of the high nobility in Castile, shared the ideology of power practiced by the monarchy. His text is a manual for those nobles who needed to be taught how to conduct themselves in a variety of social situations, and how the balance of power is maintained. "...bien se trate de educar a los jóvenes vástagos, bien se ofrezca una imagen de cómo ha de pensar y vivir" (Maravall *estudios de historia* 464). Offspring or new branches describe those recently titled who start to rise in society and become members of the lower nobility. It is to this group of *homini novi* that the *Conde Lucanor* would seem to be most specifically directed.

The fact that Juan Manuel intends to educate the illiterate nobleman (in the sense of not knowing Latin) had implications for his choice of language, and he made a conscious decision to prepare and impart his lessons in *romançe*, the language spoken daily by the people. Juan Manuel follows a movement begun in the thirteenth century that saw the translation of many authoritative works into the vernacular.[18] Juan Manuel writes in Castilian out of a need to communicate to a diverse group of people a specific set of rules, rules that would "get lost in the translation" were the text written in Latin. If the nobleman wished to teach those without benefit of his knowledge, then *romançe* would be the natural choice: it allowed for a greater dissemination of the message. Juan Manuel is always cognizant of his reader and does not deviate from his goal. The most efficient method of teaching the *lego*, he argues, is to use the language of the *lego*.

There is another implication in the use of the vernacular. Latin was the language of the Church and the vernacular that of the *seglar*. By writing his text in Castilian, Juan Manuel de-emphasizes the religious aspects of the text and highlights its secular nature. This is a mirror for princes, a treatise on political philosophy, and there is a conscious attempt to appropriate the authority of the Church and place it in the State (at least in terms of power relations). Juan

Manuel, in imitation of his uncle Alfonso X in the *Partidas*, describes this circumvention in his *Libro del caballero et del escudero*,[19]

> ca los reyes son en la tierra en logar de Dios, et las sus voluntades son en la mano de Dios....et Dios quiere que los reyes sean en la tierra, et la mantengan según los merecimientos de las gentes del su regno. (I 235)

*Kings are God's representatives on earth, so their wishes are in the hands of God...and God wishes kings to be on earth, and that they administrate it according to the merit of the people of his kingdom.*

Kings are God's representatives on Earth. It is He who wants them here, and that they care for the earth in His place. This description of a king bypasses the authority of the Church and instead argues for a separate, secular authority invested in the monarchy.

> Et por ende vos digo que el papa a poder conplido en todo lo spiritual...Otrosi, a muy grant poder en lo tenporal; mas qual o quanto es este poder, por que yo so de Castiella et los reys de Castiella et sus reynos [son] mas sin ninguna subgection que otra tierra del mundo. (I 468)

*Therefore, I am telling you that the pope has entire power in all spiritual matters...Besides, he has much power in earthly matters; but what or how much is this power? Because I am from Castile, and the king and queen of Castile as well as their other kingdoms are not subjected to anything whatsoever in this world.*

While the Pope has complete spiritual power, his temporal powers are limited. In the case of Castile, the Pope wields no recognized temporal power. Juan Manuel avoids Latin in part to avoid the authorial incursion of the Church into the secular affairs of politics, and he appropriates the authority of kingship to establish the *auctoritas* of his own text.[20]

The nobleman also avoids what Larry Scanlon defines as the sermon exemplum in favor of the public exemplum. There is a paucity of priestly or religious protagonists (three) and of sacred acts or rituals (none) in Juan Manuel's tales, characteristics of the sermon exemplum (Scanlon 70-71). The tales overwhelmingly deal with secular, political acts by kings and noblemen (twenty-one) and those tales that treat of religious themes or characters have a decidedly negative slant (XI, XXXI and XLII, for example).

Like his contemporary, the archpriest of Hita, the nobleman in the introduction to his text says in essence that he brings readers the power of understanding, "Intellectum tibi dabo...." As Giles of Rome writes in the *De regimine*, he will provide understanding in a manner that can be comprehended by those who are served and serve alike.

> E si por este libro son ensennados los príncipes como se deven haver e en cual manera deven mandar a los sus súbditos, conviene esta sciencia e esta doctrina aprenderla fasta el pueblo porque sepan cómo han de obedescer a sus príncipes. E porque esto non puede ser así, como dicho es, sino por razones superficiales e sensibles, *conviene que la manera que devemos tener en esta obra sea gruesa e figural e enxemplar.* (*Glosa* 13, my italics)

*This book teaches princes to behave and to govern their subjects. This doctrine should even be learned by the people so that they would know how to obey their princes. Since this can not happen like it has been said, but for superficial and sensitive reasons; it would be beneficial to write this book in a broad, didactic and figurative manner.*

The glossator of the *Regimine* translates Giles as saying that in order to teach vassals as well as princes, his text will be written to facilitate understanding which means broadly, figuratively and through example.[21] The *Conde Lucanor* is intended not only for a specific group of "infirm" readers in need of the power of diagnosis, but also for those, like the readers of Giles' text, who can benefit from the lessons that he will impart. Because it is designed to fit the needs of those with varying degrees of understanding, like the *Regimine*, the *Conde Lucanor* will teach by example.

There is an implicit claim of great truth value in Juan Manuel's statement that everyone will learn from his text; a claim of *auctoritas* that Juan Manuel can only make having carefully placed his text within the realm of politics or ethics.

This is confirmed in the Prologue to Book Two where the author locates his topic by telling the reader, like his contemporary the archpriest of Hita, what it is not.

> fablare en este libro en las cosas que yo entiendo que los omnes se pueden aprouechar para saluamiento de las almas et aprouechamiento de sus cuerpos et mantenimiento de su onras et de sus estados. Et commo quier que estas cosas non son muy sotiles en si, assi commo si yo fablasse de la sciençia de theologia, o metafisica, o filosofia natural, o avn moral, o otras sçienças muy sotiles, tengo que me cae mas, et es mas aprouechoso segund el mio estado, fablar desta materia que de otra arte o scienç ia. (440)

*In this book, I will speak through things I know such as how men's souls can be saved, how good use can be made out of their bodies, and how their honor and their possessions can be kept. Since these things are not so difficult themselves, I will speak of this matter as if I spoke of theology, metaphysics, natural or moral philosophy, and other very difficult sciences. I believe it will be more beneficial doing it this way.*

Juan Manuel makes no claim to special knowledge that was available principally to the educated cleric: theology, philosophy or the sciences of the quadrivium, but he shows an awareness of propriety. His text is secular, political, pragmatic, and pertains to the genre we now call 'regiment of princes' or medieval political philosophy which, as Giles claims in Castrojeriz' translation, is taught through example and not through the means of the other sciences.

> Síguese así como los fechos e las obras singulares e personales, que son materia de esta obra de la moral filosofía, son mudables e se mudan de cada día, así demuestran que devemos en ellas tener manera de figuras e de enxemplos...dice el Filósofo más adelante que de omme sabio es en tanto demandar certidumbre de cada cosa en cuanto la naturaleza de esa misma cosa lo demanda, ca semeja la naturaleza de sciencia moral del todo ser contraria a la sciencia matemática. Ca las demostraciones matemáticas son ciertas en el primer grado de certidumbre, así como dice el Comentador en el I.º libro de la Metafísica, mas las razones morales e de las otras de los ommes son superficiales e gruesas. Donde se sigue que el geométrico no ha de amonestar, mas de demostrar; el retórico e moral no ha de mostrar, mas de amonestar. Por la cual razón dice el Filósofo en el I.º libro de las Eticas que semejante e igual pecado

> es que el matemático tiene de amonestar e el retórico que ha de mostrar. *(Glosa* 12)

*This book on moral philosophy focuses on facts and on personal and particular examples. Those facts and examples are not stable and do change every day. This shows that we must have them just as examples and for guidance ... Further in the text, the Philosopher claims that a wise man is he who demands the truth of each thing to the extent that the nature of this particular thing requires it. The nature of moral science on beings is contrary to nature. Mathematic demonstrations are true in the first degree of uncertainty, as the narrator says in the first book of* Metaphysics. *Moral reasons and other reasons are superficial and vague. Where the geometrician needs not to moralize, but to demonstrate, the rhetorician needs not to demonstrate, but to moralize. Therefore, in the first book on Ethics, the Philosopher argues that a similar sin is committed when the mathematician must moralize and the rhetorician must demonstrate.*

Giles' text is inherently rhetorical in nature which means that it is devoted to practical issues of government and is the means used by the statesman to persuade others to do good works. The politician needs to reach and move a number of people of various sensibilities with regard to many difficult and diffuse matters of behavior, which, because of their variability, require figural and broad language. Juan Manuel, analogously to the statesman described by Giles, presents a text that properly reflects his area of expertise, and through the text, he will direct himself to the teaching of his readers in a way proper to his subject matter. In other words, Juan Manuel proves himself cognizant of his role as powerful statesman/politician, the responsibilities of this role (the promotion of the proper exercise of power), and the proper means of exhorting his readers in order to move them to action (through figurative language that "moves" rather than "proves"). Secular readership of the text becomes a self-constituting, self-affirming moral force. Not only does Juan Manuel establish himself as *auctor* but through the very use of the written word, his text becomes not only a model for behavior but correct political behavior in and of itself.

Juan Manuel's proposed strategy for educating the public combines what is considered to be ornamental and persuasive rhetoric.[22] Juan Manuel uses ornamental language and pleasant stories to entertain the reader. The exemplary tales plucked from tradition fulfill this role. Persuasive rhetoric in the *Conde Lucanor* comes from the application of these decorative pieces to specific problems and concerns posed by the fictional Count Lucanor. Juan Manuel proposes to attract the reader with ornament laid within a framework of persuasion designed to convince the reader of a specific course of action. The two are inseparable within Juan Manuel's rhetorical art.

Juan Manuel offers his "medicine" as a preventive, not as a corrective. In an estate society that sought and which depended upon social rigidity, the only way to maintain the status quo may have been to educate those who had recently entered the lower ranks of nobility or the court through indulgence or by fruit of their inherited title, in the hope that they would learn their rights and responsibilities and maintain the divinely ordained social hierarchy. The function of a nobleman's education was to teach the *defensor* the appropriate codes of behavior to act out within his social class, and then defend it. Those who did not inherit but nevertheless would have received titles of nobility by indulgence or worthy action lacked the proper aristocratic attitude and the codes of behavior that went with it; therefore, the new aristocrats needed a *vademecum* of how to fulfill their new social roles. Don Juan Manuel's book the *Conde Lucanor* is a response to this need.[23]

**The Social Right to Write: Building *Auctoritas***

The major character of the collection is the author whose presence at every step highlights his role in history and fiction. Juan Manuel was a well-known figure in his day. His claim to authority is backed by his person: Don Juan Manuel was the son of a prince, a prince himself (of Aragon and through marriage; he was not a prince in Castile), a duke (in Aragon), the *adelantado mayor* of the Moorish borderlands and the kingdom of Murcia, the nephew of Alfonso the Wise, an the friend and cousin of Sancho IV. He was educated at the King's court, served as the tutor to Alfonso XI, and was the son-in-law to the King of Aragon. He was for all practical purposes, without peer in his time.[24] Juan Manuel occupies a unique position in the Spanish nobility, lower than the King (although having been the tutor to one), but higher than any Duke or Count. He is a governor of huge tracts of land, powerful enough to undo his oath of fielty to Alfonso XI and war against him. Of those things which the nobleman may or may not understand, his knowledge of politics and political philosophy is undisputed. He also occupies a unique historical position within the fiction of the *Conde Lucanor* text. Not only is he author, compiler, and composer, but by virtue of his nobility and his role as co-regent and tutor to Alfonso XI (a position he occupied prior to the writing of the *Conde Lucanor*) he is able to occupy the positions of both the characters Count Lucanor (petitioner/student/nobleman) and Patronio (counselor/teacher) simultaneously. Juan Manuel represents power in a noble and simultaneously acts it out as a rhetor by articulating its function.

Don Juan Manuel used his position and reputation to insure that those who read or listened to his stories would know that they came from a very reputable, high noble, one in a position to know how to properly exercise power, how to govern, how to set an example worthy of imitation. His name, attached to the collection of exemplary tales, and again in the fifth Book, establishes its mode of discourse.[25] The name Juan Manuel, by virtue of the nobleman's position and power in history, guarantees the *Conde Lucanor* a certain status and credibility. The nobleman acts the part of author and adds title and name (Don Juan Manuel) to each exemplary tale to assure the reader that the information contained in the story is authoritative and beneficial, to the extent that Juan Manuel found the story worthy to be included in the collection. In the fifth Book Patronio cites Juan Manuel as *auctor* and his *Libro de los estados* as *auctoritas*. Juan Manuel establishes himself as the *auctor* of the text. He is the *assertor* of a passage (Don Iohan who writes the verses at the end of the tale), its editor or compiler (Don Iohan who had the story included in the collection), and he is both together: Don Iohan in the introduction to the work who says,

> yo, don Iohan...fiz este libro con puesto de las mas apuestas palabras que yo pude, et entre las palabras entremeti algunos exienplos de que se podrian aprouechar los que los oyeren.
> (28)

*I, Don Juan... wrote this book with the nicest words I was able to find, and among these words I have interwoven some examples that could be of some use to those who hear them.*

The title, name and character of Don Juan Manuel constantly enter into the fiction to reinforce the lesson with his verses and the weight of his "persona."

There are two protagonists invented by Juan Manuel to frame each story of the collection: Count Lucanor and his adviser Patronio. Juan Manuel carefully chooses a protagonist for the textual frame: the use of a count makes the social and economic status of the noble more ambiguous. Juan Manuel, in his *Libro de los estados*, defines the title of "Count:"

> otro estado ay entre los grandes omnes [a] que llaman 'condes'. Et este es vn estado est[r]anno et caben en el muchas maneras de omnes; ca en muchas tier[r]as acaesce que los infantes, fijos de los reys, son condes, et otros condes ay que son mas ricos et mas poderosos que algunos duques, et avn que algunos reys; et otros condes ay que an abes mas de çincuenta caualleros *Et asy este estado es muy extranno, por que algunos ay que son tan onrados commo los reys, et algunos ay que son de tan pequenno poder commo es dicho, pero el nonbre en todos es egual.*
> (I 384, my italics)

*There is another position among important men which is called "count". This is a strange position in which many types of men can be included. There are kingdoms where the princes, the king's sons, are counts. There are counts who are wealthier and more powerful than some dukes and even some kings. There are counts that rule more than fifty knights. There are some who are as honest as kings, and there are others who have very little power. However their title is the same and that is why this is a very strange estate.*

The ambiguity of the status of the protagonist count serves the purposes of Juan Manuel better than the less ambiguous duke or prince since dukes and princes, not to mention kings or emperors, were of such high nobility that the inability to make decisions which affected the honor, estate, wealth and soul of the nobleman found in the *Conde Lucanor*, would signal a weakness in the ruler (witness the satire in *Enxiemplo* XXXII). A count of uncertain importance and social standing would not be expected to have the same level of political knowledge or social and political standing, and, therefore, would be more acceptable as a ready listener to those readers of the exemplary tales and the overall frame. Juan Manuel proposed to educate the lower nobility on how to govern well, and the use of a count as a protagonist aided in the credibility of the lessons, since if a *count*, a member of the amorphous nobility, was in need of direction on how to govern, and the exemplary tales did not alienate or offend him, then the tales should not offend those of lower nobility in need of similar advice.

Perhaps on a different level, the contrast between the naive count and his wise counselor serves to reinforce the role that Juan Manuel, author and character, is playing. It is no accident that Lucanor is younger and hence less experienced than his older counselor, Patronio. That age equals wisdom is a commonplace in the later Middle Ages, one that Juan Manuel employs liberally in the *Conde Lucanor*. Tales 2, 21, 25, and 50 serve as examples.[26] Metaphorically, the naive count exemplifies the *hombres ricos* who are gaining more power and entering the ranks of nobility. In the same way, Patronio metaphorically exemplifies the older and wiser, established nobility who must educate inexperienced noblemen in the rules of governing. Patronio is responsible for the protection of society as it exists: he indoctrinates the novitiate and thus preserves the social order.

**Within the Oral, Medieval Literary Tradition (Exempla and Proverbs)**

In Book One, Patronio and Lucanor are involved in fifty discussions of power relations in which Lucanor presents a problem leading Patronio to cite an exemplary tale which illustrates the proper resolution of the problem of the implementation of power that, in every case, leads to a profitable outcome for the count (*et fallóse ende bien*). All the exempla are directly or indirectly related to the rhetoric of power. This process is repeated fifty times in tales that either rely on an historical account of some veracity or tales that are more fable-like in nature. Commentators and glossators of the Middle Ages often discuss the use of exempla and its value in rhetorical treatises as has already been indicated in Giles. Brunetto Latini discusses exempla specifically under the heading of arguments to prove what the speaker says. Everything is confirmed through arguments which are taken from the basis of the discussion (word or act). "Toda esçiençia es confirmada por argumentos que son sacados por las propriedades del cuerpo & por las propriedades de las cosas" (*Tesoro* 201). In his catalog of types of arguments Latini describes arguments that are similar to truth (*argumento semejante verdat*). "El argumento semejante verdat es de las cosas que acaesçen mucho a menudo o de las cosas que onbre cuyda que sean o de las cosas que an alguna semejança que sean verdaderas" (*Tesoro* 204). To "prove" his statement he divides these arguments into signs (a demonstration ascertained through confirmation of one or more of the five senses), believable notions (much like common sense statements), established notions (laws, common use or agreement), and similarity. Similarity is further divided to yield similitude, comparison and example. Example, according to Latini,

> es el argumento que muestra alguna semejante cosa por los dichos & por los mandamientos que onbre falla en los libros de los sabios, et por aquello que acaesçe a los onbres & a las cosas que fueron de aquella semejança. (*Tesoro* 204)

*It is the argument that shows the similarities between the sayings and the commands that men failed to fulfill in wise men's books. It also shows those things that happen to men and things that were of the same origin.*

Exempla are arguments that show similarity through the sayings or commands found in the *auctores*, and through those things that happened to men or things that gave rise to the similitude. What Latini describes as *example* encompasses almost any type of tale or saying that can be used to support a proposition, and in the case of Juan Manuel that includes tales and proverbs. It is probable that a learned nobleman of Juan Manuel's stature, educated at the royal court, would have been exposed to treatises like Latini's *Libro del Tesoro* (among others) that includes an opus on rhetoric and on politics. Latini was chosen as exemplary in this instance because of the established popularity of his work on the peninsula.[27] Familiarity with those treatises would have afforded Juan Manuel a variety of methods judged as successful in the art of *argumentatio* and may have led the nobleman to choose the exemplum as the most appropriate vehicle for the transmission of his lessons.

Apart from the fact that Juan Manuel was familiar with rhetorical teachings, there is another reason why the exemplary tale was a natural choice for the nobleman. The oral, medieval, literary tradition united legends, anecdotes and fables, and used them for the purpose of educating the unlearned. Juan Manuel's rhetoric of power employs an already established literary tradition and familiar tales for two reasons: since these tales were established and in use, they enjoyed a certain acceptance and they were comfortable because they were known.[28] Sandra Dolby Stahl addresses this issue in her book *Literary Folkloristics and the Personal Narrative.* She indicates that in all communications there is a shared frame of meaning. "Someone listening to a personal narrative projects this assumed meaning onto the storyteller and basks in the resultant sense of community, of *shared tradition*" (119). While Stahl refers specifically in this instance to a personal narrative, the sense of community or of shared tradition is not limited to such narrative, but is achieved through folktales in general, and in the case of *El Conde Lucanor*, the exemplary tales and proverbs in particular. The nobleman's rhetorical art uses these established and comfortable tales and fixes the tales physically in the text as well as (af)fixing their meaning. Juan Manuel avoids uncertainty by using the familiar and then frames them with specific meanings. The tales remind the reading community of its communal acceptance of the myth or legend (Frye *Myth and Metaphor* 282). The *enxiemplo* was the most efficient choice for his lectures on how to govern in a medieval society because it was popular, and was easily adapted to his social ideology.

Two other points need to be made with regard to Juan Manuel's use of the exemplary tale, and they are both structural in nature. The composition of the *exiemplos* provides a combination of oral and written traditions. Juan Manuel appropriates oral tales, transforms them into lessons on the art of good government knowing that they will once again be transmitted orally to an audience that he wishes to influence. These adapted stories, outfitted with a moralistic frame and replaced into the oral domain can, in turn, "infect" the existing oral tale with the moral attached to those stories by the nobleman. Thus Juan Manuel's frame becomes associated with the tale, and what once had no specific fidelity to any moral in its telling is now associated with Juan Manuel and his lessons on good government. The notion of "infecting" a tale or proverb is, to a certain extent, a description of *memoria ad res* which is taken up later. A modern critic's speculations may approximate the historical context of Juan Manuel's tales.

> Tanto el autor como su auditorio o sus lectores entendían lo innecesario y pedante de deslindar autorías en ese medio y en tal clase de tratados en romance, y admitían tácitamente que esa ingente masa de doctrina y ejemplos era, desde ese momento, suya por el derecho propio con que el escritor de esos siglos utilizaba el saber tradicional recreándolo al trasmitirlo.
> (Orduna *El exemplo* 125)

*The author as well as his audience or his readership thought it unnecessary and pedantic to determine authorship in that medium and in such romance treatises. They unspokenly agreed that such an immense amount of knowledge and examples were, thenceforth, theirs by the same right that any writer during those centuries used popular knowledge and recreated it by means of transmission.*

The tales that Juan Manuel appropriates for use in his *Conde Lucanor* are quite familiar to the listeners or readers of his tales and those exposed to the text tacitly recognize Juan Manuel as the author of the tales, recreating and transmitting traditional wisdom which, in this case, involves the art of good government, the proper exercise of power.

The frame establishes Patronio as the teller of the exemplary tales to Count Lucanor. The counselor tells these tales to respond to and provide illustrations of Lucanor's petitions for advice in the face of a perceived problem. Patronio appropriates the oral tale and uses it to recreate a fictional parallel to Lucanor's predicament. The tale thus becomes a specific example by reflecting the count's problems, which in turn leads Lucanor to adopt the message of the tale as his normative code of behavior. The format of the oral exchanges between Conde Lucanor and Patronio is the initial frame within which each tale is told.

The oral delivery of each exemplary tale and the hearing of each message are reproduced as written discourse. The oral tradition, employed to elicit an immediate and direct reaction to the predicament of the listener (in fiction, Count Lucanor), becomes significant to Juan Manuel's rhetorical art. The oral petition for advice and the spoken response are private and hence create for the upcoming tale a sense of immediacy and urgency. One function of the fixed framework is relevance. The written account of this same oral exchange however fixes the sense of urgency and immediacy for a different audience (the anonymous group of actual historical noblemen) and thus preserves each tale in the form of a book.

The rhetorical language of Christian virtue cloaks this urgent need for an art of government. The spiritual language of Christian morality is absorbed into the language of practical advice. The powerful Lucanor becomes, metaphorically, a sinner in search of salvation who, facing daily perils to his estate, self, honor and soul, with the help of his experienced counselor, pursues good works and charitable activities designed, as a duty to himself, to help others and, as his duty to God, to save his soul. The need for divine grace to gain worldly goods may be perceived as a corruption of the discourse of practical ends by a discourse of religious means.[29] Readers do not suspect the euphemistic discourse because it appears in straightforward exemplary language, but it highlights the ways in which religious moral conduct in fourteenth-century Castile was defined and understood. More significantly, to perform good works in the form of selfish interest, but simultaneously on behalf of Christianity, legitimized what otherwise would have been sinful. Juan Manuel envelops opportunism in the symbolism of Christian morality, making it possible for readers to transfer the meanings attributed to Christianity to the worldly ends of self-interest and gain. The goal of this disguise is to perpetuate a static societal structure in which the nobility remain rich both economically and in terms of political and spiritual power. In this case the exemplary tale serves as a mechanism or instrument through which a social institution seeks its own preservation.

Let us recall the social state of affairs during the reigns of Alfonso X, Sancho IV, and Alfonso XI. These rulers were faced with a volatile noble faction that wished to rule their holdings as kings, maintain their incomes at monarchical expense, and fought any encroachment by the monarchy on their perceived "rights." Juan Manuel, perhaps the most contentious of all Castilian noblemen, goes so far as to impugn the right of the present line of kings to rule in the *Libro de las armas* (cited above), and expresses the notion that they have no more right to do so than other nobles. In the *Libro de los estados* the character Julio addresses the issue of primogeniture, a fractious issue since the death of Fernando III, and articulates the responsibilities of the eldest son.

> si el enperador quiere fazer bien et aguisado et lo que deue en tal lugar, deue tener a sus hermanos commo a sus fijos...deue saber que commo quier que Dios dio a el la mayoria et quiso que heredase por que nasçio el primero que los otros sus hermanos, *que tan fijos dalgo son commo el, et fijos son de aquel padre et de aquella madre que el*; et que aguisado et razon es que ayan parte, et en que puedan beuir bien et onrada mente, en lo que fue de su padre et de los otros reyes onde vienen.   (I 327-328, my italics)

*Should the emperor wish to do well and in a fair manner as he should, he must think of his brothers as his own children... he should consider that God made him the oldest and wanted him to inherit, as he was the first one to be born, instead of his brothers. Even though they are noblemen as he is and are born from the same father and mother. It is only fair and common sense that they must have a part and that they should live well and honestly from what belonged to his father and other kings before him.*

Since only one son can inherit the crown, the others are left to the generosity of their brother or to fend for themselves. Alfonso X, Sancho IV, and Alfonso XI, were all eldest sons (Alfonso X became eldest due to the death of his elder brother). All were related to Juan Manuel who depended on them to one degree or another for his own inheritance and that of his children. The kings' majority is an accident of birth, and Juan Manuel reminds the reader through the character Julio that royal siblings are as noble as the one who received the crown, and should be accorded an "honor" on a par with the king's own children. Combine these two attitudes expressed in the texts (the exaltation of the manueline line and the condemnation of the alfonsine line), with Juan Manuel's historically verifiable conniving for power (which included arranged marriages, assassination, and outright war), as well as his constant reminders in all his texts of the importance of maintaining honor, and a picture emerges of a nobleman bent on keeping at all cost what he considered his due.

**The Power of Scripting Experience**

The textual evidence of how Juan Manuel communicated specific ideas about governing and maintaining social power is overwhelming. Book One contains fifty tales in which Juan Manuel employs the same dynamic structure for each tale. The first part of the *Conde Lucanor* contains the script of fictitious meetings between Count Lucanor and his counselor Patronio; fifty scripts of unscripted encounters, potential situations, through which the reader learns the problems that face a nobleman, and how those problems are resolved. Here, the term script refers to two conditions: a written text as opposed to an oral text as well as a representation of life, a fictionalized account of a real life situation. The first assumes importance because it fixes a message and the manner in which it was composed and which does not preclude various interpretations of the message, but serves the purpose of linking form and meaning. In the case of *El Conde Lucanor*, fifty myths and tales are fixed in a book within a framework designed to constrain the interpretation of those tales and myths. Juan Manuel adamantly controls transmission and reception as he argues that he is not responsible for errors in copies of his text which may distort or mutate meaning, an oft-discussed problem. According to the nobleman, the only correct text is that which he himself has amended, and it is over the original text that he maintains control. Juan Manuel exhorts his readers to check the original work before passing judgment. What he has written has a specific purpose and a specific form which he himself amended to be sure that what he chose to put in the text was in all ways correct. Juan Manuel added yet another disclaimer: if after reading the corrected text there is a question as to value, the reader should blame the nobleman's lack of wisdom and not blame his intention, a familiar rhetorical topos. In one sentence the nobleman tells the reader to blame Juan Manuel's lack of understanding in the case of faulty content. He records the suggestion as a challenge since in the next sentence God himself knows that the nobleman intends to educate the uneducated. The nobleman does not doubt his own rhetoric or the lessons he means to impart, and in the case of skepticism, his original script and God serve as the authority for form and meaning.

The other condition associated with the script is that of a representation of a life-like situation.

> En esta sçiençia dize Tullio que ha çinco partidas...Trobamiento es un pensamiento de fallar cosas verdaderas o en semejança verdadera, para provar su materia; et este es el çimiento & la firmedunbre desta sçiençia que, ante que onbre nada diga o escriva, deve fallar razones & argumentos para provar sus dichos, por fazer los creer a aquellos con quien fabla.          (*Tesoro* 179)

*Tullio claims this science has five parts... poetry is a way of finding true things or things that seem to be true in order to test their matter. This is the grounding and the foundation of this science; before any man asserts or describes anything, he should find reasons and arguments to prove his arguments in order to convince his audience.*

In order for the rhetoric of Juan Manuel to be effective in communicating advice it must be meaningful in actual daily situations. The script presents situations as if they were spontaneous activity. The narrative structure is complex in its very repetition of performance: Patronio and Lucanor observe the characters in the counselor's tale; the character Don Iohan observes Patronio, Lucanor, and the characters in the tales; the narrator observes the tale, Count, counselor and Don Iohan; and the reader observes them all. While the characters are aware that they observe another character, presentation of the script occurs in such a way as to appear unrehearsed. The scripts seem immediate even though they are delivered in past tense because judgments and observations are made as the tale unfolds. Each observer in the chain is privy to the spontaneous activity of another character, and this activity, presented as genuine, is meaningful precisely because true wisdom comes from experience. Every observer in the chain watches someone else experience a fictional situation presented as veritable. Experience proves the validity of each script.

  An omniscient narrator presents the initial script to the reader and introduces the characters of Count Lucanor and Patronio and establishes a time period in which the second script occurs: "Acaesçio vna vez que el conde Lucanor estaua fablando en su poridat con Patronio, su consegero" (33). The narrator presents minimal temporal information using traditional terms such as "It happened once" or "Once again it happened that." By establishing a general chronology, each fiction is presented as if it were a real historical event. At the same time, until Patronio begins his exemplary tale, the narrator organizes the dialogue between the count and counselor to highlight the cause of the tale-- what troubles Lucanor: "et dixol commo estaua en grant coydado et en grand quexa de vn fecho que queria fazer"(45) and report Patronio's response: "--Sennor conde Lucanor--dixo Patronio--, mucho me plazeria que parasedes mientes a vn exienplo de vna cosa que acaesçio"(45). Within the script in which the count and his counselor are introduced, Lucanor presents to Patronio a sketch of a situation that will affect either the honor, estate or well-being of the count, and then asks for advice on what to do. Don Juan Manuel scripts what Patronio tells: fifty stories in which he proposes a parallel to Count Lucanor's problem. At the close of the short story recounted by Patronio to Count Lucanor, the reader returns to the script in which the counselor draws a conclusion and the master benefits from the lesson. The second script, like the exemplary tale within it, is closed. The omniscient narrator appears again at the end of the second closure to record the results of Patronio's advice, to add Don Juan Manuel's approbation of the lesson and the accompanying verses with which he is credited, and to conclude the overall narrative frame with a pithy line which serves to tie the fifty units of three scripts into a unified whole: "Et la estoria deste exienplo es esta que se sigue" (48). This process is repeated for each of the exemplary tales of Part One and it forms part of Juan Manuel's plan for rhetorically influencing his readers.

In each of the exempla the relations which Juan Manuel elaborated between himself as author and his readers or listeners can be examined. Each tale in the collection serves to give birth to a response, guaranteed in advance by the analogy between the social predicament of the nobleman who listens in the frame story and the fictional situation of the characters in the tale itself.[30] Patronio revises each oral tale he borrows in order to reduce as much as possible its potential discrepancies, to conceal its exemplary gaps, to show its moral coherence and the practical solutions of the message. Each adaptation involves the process of adjustment to new situations. In the language of semiotics, without Patronio nothing exists to unite the signifier to the signified; no inherent symbolic relationship exists between the exemplary tale told by the counselor and the problem faced by the nobleman. Patronio's exemplarity sponsors the oral tale's potential or ideal. The tale is framed to manifest those exemplary conditions of its narrative about which, outside the frame, it is usually neutral or silent.

What has been proposed in this chapter is that the *Conde Lucanor* is a product of fourteenth-century literary theory which holds that form as well as content is meaning. How the text means is outlined specifically in the Prologue to Juan Manuel's work which highlights the importance of the use of the vernacular, the secular nature of the text, the function of exempla and proverbs, and the importance of the characters chosen to motivate the text. With this overview in mind, Chapter Three will explore more closely what Juan Manuel says in his Prologues and highlight two structural keys that inform all aspects of the text, memory and the cardinal virtue of prudence, and show how they function to impart meaning. Both play a key role in the concept and practice of power as well as in the rhetorical means of communicating subtly its importance.

## Notes

[1] Mark Johnson presented a study "Do exempla illustrate everyday life?" at the 1994 MMLA convention in which he warns against taking the quotidian details presented in exempla as verisimilar representations of medieval life.

[2] All references to and citations from any of the manueline works are based on Don Juan Manuel, *Obras Completas*, ed. José Manuel Blecua (Madrid: Gredos, 1983). All citations from *El Conde Lucanor* come from the second tome of the *Obras*.

[3] Several valuable articles that deal with the problems of the move from orality to literacy as well as medieval reliance on allegorisis are found in *Medieval Texts and Contemporary Readers*, Ithaca, Cornell University Press, 1987. The most recent book-length studies on the *Conde Lucanor* by Biglieri and Diz also deal with these issues.

[4] It is interesting to note that Alfonso, by claiming the king to be head and soul of the body politic doesn't leave room for the spiritual leader, the Pope.

[5] Alfonso's son Sancho IV in the *Castigos é documentos* illustrates the virtue of generosity. "así como la parvificencia ó la pequeña facienda abaja ó deshonra mucho á los principes...así la magnificencia é la gran facienda los ensalza é los engrandesce mucho" (180). One of the qualities of magnificence is "que el magnífico debe ser muy sábio, porque sepa cómo ha de repartir sus algos, é cómo ha de facer grandes despensas en grandes obras" (181).

[6] For an overview of this aspect of peninsular history see the historical contributions by R.B. Tate, J.H. Elliott and I. Michael in P.E. Russell's *Spain: A Companion to Spanish Studies* esp. pp 78-94. See also O'Callaghan's *A History of Medieval Spain*.

[7] It is ironic that Sancho, who did not inherit the sword passed down from Fernando to Manuel, would define the importance of a king's sword in his "mirror" written for his son. "En la su mano derecha tiene aquel rey una espada, por la cual se demuestra la justicia en que debe mantener su regno; que así como la espada taja de amas partes, así las justicia debe tajar igualmente á unos é á otros sin toda bandería é sin toda mala cobdicia...Ca el poder del rey todo es en tres cosas...la tercera, la su espada con que apremia á los sus enemigos é con que face justicia á los suyos; ca la espada taja por premia é por justicia las cabezas de los que mal facen" (*Castigos* 111).

[8] Juan Manuel's relationship with Alfonso XI as well as his problematic relationship with Murcia are commonplaces in the corpus of scholarship on Juan Manuel. An article summarizing the topic is Juan Torres Fontes' "Murcia y don Juan Manuel: tensiones y conflictos" found in *Don Juan Manuel: VII Centenario*, pp353-383. An essay highlighting an opposing view (although not associated with Murcia in particular) by Aurelio Pretel Marín can be found in the same book. See also María Celia Ruiz' *Literatura y política: el Libro de los estados y el Libro de las armas de don Juan Manuel* for the bitter relationship between Juan Manuel and Alfonso XI.

[9] Ezequiel González Mas: "De las cinco partes que comprende, sólo la primera y mayor...acusa mérito relevante" (127). de Looze (1995) justifies the limited parameters of his study on the fact that the first Book is "the most important" (342). These are typical views.

[10] Ana Marta Diz' monograph is a notable exception. It examines all the books of the *Conde Lucanor*.

[11] *The Qur'an* in *Sacred Writings* vol. 3, Islam: The *Qur'an* lists The Cow, The Cattle, The Bees, The Spider and The Elephants as chapters.

[12] The period in which Juan Manuel lived and wrote has been by no means ignored by scholars. Joseph F. O'Callaghan's *History of Medieval Spain*, José Antonio Maravall's *El concepto de España en la edad media*, or Americo Castro's *The Structures of Spanish History* are important contributions to any understanding of medieval Spain. Others like Julio Valdeón Baruque, Luciana de Stéfano and R. B. Tate have also dedicated their efforts to historical research.

[13] For a definition of royal and pastoral power I have relied on Michel Foucault's "Afterword" in Hubert L Dreyfus and Paul Rabinow, *Michel Foucault: Beyond Structuralism and Hermeneutics* (Chicago: The University of Chicago Press, 1982). "It is a form of power whose ultimate aim is to assure individual salvation in the next world. 2) Pastoral power is not merely a form of power which commands; it must also be prepared to sacrifice itself for the life and salvation of the flock. Therefore, it is different from royal power, which demands a sacrifice from its subjects to save the throne. 3) It is a form of power which does not look after just the whole community, but each individual in particular, during his entire life. 4) Finally, this form of power cannot be exercised without knowing the inside of people's minds, without exploring their souls, without making them reveal their innermost secrets. It implies a knowledge of conscience and an ability to direct it" (214).

[14] Biglieri attempts a poetics of the didactic tale in his 1989 monograph, however, the focus of the text is on how the text imparts meaning rather than on how it teaches nobiliary codes. Diz' earlier work does the same thing, both scholars employing semiology to illuminate the text. While I draw similar conclusions at times to those they express, the object of the study is radically different. Furthermore, both studies ground themselves in 20th century exegetical theory at the expense of medieval literary theory. This study shows how contemporary medieval literary theory informs Juan Manuel's writings, the methods the nobleman employed to give form to his text, and how that form itself teaches.

[15] An illustration of contemporary theory highlighting the importance of simplicity of understanding is Brunetto Latini's *Li Livres dous Tresor*. This is by no means the only text in which the notion is emphasized but it is a text most probably well known to Juan Manuel. The *Libro del tesoro* and its author were both very well known in Spain. See Baldwin's edition of the *Tesoro*.

[16] The *Castigos é documentos* discusses dicing in detail in Chapter LI. It highlights five particular "sins." "los que juegan á las tablas é á los dados...pecan; é allí pone cuáles son los pecados destos. Es el primero, deseo de ganar lo ajeno. El segundo, voluntad de despojar á su prójimo. El tercero, es usura. El cuarto, mentiras. El quinto, es palabras ociosas é vanas" (179).

[17] Recall the description of the body politic by John of Salisbury and his reference to the diseases that can infect it.

[18] Erich Auerbach provides an informative essay on the movement in "The Western Public and Its Language" in *Literary Language and Its Public in Late Latin Antiquity and in the Middle Ages*, pp. 235-338.

[19] In the *Castigos é documentos*: "E para mientoes al estado que tienes, é despues que veas que eres rey ó emperador, verás é concoerás que tienes logar de Dios; é pues que el su lugar tienes, has á semejar á aquel cuyo logar tienes" (114).

[20] He explicitly attains the rank of *auctor* in the seventeenth-century *Tesoro de la lengua castellana o española* where vocabulary that he employed in the *Conde Lucanor* is cited nine times by Covarrubias. See José Romera Castillo in *Juan Manuel VII Centenario* pp. 313-324.

[21] See Aristotle's *Ethics*, B,2 "all statements concerning matters of *action* should be made sketchily and not with precision, for, as we have said at first, our demands of statements should be in accordance with the subject-matter of those statements; in matters concerning *action* and expediency, as in those of health, there is no uniformity" (22-23).

[22] "These two things seem psychologically opposed to each other, as the desire to ornament is essentially disinterested, and the desire to persuade essentially the reverse....Persuasive rhetoric is applied literature, or the use of literary art to reinforce the power of argument. Ornamental rhetoric acts on its hearers statically, leading them to admire its own beauty or wit; persuasive rhetoric tries to lead them kinetically toward a course of action. One articulates emotion; the other manipulates it" (Frye *Anatomy* 245). There seems to be a vague reference by Northrop Frye to what John of Salisbury articulates in the *Metalogicon* about the types of exempla "Induction advances deliberately from several instances to a universal or particular proposition, or leaps across by inference from one thing introduced by way of example, to another. This method is more suitable for orators, although from time to time the dialectician also employs it for ornamentation or explanation. For it serves more to persuade than to convince. Socrates generally used this kind of argumentation" quoted in Peter Von Moos "The Use of Exempla in the Policraticus" (220-221).

[23] Pertenecer plenamente a un estamento significaba adquirir ... unas determinadas formas de vida, más exigentes cuanto más alto era el estamento o el grado que se ocupaba dentro de él. Estas formas estaban orientadas a la configuración de un *ethos*, y se adquirían mediante una educación destinada, no tanto a la obtención de conocimientos objetivos, como a la formación de una personalidad dotada de un sentimiento aristocrático en el sentido originario de la palabra. (de Stéfano *sociedad estamental* 114)

[24] Francisco Javier Diez de Revenga y María Concepción Ruiz Abellan: "Denominación y títulos de don Juan Manuel", en *Miscelánea Medieval Murciana* VIII, Universidad de Murcia, 1981, pp. 9-30.

[25] See Foucault (*Author* 982), "The author's name serves to characterize a certain mode of being of discourse: the fact that the discourse has an author's name...shows that this discourse is not ordinary everyday speech that merely comes and goes, not something that is immediately consumable. On the contrary, it is a speech that must be received in a certain mode and that, in a given culture, must receive a certain status."

[26] "Aristotilis dixo que por luenga prueva de muchas cosas se faze onbre sabio, et ninguno non puede aver luenga prueva si non por luenga vida. Por que paresçe que onbre mançebo non puede ser sabio, maguer que aya buen engeño para saber." (*Libro del Tesoro* 218).

[27] Manuscript 685 of the National Library in Madrid for example credits Sancho IV with having ordered the translation. While Baldwin notes in his edition of the text that that particular manuscript shows a fifteenth-century hand, there is nothing to suggest that it is not a copy of an original thirteenth-century translation. Latini's work may well have been known by Don Juan Manuel.

28 Estos repertorios de material moralizable, que a las veces sabían trasmutar "a lo divino" relatos nada edificantes por cierto, aunaba en sí leyendas, anécdotas, fábulas...que tuvieron dilatada difusión y fueron frecuentada lectura de clérigos y autores medievales, llegando al conocimiento de los indoctos a través de la exposición oral de las órdenes predicantes.

(Barcia 12)

29 Sancho IV in the *Castigos é documentos* expresses it this way: "Para mientes cuánt bienandante es el home á quien Dios da bienandanza ó buenas andanzas. E muy bienaventurado es el que las bien sabe guardar é mantener. Bienandanza es ganar el home el bien de primero, é mejor andanza es desque lo ha ganado saberlo guardar é mantener que lo non pierda; ca desque lo pierde, asimismo pierde en ello" (174).

30 Biglieri refers to it as '*sentencia* first": "la literatura didáctica parte de una sententia de la que han de depender la estructuración de la significación en el discurso y la presentación y tratamiento de los hechos, personajes y circunstancias espacio-temporales de la historia" (71).

## Chapter 3: Organizational keys to the *Conde Lucanor*

Juan Manuel appropriates for his rhetorical purposes specific rules that governed teaching and learning in the late Middle Ages. In the case of the *Conde Lucanor*, the nobleman recognizes the importance and function of the Prologue with its relationship to the rest of the text. As early as the XII century, Conrad of Hirsau (1070-1150), as translated by Minnis and Scott, had defined "prologue" as...

> a preliminary statement before a discourse. The difference between a prologue and a title is that the title briefly indicates the author and his subject-matter but the prologue makes the reader or listener readily taught, attentive, and well disposed. Every prologue is either apologetic or else commendatory. For the writer either excuses himself, or tries to commend himself [to his readers]. Finally, the title prefaces all books, while the prologue prefaces comic and prose-writers and explains what each work is, why or how it has been written, or how it should be read.
> (Minnis *Medieval Literary Theory* 43)

According to Conrad and as later manifested in Juan Manuel's Prologue to the *Conde Lucanor*, the prologue serves a variety of functions which include preparing readers to be taught, in part by informing them of the purpose of the text and how it should be read. Juan Manuel maximizes his rhetoric of power by preparing the reader to learn the lessons that the book contains, in part through his prologue to the work.

Keep in mind that in medieval pedagogy, learning is equated with memory, and Juan Manuel imparts his rhetoric of power by emphasizing the importance and exercise of memory. The lessons in the *Conde Lucanor* are structured in such a way so as to be made memorable-to facilitate their acquisition

62

through various mnemonics that allow the reader to "gather" the lessons, put them in a "place", and allow them to be recalled easily for future reference.

Juan Manuel is also aware that because his text deals with politics it must be properly rhetorical. The text therefore centers on the virtues and vices (epideictic), most specifically the virtue of Prudence. By adopting the virtue of Prudence as the chief structuring agent and guide for noble behavior, Juan Manuel creates a text designed to teach others how to behave "properly" with the end result that the reader learns how to govern well. Explicit in the notion of "govern well" is first governing oneself and thereby acquiring the ability to govern others. This chapter examines tales, proverbs, and the final book in detail in order to elucidate what it means to know (and therefore govern) oneself and others. It is a way of exposing Juan Manuel's rhetoric of power. (1)

**Aristotelian Causae and the Prologue to the *Conde Lucanor***

The prologues in the literary corpus of Juan Manuel have been given relatively short shrift in terms of scholarship, even though they form a fundamental part of the nobleman's literary art. Brunetto Latini emphasizes the importance of prologues in his *Tesoro* by dedicating some 19 chapters to its proper use.

> Por que prologo es señor & cabdiello de cuento, segund que Tullio dize & lo prueva en su libro, es bien derecho que sobresto oyades algunos enseñamientos...devedes saber que quando quieres bien fazer tu prologo, convienete saber primero tu materia & conosçer la natura del fecho & su manera, & despues adozir enxienplo de aquel que quiere fazer casa, que non corre apresuradamente a labrar, ante la mesura toda & la eguala en su coraçon, et conprende en su memoria todo el ordenamiento & la figura de la casa. (187)

*According to what Tullio says and proves in his book, the preface is the lord and the knight of the book. It would be good for you to hear some teaching about this... you must know if you wish to write a nice preface that, first, you need to know the subject matter, its nature and its ways. Second, you need to present the example-plan from which you want build your house. You do not need to elaborate hurriedly according to the measure and figure of the house.*

The prologue is the lord and head of the story. The author, like a builder, must know his material, and how it is to be used. The prologue serves as the blue-print for the text-as-house. It shows the reader what the text will contain, as well as how and why the author/builder plans to erect his house. The Prologue of the *Conde Lucanor* does just as Latini describes. It is written in first person by Don Juan Manuel, and it is apparent that the author was aware either directly or indirectly of the contemporary method of literary exegesis, the *accessus*, which employed the use of the Aristotelian causes. Juan Manuel was educated in Sancho IV's court, knew Latin, and would therefore fit Minnis' description of those with at least a grammar-school familiarity with that language: "Anyone with any education at all...would have been familiar with the standard method of analysing the intentions, objectives, styles and literary structures of authoritative writers, the *auctores*" (Minnis 'Moral Gower' 50). Juan Manuel includes the information that such exegesis would require to explicate the work and prepare the reader for what is to come: a rhetorical treatise on the proper maintenance of power. The four Aristotelian causes accomplish this through a four-step revelation: the *material* cause which describes the materials employed; the *formal* cause, in which the style and structure of the text are elucidated; the *efficient* cause which pertains to the author; and the *final* cause or the objective in writing. Juan Manuel does not use these terms in the prologues. Nor does he employ these *causae* in any particular order. However, the four causes are there and are well defined. The information that they provide is of paramount importance for a reading of the medieval text because they prepare the reader for the text and the lessons, the first of which, already revealed in the Prologue itself, is the correct exercise of power.

## The efficient cause

The author of the *Conde Lucanor* begins with a prayer "En el nonbre de Dios: amen," which is at the same time tacit recognition of the first efficient cause: God. God is the prime moving cause who is responsible for the existence of men and all their incredible differences.[1] The author of the text amplifies these differences to include the variety of means to serve God and he notes that all of the means that exist to serve have one thing in common: that men are motivated to use, desire and learn those things which are satisfying to them and ignore those which are not. "...todos se semejan en tanto que todos vsan et quieren et aprenden mejor aquellas cosas de que se mas pagan que las otras" (I 27). Recognizing the fact that man uses, desires and learns best those things which are most satisfying, the author names himself as the second, instrumental efficient cause, moved by God to serve him and edify others by writing a book: "Por ende, yo, don Iohan, fijo del infante don Manuel, adelantado mayor de la frontera et del regno de Murçia, fiz este libro..." (28). The efficient cause (Juan Manuel) constructs a thing in accordance with its end. For this reason, a work of art (in this case the *Conde Lucanor*) is beautiful if it is functional, if its form is adequate to its scope.[2] In the text, the *palabras* are *apuestas* because they are useful (28). The notion of the *duplex causae* lends substance and provides structure to the rhetorician's 'modesty formulas.' It also underscores the importance of the text to the reader: one that was created through the motivation of God with the intention of teaching the reader valuable lessons on how to properly maintain and exercise power.

The Prologue to the second book adds a third efficient cause which Juan Manuel places between himself, the instrumental cause, and the first moving cause which is God. The third author of the text is Don Jayme of Xérica who moved Juan Manuel to write the second through fifth parts in a manner that would be more beneficial to those who have a more profound ability to understand and who, because they are so *sotil*, find ideas expressed simply as evidence of a lack of wisdom.[3] Whereas in the Prologue to Part I Juan Manuel defers any accusation of fault that may be found in the text until the original is examined for errors, allowing for the possibility of an error of his understanding but not of his intention, in the second and continuing parts, fault, if found, is to be placed either on a friend of Juan Manuel's, Don Jayme de Xérica, who moved the author to write the book, or on the reader himself who is not sufficiently capable of understanding the material contained within.

> et los que non las entendieren non pongan la culpa a mi, ca yo non lo queria fazer sinon commo fiz los otros libros, mas pongan la a don Jayme, que me lo fizo assi fazer, et a ellos, por que lo non pueden o non quieren entender. (441)

*Those of you who did not understand it should not blame me. I only wanted to do it according to the other books. Blame don Jayme, who made me do it as such, and blame yourselves, because you could not or did not want to understand.*

Those ignorant people who cannot or do not want to understand what is written are dangerous and should be avoided.

> non te pagues nin quieras en tu compañía home nescio, que en todo el mundo non ha tan mal home como el nescio. E el que fuere nescio, cuidando en su corazon que face bien, fará aína una grand traicion, por la cual te fará perder el cuerpo é cuanto hobieres, é terná que face en ello lo mejor, é non sabrá della guardar á tí nin á sí mesmo, é terná que la traicion es lealtad, é non conoce su yerro ante que lo faga, nin lo entiende despues que lo ha fecho.
> (*Castigos é documentos* 166)

*Do not want an ignorant man as your company, because there is not a man more dangerous than an ignorant man. An ignorant man, thinking that he is doing you good, will betray you immensely; he will make you lose your body and anything you may possess. He will be thinking that he is doing the best, therefore, will not protect you or even himself and will believe this treason to be loyalty. He will not understand his mistake before or even after making it.*

The author of the *Conde Lucanor* claims that except for Don Jayme's petition he would have written the following book like the others he has written: in language easily understood. Unlike the other books, this one is comprised of difficult words that only those with superior understanding will be able to decipher. Like the first part, Parts II, III, IV and V are written with the help of God's grace, and through his mercy and pity, will be beneficial to those who know how to read them. The words used in his book are elements of the material cause.

## The material cause

Juan Manuel moves from the efficient to the material cause by saying that his book is composed of elegant words into which are mixed some exemplary tales "...conpuesto de las mas apuestas palabras que yo pude, et entre las palabras entremeti algunos exienplos..." (28). What is implicit in this statement is stated boldly in the General Introduction to the work: Juan Manuel is cognizant of his dual role in the creation of his book. He is at once compiler and author. In the General Introduction the narrator, exhorting the reader who may question what is found in the text at hand to first read the original before passing judgment, defines which books he is describing: "...ruega a los que leyeren qual quier libro que fuere trasladado del que el *conpuso*, o de los libros que el *fizo*..." (23, my italics). *Componer* is not just another way to say "write", it means "to compile" and in the later Middle Ages there is a difference between a compiler and an author. Juan Manuel is aware of the difference, shown by his invective against copyists, similar to that by Vincent of Beauvais or Chaucer, in which the narrator cites the problems that come with untrustworthy copies (Minnis *Authorship* 202-203).[4] The preoccupation with the original text placed, according to the narrator, in the monastery at Peñafiel mirrors current fourteenth-century literary trends to work from or cite the uncorrupted work (as opposed to the collections and compilations so popular at the time) and points to a consideration on the part of Juan Manuel of himself as *auctor* and his text as *auctoritas*. The power inherent in an *auctor* when determining truth was considerable. If Juan Manuel were to achieve authorial status, his rhetoric of power as articulated in the *Conde Lucanor* would by nature of its status as *auctoritas*, also be endowed with the weight of truth ceding it great power indeed. Many scholars have noted the absence of authorial citations in Juan Manuel's texts. María Rosa Lida de Malkiel shows that even when the nobleman does cite others, he often confuses author and text. When Juan Manuel has his own words included in the text, it is so noted and the notation becomes part of the formulaic frame of the exemplary tales, repeated fifty times. This so-called scholarly "laziness" on the part of Juan Manuel is not unique to him nor would he have considered it a deficiency.[5] Both means and ends in the text are geared to the same rhetorical end: the exercise of power. Juan Manuel makes this clear in the Prologue by telling the reader why he has written his book.

## The final cause

The nobleman identifies his objective in writing or the final cause as the edification of his reading audience: "...de que se podrian aprouechar los que los oyeren" (28). His objective is followed by the formal cause or a metaphorical definition of style and structure: "Et esto fiz segund la manera que fazen los fisicos..." (28). It is significant that Juan Manuel employs the "spoonful of sugar" metaphor, analogous to what Glending Olson calls the "hygienic" or "therapeutic" justification for pleasurable literature, to describe how his text will teach through elegant words and pleasing tales, and, reiterating the final cause, that those who read the text will learn from it, some because they understand the meaning of the tales and others who are moved by the elegant words and sweet tales. The nobleman is aware of the interrelationship between pleasure and profit or work and play; both have a function in the learning process, a commonplace in medieval literary criticism found, for example, in Horace's *Ars poetica* and Aristotle's *Ethics*. Horace's view was perhaps more influential than that of Aristotle, and his views comprised one of the best known medieval commonplaces adopted by Juan Manuel.

> aut prodesse volunt aut delectare poetae, aut simul et iucunda et idonea dicere vitae. quidquid praecipies esto brevis, ut cito dicta percipiant animi dociles teneantque fideles: omne supervacuum pleno de pectore manat. (*Ars* 35)

*The poet's aim is either to profit or to please, or to blend in one the delightful and the useful. Whatever the lesson you would convey, be brief, that your hearers may catch quickly what is said and faithfully retain it. Every superfluous word is spilled from the too-full memory.*

Horace poses three literary intentions...profit, pleasure, and the combination of the two, elevating the third as does Juan Manuel. He adds the benefits of *brevitas*, a short pithy lesson that aids comprehension and retention, making it possible for the reader to learn the lesson well. Aristotle notes the benefits of such a combination.[6]

> to amuse oneself for the sake of serious work seems, as Anarchasis put it, to be right; for amusement is like relaxation, and we need relaxation since we cannot keep on working hard continuously. Thus amusement is not the end, for it is chosen for the sake of serious activity. (K 6, 33-37)

Those who read the tales as a source of amusement or recreation will be moved to act, or learn, because play causes joy, not in its relation to its entertainment value but in relation to the virtuous activity that it inspires. The virtuous activity in which Juan Manuel indulges through the writing of the *Conde Lucanor* is a manifestation of his stated intention in the Prologue.

Juan Manuel addresses the question of authorial intention and based upon his *duplex causae* with God as the first efficient cause, denies responsibility for what is found to be wanting in the text, although he accepts his humanity and the possibility of human error: "Et lo que y fallaren que non es tan bien dicho, non pongan la culpa a la mi entençion, mas pongan la a la mengua del mio entendimiento" (28). Juan Manuel places the emphasis here on intention and he shows an awareness of contemporary moral philosophy which holds that intention is the beginning of the complete act, in this case the writing of his book, and if the intention is good, then the complete act is good.[7] Juan Manuel indicates that there is only one way to read the text and that is to look for the good and abhor the evil. God: "es aquel por quien todos los buenos dichos et fechos se dizen et se fazen" (28). There is a similar denial of authorial responsibility in the General Introduction: "...que si fallaren alguna palabra mal puesta, que non pongan la culpa a el, fasta que bean el libro mismo que don Iohan fizo, que es emendado en muchos logares, de su letra" (23). This disavowal of responsibility without checking the original lies side by side with what is a tacit claim of *auctoritas*; it is an authority that lies outside of the Church and within the secular realm as will be seen.

**The formal cause**

In an explanation of style (*forma tractandi*) and structure (*forma tractatus*), Juan Manuel's use of exemplary tales has definite implications for the reception of his rhetoric of power. By choosing examples and proverbs, Juan Manuel employs the *modus parabolicus* which treats of the historical sense of things to the extent that in speaking of history, one can refer either to real things, as in historical events, or to the similitudes of things as in examples (Minnis *Authorship* 131). This harks back to the Augustinian notion of words as signs and the fact that words may signify literally or figuratively. By using examples, Juan Manuel lets his readers know that there are various ways of reading the text, and that care must be taken in extracting the message. That this is so is manifested by the use of the frame tales and the summary verses that Juan Manuel employs to control (as much as possible) the interpretation of the text. While Juan Manuel insists that he will speak openly, he chooses one of the methods judged least amenable to such simple interpretation.

Fulfilling the nature of the *forma tractatus*, Juan Manuel tells his reader how the text will be organized. The text is divided into three parts: it is dedicated to the service of God, the salvation of the soul, and to the health of the body of the reader.

> Et Dios, que es conplido et conplidor de todos los buenos fechos, por la su merçed et por la su piadat, quiera que los que este libro leyeren, que se aprouechen del a seruicio de Dios et para saluamiento de sus almas et aprouechamiento de sus cuerpos; asi commo el sabe que yo, don Iohan, lo digo a essa entencion.
> (28)

*God, who is the doer of all good deeds, may for his favor and his mercy, want those who read this book to benefit from the doings of God, this may be saving their souls and benefiting their bodies. The same way he knows I, don Iohan, say it with that intention.*

The emphasis in the Prologue is placed on spiritual advantage and the physical is subordinated (in the General Introduction to the text the *Conde Lucanor* is divided into four constituent parts with the first three emphasizing the physical and the fourth the spiritual). Juan Manuel takes a page from Aquinas' commentary on the *Ethica* where St. Thomas describes literary *ordinatio* as the disposition and arrangement of material to an end or objective (6).

### The question of "order" in the *Conde Lucanor*

Much scholarly criticism of the *Conde Lucanor* has focused on the problem of order in the text: that the various extant manuscripts do not all follow the same numerical order of exempla, the question of the exact number of exempla that the text contains, the problem of the summary line in Book One "Et la estoria deste exienplo es esta que se sigue," and the problematic relationship between the proverbs in the succeeding books. The author himself is tremendously preoccupied with the question of order and he emphasizes this by including a table of contents, the division of the text into five different books or parts, a careful count and articulation of the numbers of tales and proverbs that he has included within the various books, and within the enigmatic fourth book itself where the order of the proverbs is intrasententially rearranged. Juan Manuel is a typical medieval writer preoccupied with organization because "...before *collectio* or ratiocination could take place, one had to engage in *definitio* and *divisio*: Only then could conclusions follow logically from propositions, and points of doctrine be proved or disproved" (Minnis *Authorship* 146). While Minnis is discussing Scriptural exegesis in particular, the order of the parts emphasized by Don Juan Manuel is inextricably related to the order of the whole text, to the objective intended by the author of the *Conde Lucanor*. In other words, any reading that does not take into consideration the order of the parts or that focuses on one or another part (tale, verse, proverb or book) at the expense of the text as a whole is necessarily incomplete.[8]

Juan Manuel's preoccupation with order has to do with the didactic function of the text. Teaching and the division of knowledge into parts in order to make the text more accessible go hand in hand. Therefore the practice of division and the function of memory cannot be ignored.[9] According to the late medieval ethical poetic elucidated by Judson Allen, a literary work belongs to the branch of philosophy that treats of ethics; within the process of construction and *memoria* is praxis, which as will be seen, is equivalent to the medieval conception of prudence.[10] Juan Manuel emphasized his desire to make his text accessible to an unlearned (not knowledgeable in Latin), diverse audience, and the breakdown of the text into digestible chunks, to borrow from his metaphor, helps fulfill this desire. He says in the Prologue to the *Libro Enfenido*: "Et por que sea mas ligero de entender et estudiar es fecho a capitulos" (I 148). There is an implied relationship between division by chapter and one's ability to understand as well as to facilitate study. The relationship is expanded in the first part of the *Libro de los estados* to include the relation of chapters to books: "...et es puesto en dos libros: el primer libro fabla de los estados de los legos et el segundo fabla de los estados de los clerigos. Et [en] el primer[o] ha çient capitulos, et en el segundo..." (I 195).[11] He goes on to name all the chapters in each of the books. In the *Conde Lucanor* the division of his text into parts is reiterated in the prologues to the various books, such as in the *Razonamiento* of the fourth book:

> trabaje de vos dezir algunas cosas mas de las que vos avia dicho en los enxienplos que vos dixe en la primera parte deste libro en que ha çinquenta enxienplos que son muy llanos et muy declarados; et pues en la segunda parte ha çient prouerbios et algunos fueron ya quanto oscuros et los mas, assaz declarados; et en esta terçera parte puse çinquenta prouerbios, et son mas oscuros que los primeros çinquenta enxienplos, nin los çient prouerbios. Et assi, con los enxienplos et con los prouerbios, he vos puesto en este libro dozientos entre prouerbios et enxienplos... (461)

*I attempted to say a few more things, other than those I already discussed in the examples presented in the first part of this book, which contains fifty simple and clear examples. I included 100 proverbs in this second part; some were very difficult and others easily understood. In the 3rd part I added 50 proverbs and these are more difficult than the fifty examples and the hundred proverbs. Thus, I have included two hundred proverbs and examples altogether in this book...*

Juan Manuel writes his book based on certain foundations: it is divided into parts and the parts contain different numbers of items of increasing difficulty; it is divided so as to make the text more accessible. He creates an architecture to enable understanding, to facilitate study, to enable the reader to remember what has been written. If his rhetoric of power is to succeed, it must move the reader to act, and action can only come if the reader understands and remembers the lessons.

It is apparent from an examination of the prologues of Don Juan Manuel's books that the author is aware of a need to organize his material, and divide it into accessible and definable units. This need finds its genesis in the desire to teach the reader how to exercise power correctly. Juan Manuel teaches in part by modeling correct behavior which in the *Conde Lucanor* is to understand the lessons and act on them. To date, and as has already been shown, many scholars have debated Juan Manuel's ability to count correctly rather than examine the function of Juan Manuel's division of the text.

**The function of Memory**

Mary Carruthers in *The Book of Memory* sheds light on Juan Manuel's practice of dividing his texts into units and the emphasis he places on specifying the numbers of elements in the texts.[12] As María Rosa Lida de Malkiel has demonstrated, Juan Manuel was heavily influenced by the Dominicans. It is his structuring of his texts that shows him to be most influenced by the Order of Preachers who were influential in the creation and proliferation of writing tools as well as the dissemination of the architectural mnemonic (citing by book, chapter number, and number or letter) (Carruthers 100-101).

> reading and memorizing were taught as they were in antiquity, as one single activity, and further, that the monastic understanding of what one does in reading...not only persisted but became part of general culture in the thirteenth, fourteenth, and later centuries, for reasons that had as much to do with the moral value of *memoria* in meditation and prayer as with its utility. (Carruthers 101)

The notion that Juan Manuel sees reading and the exercise of the memory as a single activity is reflected in the line from the Prologue to the *Libro Enfenido* in which he justifies the division of the text so as to facilitate understanding and study. "Et por que sea mas ligero de entender et estudiar es fecho a capitulos" (I 148). The book is divided into chapters with the purpose of making understanding and study of the text easier.

### The three levels of Hermeneutic Dialogue

In the first book, the collection of exemplary tales, various mnemonics are employed by Juan Manuel to enable understanding: the use of dialogue, the exemplary tale itself and Juan Manuel's summary verses. The use of dialogue and the exemplary tale are inextricably linked. Carruthers defines medieval reading as a "'hermeneutical dialogue' between two memories, that in the text being made very much present as it is familiarized to that of the reader" (*Book* 169). In the *Conde Lucanor*, this dialogue occurs on the following three different levels. In response to a petition for advice from his lord, Count Lucanor, Patronio illuminates the Count's problem by telling a story.

> se que mi consejo que vos faze muy pequenna mengua; mas pues lo queredes, dezir vos he lo que ende entiendo. Sennor conde Lucanor -dixo Patronio-, mucho me plazeria que parasedes mientes a vn exienplo de vna cosa que acaesçio vna vegada a vn omne bueno con su fijo. (45)

*I know you are in very little need of my advice, but, since you want it, I will give it to you. Sir count Lucanor --said Patronio--I would like you to pay attention to an example of an event that happened to a good man with his son.*

As a response to Count Lucanor's petition for advice, Patronio says that he will tell him what he understands of the situation. He does this by recounting a story which serves to create parallel or analogous situations. These stories are *florilegia*, extracts and maxims from the past, the contents of the fictional Patronio's memory, and are presented as a guide to aid in the formation of Count Lucanor's memory; they are commonplaces, tales told from the pulpit, or recounted by the fire, not original or unique to the teller, but already established and in use. The tales enjoy a certain acceptance, and they were comfortable because they were known; they are the norm, presented by Patronio not to normalize an occasion, but to "occasionalize a norm" (Carruthers 181). The importance of using relevant, familiar exempla is the subject of some discussion in John of Salisbury's *Metalogicon*.[13]

> When examples are adduced to prove something..."they should be relevant, and drawn from things with which we are well acquainted"...If examples are taken from the [classical] authors, a Greek should quote Homer, a Latin, Vergil and Lucan. Familiar examples have greater cogency, whereas strange ones lend no conviction concerning what is doubtful. (*Metalogicon* 193)

John highlights relevancy and familiarity as key ingredients of the exemplum used to prove a point. The relevancy of the exempla are made apparent through Patronio's framing of the tale, their familiarity is reflected especially in such tales as XIV, XV, XVI, XVIII, XXVII, XXVIII, XXX, XXXIII, XXXVII, XLI, and XLIV which all feature either Spanish heroes or Arab kings (one of Córdoba and one of Seville). In other words, Patronio's telling re-presents the tales, elements of public memory, and makes them signify in a particular situation thus providing the counselor with a means to describe Lucanor's problem (through Patronio's memory) in the present. This re-presentation of a tale is also a demonstration of Patronio's ethical nature in that he takes a tale from another time and place and makes it mean in a new situation. He has made the material his own. Lucanor likewise makes the material his own by following the advice and profiting from it. "El conde touo por buen consejo lo que Patronio le consejaua. El fizo lo assi, et fallose ende bien" (48). Patronio's counsel is not contained exclusively in the tale, he summarizes the tale and tells the Count what he believes is the proper course of action, but the advice is made memorable through the exemplary tale. Juan Manuel makes the material his own by re-writing it in verse form, (answering the critics who condemn him for misreading the tale).

Within the fiction, this "hermeneutic dialogue" takes place not only between Patronio and Count Lucanor but also between them and Don Iohan, who after hearing the tale framed in its circumstances, writes a verse to summarize what the story means to him, thereby interpreting Patronio's memorial tale and making it his own. "Et quando don Iohan fallo este exiemplo, mandolo escriuir en este libro, et fizo estos viessos en que esta avreuiada mente toda la sentençia deste exienplo" (48).[14] This step in the memorial chain is fundamental.

> Lay hold upon the source and you have the whole thing. I say this because the memory of man is dull and likes brevity, and, if it is dissipated upon many things, it has less to bestow upon each of them. We ought, therefore, in all that we learn, to gather brief and dependable abstracts to be stored in the little chest of the memory, so that later on, when need arises, we can derive everything else from them. (*Didascalicon* 94)

Because men's memories are not efficient they rely upon brief summary statements to recall a particular lesson. The ability to get to the pith of the lesson through synthesis is to show that the lesson is truly understood. Don Iohan understands what has been said and synthesizes the information in a short verse that contains the sense of the tale. In the *Conde Lucanor* Patronio, Lucanor, and Don Iohan focus on the example, Lucanor and Iohan in particular act in imitation of it, and they both internalize the imitation, transforming it, making it their own (Patronio, in applying the story to the situation has already done the same); Lucanor through his fictional action on the advice and Don Iohan by rewriting the tale through his verse. They all provide a model for the outside reader for they have read completely, properly. This hermeneutic dialogue also occurs between the three characters in the text and the reader outside of it. The reader, encouraged by the appropriation of the memory by the fictional count and Don Iohan, is engaged to do likewise, to train and form his memory with the result that Juan Manuel prevails in his intention. The moral lesson is reiterated by the lord and his counselor, repeated in the maxims of Don Iohan, and reiterated again as the reader ingests each of the fifty tales and their frames. At each level, memory is re-presented and interpreted because the medieval mind conceived of "knowledge as a collection of truths...expressed not singly but 'copiously'" (Carruthers 26). Patronio's rhetoric succeeds in persuading when the reader, following the model established by the ideal reader Count Lucanor, receives his memories and makes them his own.

**Memoria ad res**

Consonant with the importance of division and the breaking down of information into chunks is the concept of *memoria ad res*, memory of generalized content as opposed to word-for-word memory (Carruthers 91). Juan Manuel incorporates this into the text through himself as character. After the presentation of the problem, its illustration and solution through story, and its "actual" fictional solution, Don Iohan decides that the story is good, has it included in his book and writes summary verses.

> et fizo estos viessos en que esta avreuiada mente toda la sentençia deste exienplo. Et los viessos dizen asi:
> > *Por dicho de las gentes,*
> > *sol que non sea mal, al pro*
> > *tenet las mientes,*
> > *et non fagades al.* (48)

*and composed these verses in which the core of this example is abbreviated. These verses go as follows:*
> > *According to what people say,*
> > *as long as the sun is not bad,*
> > *it does good to the mind,*
> > *and does it no harm.*

The verses that Don Iohan includes in the text abbreviate the frame and tale just told, but they retain the entire lesson; they break down the larger frame and story unit into a manageable whole. Alan Deyermond has erroneously pointed out that these verses written by Juan Manuel are less than worthy of the nobleman's art, they are poor verses. Such evaluative critiques ignore their function in the text.[15] They are not meant to serve as elegant poetry, their function is as a hook that the reader can use to remember the story and thereby the lesson of the tale, and to that end, they obtain.

**Illumination as memorial mnemonic**

There is one more link in the memorial chain constructed by Don Juan Manuel in the collection of exemplary tales: the enigmatic "Et la estoria deste exienplo es esta que se sigue" that joins all fifty tales to one another. Scholars have debated the meaning of the lines and seem to have settled on José Manuel Blecua's hypothesis that they introduced an accompanying illumination that, along with the original text, has been lost to us.[16] The hypothesis of emblems or visuals is appealing from a point of view that privileges the relationship between reading and memory. Along with the other mnemonics already suggested, the use of an illumination would have served as an additional cue on which the reader could draw to place the tale in his memory.

> "Representation"... was understood not in an objective or reproductive sense as often as in a temporal one; signs make something present to the mind by acting on memory. Just as letters, *litterae*, make present the voices (*voces*) and ideas (*res*) of those who are not in fact present, so pictures serve as present signs or cues of those same *voces* and *res*. (Carruthers 221-222)

Understood in this manner, the supposed lost illuminations would have functioned not as imitations of what was written, but as emblematic texts themselves. The "*estoria* deste exienplo" hypothesized by Blecua would have functioned as written text, recalling the past to memory, not as something analogous, the same as the written text but in a different format, but as original text that would have communicated to those unable to read the written text.

**Brevitas**

The succeeding books, the collections of proverbs and the fifth part, do not offer the probability of illuminations (Manuscript "S" contains one blank page between each exemplary tale, supporting Blecua's hypothesis), but they do contain the other elements of memory already discussed: division and composition and emphasize a third, *brevitas*. Whereas Don Iohan judges the stories in the first book worthy of inclusion in his text and structures this addition by writing a verse to summarize them, the nobleman does not enter into the succeeding books. Nevertheless, the verse activity used to inspire memory continues, and they are the verses that Patronio recollects and proffers to train the memory of his lord. The value of the refrains that Patronio articulates is not less than that inherent in the tales, but is in fact, greater.

> Et commo quier que en esto que vos he dicho en este libro ay menos palabras que en el otro, sabet que non es menos el aprouechamiento et el entendimiento deste que del otro, *ante es muy mayor* para quien lo estudiare et lo entendiere.
> 
> (453, my italics)

*The things I have told you in this book contain fewer words than the previous book. However, know that the benefit and understanding of this book is no lesser than the other book's. Those who study and understand the second book will benefit more than they would by studying and understanding the first one.*

Refrains are greater in value than the *exempla* due to the authority granted a proverb or maxim (generally accepted as true as well as having the effect of a command as will be seen in Chapter 4). Patronio has distilled his advice into the maxims that he presents to the Count, each one worthy of recollection, imitating Don Iohan in the first book. He has divided his memories into smaller and briefer but pithier pieces and re-presented them in a given order. Scholars have noted a tendency to group the maxims into units that share some common theme: *seso* or *fazer* or *obrar*, although apart from that general tendency no specific order or rationale for the linear presentation of the proverbs has been discovered, and as Patronio says in one of his maxims, "Qui ha de fablar de muchas cosas ayuntadas es commo el que desbuelve grand oviello que ha muchos cabos" (455). Whoever talks about many things raveled together is like one who unravels a huge ball of thread comprised of many pieces. Despite the apparent lack of a direct notional/ideological/thematic relationship between each refrain, they do, nevertheless, all fit together, tied end-to-end by Patronio to create a cogent whole. Patronio in parts II, III, and IV, presents the unraveled pieces of his memory leaving it for Lucanor and the reader to weave their own tapestry from his memories. Patronio tells Count Lucanor how to put the sayings into his own memory by reminding the Count of the numbers of items he has supplied in each book thus providing him with a numerical schemata in which he can store the bits of information for later recollection.

The fifth part of the *Conde Lucanor* is a departure from the previous four sections in which Count Lucanor initiates the telling of tales or the reciting of proverbs with a petition for advice (Part I), or that Patronio tell him more so that he may learn (Parts II, III, IV). The first book contains the active participation of three fictional characters, Count Lucanor, Patronio and Don Iohan. Patronio and Lucanor participate in the second through fourth books, but in the fifth book there is only Patronio (although he addresses himself to Count Lucanor).

The fifth book of the *Conde Lucanor* is an extended narrative on the part of the character Patronio in which he highlights the importance of doing good works. The structure of the text is interesting when compared to the previous books because it is most similar to medieval disquisitional or exegetical texts and less like the florilegia or exemplum collections. Nowhere in the previous four books are what may be considered "traditional" types of division employed, in this case, division by four.

et estas buenas obras para guardar las almas et guisar que vayan a
Parayso ha mester y estas quatro cosas: la primera, que aya omne
et biua en ley de saluaçion; la segunda, que desque es en tienpo
para lo entender, que crea toda su ley et todos sus articulos et que
non dubde en ninguna cosa dello; la terçera que faga buenas obras
et a buena entençion por que gane el Parayso; la quarta, que se
guarde de fazer malas obras por que sea guardada la su alma de yr
al Infierno. (469)

*And these good acts performed to save souls and ensure they go to paradise need to fulfill these four conditions: first, there needs to be a man who lives a life that deserves salvation; second, he must have the time to understand this; third, he must do good acts and have good intentions so he can earn paradise; forth, he must keep himself from wrongdoing so that he will avoid having his soul being sent to hell.*

The topic is divided into four parts which, after their division, are defined and then subdivided in the same manner as in a typical medieval sermon, for example. This offers the reader a model for storage of information in the memory (Patronio as ideal orator), a means of following the discourse (organizational skill of the rhetor) as well as breaking up the material into pieces that can be stored in one's memory (outside the text, the practical application of the fiction). Although the narrative structure of the fifth book is unlike that of the others, it still follows the model proposed for all: a text designed to facilitate learning of which memory is an integral, fundamental structuring agent.

**Virtue and the *De regimine principum* of Giles of Rome**

The *Conde Lucanor* treats of moral behavior, and memory in the Middle Ages is identified with the formation of moral virtues (Carruthers 156). Moral virtues and their relationship to the education of princes in the subject of Giles of Rome's *De regimine principum* as it is that of the *Conde Lucanor*.

In Chapter IV of the *Libro Enfenido*, Juan Manuel, addressing his son, cites Giles of Rome and his book *De regimine principum* as a repository of the characteristics of good kings and tyrants:

> Et si quisieredes saber quales son las maneras et las costumbres de los buenos reys et las maneras [et las costumbres] de los tirannos, et que deferençia ha entre ellos, fallar lo hedes en el libro que fitzo fray Gil, de la orden de sant Agostin, que llaman *De regimine principum,* que quiere dezir *Del gouernamiento de los principes.*
> (I 159)

*If you wish to know good kings' ways as well as practices and tyrants' ways and practices, and the differences among them, you should find it in the book written by Brother Gil, from the Saint Augustine order. The book is called De regime principum, which means On government by princes.*

The manners and customs of a good king and those of the antithesis, a tyrant (the correct and incorrect uses of power), in *De regimine* are organized around the celebration and acquisition of the cardinal virtues and the avoidance of vice. The first part of Giles' text serves to describe the benefits and importance of self government, that which should be avoided by the good king (vice), and the importance of doing good works.

Men are endowed with certain degrees of *Understanding*, one of the powers of the soul which links Man with God through similitude. "Otros poderíos hay muy altos e muy nobles, en los cuales semeja el omme a Dios e a los ángeles, como son el entendimiento e el apetito intelectivo que llamamos voluntad" (*Glosa* 72).[17] In order for Understanding to work properly, it must be able to use components that pertain to it, such as wisdom, science and prudence.[18] The degree to which an individual is prudent, versed in the sciences (human knowledge), and wise will, in turn, determine his degree of understanding. Since all men are endowed with understanding to one degree or another, one's happiness (*bienandanza*) is not determined by his possession of the powers of the Soul nor virtuousness; it is determined by (virtuous) works (*obrar*).[19]

There are two types of *bienandanza*: civil/political and contemplative/celestial. The individual must place this *bienandanza* in virtuous acts. In the case of political life, virtuous acts pertain to prudence and in the case of contemplative life, virtuous acts pertain to wisdom. He who knows how to govern himself and others prudently is successful is this life, and in the next if he is wise enough to contemplate God and keep his commandments.

## The function of Prudence

Giles introduces the main structuring unit of the text, a life ruled by the virtue of Prudence: "...aquel es bienandante en este mundo que sabe bien governar a sí e a los otros, según la virtud de prudencia" (*Glosa* 61). Wisdom and understanding, the defining characteristics of a good governor, are concomitant with prudence.

The second part of the first book defines the virtues and their function in relation to one another. After discussing Prudence, Justice, Fortitude and Temperance, Giles places them in a hierarchy where chief among them is Prudence. "E por ende conviene dar una virtud principal que nos muestre facer buenas razones de todas nuestras obras, cual es la prudencia" (*Glosa* 87).[20] According to Giles, Prudence is a unique virtue in that it is practical and mediates between the speculative and moral intellect which together comprise *Understanding*; all other virtues are subject to Prudence.[21] This is because Prudence guides the other virtues "e a ésta pertenesce consejar e ensennar lo que las otras tres han de facer, ca el consejo ha de venir antes de la obra" (*Glosa* 89). Echoing notions held from antiquity, Giles privileges Prudence because one must look before he leaps.

## Advice and action as they relate to prudence

Implicit in the notion of looking before leaping are the elements of *consejar*, (to advise) and *obrar*. The two elements are related in that one must have knowledge (understanding) of consequences in order to counsel wisely, and the logical conclusion to advice is action. In addition, to counsel is to act.

> Ca más facen los que dan buenos consejos en todos los fechos que los otros, ca son semejantes a los governadores de la nave, que con pequenno governalle salvan a todos los otros. *(Glosa* 105)

*Those who give good advice do more good in all areas than others who do jobs like the captain of a ship. These captains save other people with just an order.*

Those who give good advice do more good than others. According to Giles they are like ship's pilots who, by providing some direction in a storm, save all those on board. Providing direction on how to behave properly, that is, counseling and performing good works, as components of Prudence the structuring agent of the *De regimine* and the *Conde Lucanor*, is manifested in every aspect of Juan Manuel's collection of tales and proverbs.

In the Prologue to the collection of tales, Juan Manuel uses the topos of text-as-medicine, placing himself in a position of one-up; he is the doctor to the reader-as-patient. In other words, he has the necessary knowledge or understanding (informed by prudence) to be able to perform an accurate "diagnosis" and thus counsel those who will read his book (who necessarily lack his knowledge). The act of writing his books is a measure of his prudence.[22] By writing a book of advice, Juan Manuel shows himself to be a good governor, to exercise power properly: he possesses both wisdom and understanding, and places his *bienandanza* in virtuous works (recall his reaction to those who criticized his writing of books, contrasting his act of writing with those who act by play dice).

To impart his wisdom and understanding, Juan Manuel will use a dialogue between a great lord and his counselor. The first three tales emphasize the relationship of *consejar* to *obrar* in the frame and in the exemplary tale. In the case of the first tale, Count Lucanor asks for advice from his counselor, Patronio, who employs a modesty topos and exclaims that the Count has no need of his advice (being sufficiently endowed with true understanding). Since he asks it, though, Patronio will provide it. The exemplary tale focuses on the importance of good advice, and underscores that fact by telling of a counselor to a king whose own counselor advises the *privado* on what advice to give the king. The importance given to *consejar* reappears at the close of the frame where the narrator reports Count Lucanor's reaction. "El conde se fallo por bien *aconsejado* del *consejo* de Patronio, su *consejero*, et fizo lo commo el le *consejara*, et fallose ende bien" (37).[23] The repetition of the various word forms of *advice* serves as a rhetorical crescendo which comes to a climax with the resultant good that Count Lucanor receives by taking Patronio's advice (*et fallose ende bien*). The importance of good advice is reiterated once more in the verses composed by Juan Manuel that summarize his take on the point of the story.

The second and third exemplary tales provide a similar crescendo as they reemphasize and amplify the lesson of the first example. The frame of the second story mirrors the first in which the Count asks for advice, Patronio employs the modesty topos but advises his lord anyway. Patronio's exemplary tale focuses on those with understanding but without prudence (the "average" human being); those most in need of advice in order to know how to act. Patronio's conclusion at the close of the frame, filled with synonyms for advice, is to seek advice, to find a good counselor before acting.[24] The third tale completes the metaphor used earlier about looking before leaping in a literal fashion (*Del salto que fizo el rey Richalte de Ingla terra en la mar contra los moros*). Whereas the first tale stresses the importance of good advice, and the second tale highlights the benefits of a good counselor, thus preparing the good governor to act (to look), the third tale underlines the importance of acting properly within one's estate, doing good works, or in the language of the tale, leaping.[25] The frame highlights the importance of (proper) acts as opposed to words: one cannot earn salvation through oral justification of one's life on earth; it is earned by doing good works. Patronio's advice is that, as a nobleman, Count Lucanor must fulfill the divinely ordained role of nobleman which is to war against the Moors or defend the Faith (See, for example, Tale 33). Any other act (such as forsaking his estate for that of *orador*, for example) is imprudent and potentially life- and afterlife threatening.

Anecdotally, the collection of tales ends as it began: with tales that focus on good works and the value of good advice.

As the text progresses from tales to proverbs, Juan Manuel, in the Prologue to the second part, presents the opinions of another historic Castilian, Don Jayme of Xérica who passes his judgment on the tales and asks for subtler counsel for those of sharper wits. Each of the three successive collections of proverbs contain multiple, explicit references to advice and good works. References to *seso, fechos, fazer, consejo, obras,* and *saber,* for example all point to the elements of prudence highlighted, to wit, to counsel and to act.

In the fifth part of the *Conde Lucanor*, the character Patronio continues to advise his lord. Patronio dedicates significant time to the importance of doing good works and the avoidance of evil (works) as a manifestation of true understanding.

> deuedes entender por estos enxienplos la razon por que las obras para que el omne vaya a Parayso es mester que sean buenas, et bien fechas, et por escogimiento; et las por que el omne ha de yr al Infierno conuiene que sean malas, et mal fechas et por escogimiento. Et esto que dize que sean bien fechas, o mal, et por escogimiento es en la entencion; (483)

*You should understand through these examples the reason things done to go to paradise need to be good, well done and well chosen. The deeds that send a man to hell need to be bad ones, poorly done and by his choosing. Those deeds being well or poorly done and by their choosing refers to the intention;*

Patronio ties the entire text together by returning to the beginning: the good governor is endowed with understanding, one whose happiness (*bienandanza*) is determined by good works, the province of prudence.

In every case, Don Juan Manuel (author and character), Don Jayme of Xerica, Patronio (as well as many of Patronio's characters in the exemplary tales), and Count Lucanor show themselves to be prudent, endowed with certain knowledge that allows them to guide others to do good works (*obrar*), and in guiding others, performing good works themselves. To that end, the book itself is a physical exemplar of Prudence, containing and manifesting the elements necessary to behave wisely.

### Prognostication and memory as components of Prudence

Two other important aspects of Prudence are to be not quite omniscient, but somewhat omni percipient so as to be able to foretell the future based on given circumstances, and to use one's memory of past rulers, experiences, customs, and laws that can likewise illuminate the future.

> Prudencia es conoscimiento presente que cata a las cosas que han de venir, cuyo oficio es por las cosas presentes entender las que son de venir e aconsejarse e tomar remedio contra los males que pueden acaescer; e esta virtud fué mucho en los reyes antiguos...
> (*Glosa* 80)

*Prudence is knowledge of the present that looks at things that are yet to come. The task is to understand those things that are yet to come by obtaining advice and looking at solutions for things that are currently happening. Former kings very often practiced this virtue.*

One of the characteristics of prudence is the ability to determine what is to come based on present knowledge.[26] Memory proves the validity of the statement since it has been determined that those who governed before were endowed likewise with the ability to prognosticate. "La memoria es virtud por la cual el ánima repite las cosas que fueron, así como la inteligencia cata e entiende las cosas que son presentes" (*Glosa* 80). The prudent man is like a meteorologist who, based on contemporary conditions, is able to make a prediction of likely consequences, and is able to recall the past to recognize the qualities and rules of good meteorology and apply them as well to his prognosis for the future. Prognostication, then, is an important element in one's "governmental" repertoire, and it can be found in the here and now and confirmed through the past.

The question of the future is explicitly at issue in each of the fifty exemplary tales in the *Conde Lucanor*. Faced with various present socio-economic conundrums, Count Lucanor asks his counselor what should be done.

In each case Patronio recognizes the problem, presents an issue which is analogous to the Count's problem through the telling of a story, and shows him the ramifications of acting in one way or another by tying the story to the Count's particular situation. Patronio recognizes the future consequences of (in)action and guides his charge to a profitable decision.

Outside the fiction the reader sees that Patronio never errs, always recognizes possible consequences, and advises his lord to a profitable end. He proves to be the epitome of a good counselor. Inside the fiction, the fragility of what constitutes "good" advice, the ability to understand possible consequences, is made palpable through two specific reminders. In tale XII Patronio presents the problem of giving "good" advice and the consequences of failing in the attempt.

> en los grandes fechos et muy dubdosos son muy periglosos los conseios, ca en los mas de los consejos non puede omne fablar çierta mente, ca non es omne seguro a que pueden recodir las cosas; ca muchas vezes viemos que cuyda omne vna cosa et recude despues a otra; ca lo que cuyda omne que es mal, recude a las vegadas a bien, et lo que cuyda omne que es vien, recude a las vegadas a mal; et por ende, *el que va a dar consejo, si es omne leal et de buena entençion, es en muy grand quexa quando ha de conseiar, ca si el consejo que da recude a bien, non ha otras gracias sinon que dizen que fizo su debdo en dar buen consejo; et si el conseio a bien non recude, sienpre finca el conseiero con danno et con vergüença.* Et por ende, este conseio, en que ay muchas dubdas et muchos periglos, plazer me ya de coraçon si pudiese escusar de non lo dar, mas pues queredes que vos conseie, et non lo puedo escusar, digo vos que querria mucho que sopiesedes como contesçio a vn gallo con vn raposo.
> (109, my italics)

*Giving advice is very dangerous when dealing with important matters, as most of the time, one can not be completely certain when giving advice. One can not foretell the things that are bound to happen. Sometimes, things that are predicted to be good turn out to be bad and vice versa. Therefore, the person who gives advice, whether or not he is an honest man with good intentions, is always in a compromised position; if the advice turns out to be good advice, he is not thanked because he only did his job. However, if the advice turns out to be bad advice, the counselor has earned himself shame and damage. Consequently, I would be delighted not to advice on this particular matter because it is especially uncertain and dangerous. Since I can not avoid my duties, I would like to tell you about what happened to a rooster and a fox.*

Advice is very dangerous because of the inherent incertitude of life itself. Some things do not go as anticipated and what one sees as a potential evil may actually be good (recall the Spanish proverb: No hay mal que por bien no venga). Conversely, what is viewed as good may turn out to be evil. Because the counselor can never really be sure of the outcome of his advice, it puts him in a dangerous no-win position. The *Castigos é documentos* of Sancho IV reiterates what Patronio describes as an outcome of advice that turns out to be bad. "demanda consejo á homes buenos é entendidos é sabios que te sepan consejar sobre tal cosa, é así fallarás y lo mejor, é aunque aquellos lo errasen, suya seria la culpa, que non tuya" (*Castigos* 102). On the one hand, if advice proves true or profitable, the counselor is seen to have done only that which is expected of him. If, conversely, his advice leads to a bad end, the counselor has failed in his duties, and has brought himself and his lord shame and potential damage.[27] Patronio says that he would rather not have to give advice in this case, but since it is his duty, he will fulfill his lord's petition. He shows himself to be what is, by his definition, a good counselor: he is both loyal and well intentioned.[28]

Patronio's discourse on the dangers of advice comes as a response to a situation in which Lucanor confesses himself fearful due to the advice he has received from others. Patronio addresses this fear by telling the story of a rooster and a fox in which the rooster, through unwarranted fear, makes a poor decision and loses his life to the wily fox. Patronio's advice is to enter into every situation with one's eyes open and as well informed as possible. Once it is time to act, one must act boldly because unwarranted fear kills. Patronio provides the answer to both his lord's as well as his own fear of uncertain outcomes. Neither the adviser nor the advised can act fruitfully out of fear. They must, on the other hand, inform themselves well and once prepared, act with resolve. The reader outside the text sees that Patronio is a perfect counselor; in every case he always offers the right advice (his recitation of 180 proverbs are also cases of correct advice).

He is so because within the fiction he takes his own advice, realizing that nothing is certain except that those who flee their duties and responsibilities invariably fail while those who do what must be done, once prepared properly, will succeed.

One fulfills his duties and responsibilities in the case of a counselor if he is loyal and well intentioned. These qualities are not apparent in the individual but must be divined through trial; this has been apparent from the very first tale. The test or trial goes to the heart of one's ability to prognosticate. In tale XXIIII, Patronio reiterates the problem of giving advice: "esto que me vos dezides es muy fuerte cosa de vos lo dezir ciertamente, ca non se puede saber çiertamente ninguna cosa de lo que es de venir; et esto que vos preguntades es por venir, et por ende non se puede saber ciertamente" (181). This observation is in response to Lucanor's desire to know how to identify youths who will prove to be the best men. Patronio provides some physical clues but concludes that they are uncertain.

> Et con todo esto, estas son sennales, *et pues digo sennales, digo cosa non çierta, ca la sennal sienpre es cosa que paresçe por ella lo que deue seer; mas non es cosa forçada que sea assi en toda guisa.* Et estas son las sennales de fuera, que sienpre son muy dubdosas para conosçer lo que vos me preguntades.
> (181, my italics)

*Despite all this, these are signs. I label signs as something that is not certain. The sign is something that represents what it appears to be, but does not necessarily represent what it should be. These are the outer signs, which are always dubious to know what you are asking me.*

The "medieval" reasons: outer signs and inner realities do not always coincide. Hence the danger. Signs are unreliable and uncertain and one cannot use them exclusively to determine what will be (this is the lesson in tale XII; the rooster reads the signs, but they are unreliable, and on the basis of unreliable information, the rooster commits a fatal mistake).[29] The illustration that Patronio now applies to judging children applies equally to the problem of giving advice; there are signs that are available that will point in one direction or another, but they are unreliable. Success will come from testing the evidence to see what holds up and what fails. Patronio provides a tale in which a king tests his three sons to determine which is most capable of succeeding him. The question of reliability is not determined by the behavior of any one of the three, but by reading all the signs and comparing them. In this way the king determines his heir, and Patronio his advice. The counselor does not rely on appearances alone; he tests the evidence and when found sound, uses it to give advice to Count Lucanor. Through this process, the counselor can face an uncertain future and give his advice successfully.

The socio-economic problems that Lucanor faces are the tests that both a good governor and a counselor must confront. The exemplary tales that Patronio uses serve as the test by which current evidence is weighed and a decision about future behavior or consequences is made. They serve to highlight the problem from different perspectives, to clarify hidden traps and expose the truth behind a (not so) disguised conundrum. As counselor, Patronio subjects Lucanor's problems to a test, never relying on appearances, and after examining the results of his test, advising his lord on a course of action. The tests that Patronio employs come from his memory; they are stories that belong to common memory and he "occasionalizes a norm" for the purpose of illustrating the true nature of Lucanor's problem and thereby providing a solution to the problem.

The function of memory as a structuring element in the *Conde Lucanor* has already been discussed, and it only remains to illuminate one other perspective presented specifically (but not exclusively) in Giles. Enumerating the components of prudence, Giles defines the function of memory as "...acordarse de los tiempos pasados en que fué mejor governado el reyno e facer porque sea así governado en el su tiempo..." (*Glosa* 104). This reinforces the notion expressed earlier relating the training of the memory to praxis, and praxis, as has been shown, is prudence. Memory looks at *what was* in order to decide *what should be*. Of the fifty exemplary tales in the *Conde Lucanor*, Patronio uses 6 anonymous, fictional kings and 16 historical figures as protagonists of his stories.

Not all of the fictional kings are worthy of emulation, but all perform works *in bono* or *in malo*, and Patronio uses these kings and heroes to illustrate what Lucanor should do to govern well in the future.[30]

**The qualities of a nobleman**

In the *Libro del cauallero et del escudero* Juan Manuel, through an old knight, defines the estate of nobleman and how a true nobleman must behave. The old knight, responding to questions by a squire, tells him that the highest and most honorable estate in the secular world is that of *cauallero*, "ca los caualleros son para defender et defienden a los otros" (I 44). To the nobility belongs the defense of society. The knight goes on to compare the estate to a sacrament, noting that each sacrament is comprised of parts without all of which the sacrament cannot be completed. It is the same with knighthood. "Otrosi, la caualleria a mester que sea y el sennor que da la caualleria et el cauallero que la reçibe et la spada con que se faze. Et asi es la caualleria conplida...Et por [que] semeja mucho a los sacramentos...es [el] mas onrado et mas a[lto] estado que entre los legos puede ser" (I 45). The nobility obtain a sacred position akin to the sacraments through similitude. Because it is so related it is the most honorable estate to which the non-clergy can belong.

In the following chapter, the old knight describes the qualities necessary to receive and maintain nobility, grace, reason, and shame.

> *et la gracia de Dios le ha de mantener la onra que deue ganar por sus obras*, et [le] a de guardar et de defender el cuerpo et el alma de los periglos en que anda cada dia, mas que ningun omne de mayor otro estado; *et la gracia de Dios [le] ayuda[ra] et le fara auer seso para fazer [sus] fechos commo deue, et quer[r]a que aya uergüença de fazer lo que non deua.* (I 46, my italics)

*More than any other man of high position, God's grace will make him do the good deeds he must do, and it will help him deliver his body and his soul from the daily dangers. God's grace will help keep him in the mind to complete those good deeds in a proper manner. God's grace will also ensure that he is ashamed for his wrongdoing.*

God's grace makes it possible for the knight to maintain his honor through (good) works, helps him have the knowledge to do properly the things that he must do, and helps him to avoid through shame those things that he should not do. The focus is on proper acts.[31]

The old knight goes on to amplify the functions of reason and shame. Through reason, a nobleman knows how to manage all aspects of society in general, himself, others, his household, and his holdings in time of peace and in time of war.[32]

> Otrosi, el buen seso le es muy mester, ca el seso le amostrara quien es el que puede et lo deue fazer cauallero; et otrosi el que a de reçebir la caualleria...Et otrosi el seso le dira commo se deu[e] mostrar por sennor a los suyos, et commo los deue seer buen conpanno, et commo deue fazer en el tiempo de la guerra o de la paz, si fue[re] muy rico o abon[d]ado; et commo quando lo non fuesse tanto, o quando obiesse desto alguna mengua. Et otrosi el seso le mostrara commo deue fazer quando ouiere buena andança, et quando el contrario; et commo deue partir las ganancias que Dios le diere. (I 48)

*Besides, good judgment is very much needed, because good judgment will show you who can be and should be a good knight. Also, it will tell you who should be bestowed a knight. Good judgment will tell you how to behave with your people and how to be a good master. It will tell you how to behave in times of war or peace, regardless of whether you are rich, poor or abandoned. Good judgment will tell you what to do when luck is on your side and when it is not. It will tell you when to do good deeds and how to distribute the gains that God has granted you.*

Reason shows a nobleman how to behave as lord of his household, what should be done in time of war and in time of peace, with riches or without, what to do when fortunate or down on his luck, and how to divide his goods. Reason in all its manifestations guides the nobleman's daily life.

Shame is the most important quality that a nobleman may possess because, like prudence, it mediates all acts, it puts them into perspective. It is a quality of goodness. Shame, like humility, is the ability to know oneself, and through shame a nobleman does what he should and avoids doing what he should not.[33]

The combination of grace, reason and shame as qualities of the good nobleman are reflected time and again in the stories and proverbs of the *Conde Lucanor*. While nowhere does Juan Manuel or his characters say that they have the qualities of past rulers and are therefore worthy of emulation, he does put issues of grace, reason and shame into the tales with rulers as protagonists. The tales that feature fictional or historical rulers are not limited to these three specific issues. However, it is a fact that these characteristics manifest themselves in the tales either explicitly or implicitly as exemplars of reason in particular (when to make war, when to be friendly and when to anger, what to give and what to keep, etc.).[34] They are the qualities that the old kings and heroes possessed and that tyrants, unworthy rulers because they abused their power, lacked.

The first and third exemplary tales in the *Conde Lucanor* which deal with an anonymous fictional king and Richard the Lionhearted respectively have already been discussed to some degree. Of these two, the third tale in particular serves as an example of Patronio's appropriation of the experiences of past governors to illustrate how to behave in the future because it illustrates all three of the characteristics just highlighted. In the tale, Lucanor recognizes that he is a sinner and that the only way to atone for sin is through good works. He asks Patronio what he should do to gain God's grace thereby showing himself to know the importance of grace to his estate, to possess the necessary reason to ask for counsel, and to have self-knowledge/shame leading him to pursue a right course of action. Patronio recounts the tale of Richard and his fictional leap. The tale contains another frame within that established by Patronio and Lucanor in which a hermit, through his good works, is assured by God a place in Paradise. The hermit asks to know who his companion will be in Heaven, and God, through an angel, tells him that it will be King Richard. The hermit is upset at the news, believing Richard to be a less-than-ideal companion much less a candidate for salvation. The hermit is assured that through the singular act of leaping, Richard would merit salvation more so than the hermit and all his good works. Patronio privileges a single act by a monarch/nobleman over the myriad deeds of a holy man.

The angel who brings the hermit the news of his heavenly companion tells him about King Richard's leap. The kings of France, Navarre and England, having arrived in the Holy Land by ship, find themselves facing the daunting task of making it to shore and facing a huge Moorish army. The French king sends an emissary to Richard, inviting him to the French ship so they can discuss a proper course of action. Richard, mounted, answers the messenger by telling him to tell the king of France that he (Richard) has put his affairs in order, made his peace with God, and knows that he would do God a great service by warring against the Moors. With that, he puts spurs to his horse and leaps from the ship into water too deep for armored knight and horse to manage. God saves them, and his soldiers, seeing this, follow Richard into the water and charge the Moors. The French follow suit. The Moors, seeing that the armies do not fear death, flee, and the Christians vanquish the Moors doing God great service.

Rather than the importance of Richard making a "leap of faith," first Patronio, then the hermit, then Don Iohan highlight the importance of bearing arms against the Moors. In other words, a nobleman must behave like a nobleman, and the lesson comes from a past king known for his bravery. Patronio, after hearing Lucanor's petition for advice, prepares his lord for the tale by privileging Lucanor's estate over any other.

>   ca çiertamente, sennor conde Lucanor, si vos quisieredes *dexar vuestro estado et tomar vida de orden* o de otro apartamiento, non podriades escusar que nos non acaesciesçen dos cosas: la primera, que *seriades muy mal judgado de todas las gentes*, ca todos dirian que lo faziades con mengua de coraçon et *vos despagavades de beuir entre los buenos...*  (56, my italics)

*Certainly, my lord Count Lucanor, should you wish to leave your current life and enter a religious order or some other sort of life, you will not be able to help the following two things from happening to us: first, people will not judge you nicely; since everyone would think you a coward and that you willingly decided not to live among the good people...*

Patronio compares the religious estate none too favorably to Lucanor's own. Leaving his estate to enter a religious order would cause people to judge Lucanor a coward and conclude that he chose not to live among the good. The term *los buenos* is sufficiently ambiguous to allow for various interpretations, but *vida de orden* does not enjoy similar ambiguity. Patronio, anticipating the exemplum he is about to recount, makes it very clear that any interpretation that would include privileging the religious life or behavior particular to that estate at the expense of the life or proper behavior of a *defensor* would be erroneous. The tale to come will relate behavior proper to a nobleman.

The hermit, after hearing the tale told by the angel, changes his mind about Richard. "...entendio quel fazia Dios muy grant merçed en querer que fuesse el compannero en Parayso de omne *que tal seruicio fiziera a Dios, et tanto enxalçamiento en la fe catholica*" (58, my italics). The story moves the hermit to recognize the mercy that God was granting him by providing him with such a man as Richard as a companion in Heaven who exalted the catholic faith and did God such great service through his act of leaping. Recall that the act of leaping is not interpreted as a religious act but as the bold, brave and responsible move of a worthy monarch. Like the ideal nobleman outlined by Juan Manuel in his *Libro del cauallero et del escudero*, the Richard the Lionhearted of Patronio's exemplum shows himself to possess God's grace (having made amends to those he had offended and having put his affairs in order), reason (knowing the honor he must pay to his God and the honor that he must provide for himself, knowing how to make war when the odds are not in his favor, etc.), and shame (doing what he must do). His exploits are culled from Patronio's memory to illustrate how Lucanor is to behave in the future.

Don Iohan in his verse summary reiterates the error that one commits by leaving the noble estate to serve God as an *orador*; to serve through prayer as opposed to arms (it is presumed that leaving the second estate for the third would be unthinkable). "Qui por cauallero se toviere, mas deue desear este salto, que non si en la orden se metiere, o se ençerrasse tras muro alto" (59). He who considers himself a nobleman should wish to make a leap like that of Richard the Lionhearted, and not join one of the mendicant orders to enclose himself within the walls of a monastery. The comparisons that are made between the religious and noble estates lower the estate of *orador*, and elevate that of *defensor*.[35]

The concrete comparison that Patronio makes to Lucanor's fictional problem illustrates how, through Patronio's memory of past kings and their exploits, real or legendary, an action of uncertain outcome (Lucanor's desire to make amends to God and gain his grace) is compared to a similar action from the past (Richard's leap), whose positive outcome is known, and so proved to be recommendable.[36]

## Notes

[1] The importance of beginning the *Conde Lucanor* with recognition of God as prime mover of the work recognizes as true what Sancho IV describes in the *Castigos é documentos*: "los dones de Dios valen mas que los otros. E conosciendo los sus dones que te él da conoscerás á él, é conosciendo á él, conoscerás á tí mesmo, é conoscerás el estado en que estás, é saberlo-has guardar; é conosciendo el tu estado conoscerás á lo que has de venir; é conosciendo á lo que has de venir guardarte-has de non caer en yerro, é guardándote de yerro non caerás en perdon" (*Castigos* 143).

[2] See Minnis 78.

[3] See the *Castigos é documentos*, Chapter XLII. "El nescio non puede facer cosa de que el entendido se pague. El home entendido olvida lo que sabe é lo que entiende cuando fabla con el nescio, é non vee la hora que se parta dél. E el entendido gran sabor toma cuando falla otro entendido con que fable en su entendimiento, bien así como el que es letrado que se paga mucho de fablar en letradura con letrado" (166).

[4] In addition, supporting the argument that memory functions as a structuring agent in the text, the denunciation of the copyist places credibility in the memory of the reader/teller and less in the text itself. In Carruthers, discussing the issue with regard to Richard de Bury notes: "Bury is saying that he regards the memorial transmission of a trained cleric as more reliable than the written copy produced by one of these scribes" (*Book* 162).

[5] Peter Von Moos highlights the same tendency in John of Salisbury. "The credibility of tradition has more importance than authenticity...In accordance with a commentary on Lucan he claims that the *imago Romae* really appeared in a vision to Caesar on the Rubicon. On the other hand the famous fable ascribed to Menenius Agrippa about the conflict between the stomach and the limbs must have seemed too apocryphal; John changes period, author and witness transforming the *apologus*, as he calls it, into a contemporary bon mot told to himself in a private conversation by Pope Adrian IV. To prove the authenticity of the same papal apophthegm, Petrarch refers to a certain reliable witness, who has heard the story with his own ears. This witness is none other than our John of Salisbury!" (pp224-225).

[6] See *Literature as Recreation* especially Chapter 3: "The Recreational Justification" (90-127).

[7] A moral act, therefore, always gains by being inspired by a good intention, for, even if failing in the accomplishment of its object, it retains none the less the merit of having intended to do good, and often even deserves more than it accomplishes. (Gilson *Thomas* 319)

[8] "However interestingly developed or richly wrought the individual stories or fables may be, they may never be allowed to become independent of the whole. Whatever brilliance they may have is contributory to their function, which is to represent the variety and openness of the world, and to present this world to a mind which is capable of reflecting on it." (Dunn 53) Peter Dunn recognizes that Juan Manuel employs a strategy in the text in which a variety of literary forms are encased in a central dialogue. Unfortunately, Dunn's article treats *El Conde Lucanor* only in the light of the first part. This study argues that where Dunn emphasizes the inseparability of parts to whole in Part I, the same is true not only for the first, but also the four succeeding parts, and must

be so in order for Juan Manuel to obtain his objective. It cannot be achieved by reading the first part alone.

[9] Hugh of St. Victor: "Concerning memory I do not think one should fail to say here that just as aptitude investigates and discovers through analysis, so memory retains through gathering...Now "gathering" is reducing to a brief and compendious outline things which have been written or discussed at some length"(93). In ad Herennium, III. xx. 33-34: "Often we encompass the record of an entire matter by one notation, a single image" (215).

[10] The choice to train one's memory or not...was not a choice dictated by convenience: it was a matter of ethics. A person without a memory...would be a person without moral character and...without humanity. *Memoria* refers not to how something is communicated, but to what happens once one has received it, to the interactive process of familiarizing-or textualizing-which occurs between oneself and others' words in memory. (Carruthers 13)

[11] Very similar to the outline given by Juan Manuel in the *Libro de los estados* is that provided in the 13th-century *Poridat de las poridades:* "En esto mio libro a .viii. tractados: el primero tractado es en maneras de parte de los reyes. El segundo es del estado del rey et en su manera et commo deue faxer en si mismo et en su auer et en sus ordenamientos. El tercero es de la manera de las iusticias..." (*Poridat* 32).

[12] Frances Yates' informative study, *The Art of Memory* provides much valuable information on medieval memorial arts as well.

[13] The *Castigos é documentos* provides a synthesis of what John elaborates about exempla: "Non cae al rey decir enjiemplos que non tangan á aquella cosa en que está fablando; mas cáele bien decir aquellos que semejen é den firmeza á aquellos que dice" (113).

[14] Note Juan Manuel's power to command and act. Discovering an appropriate exemplum for his text, he orders it written in his book and he then makes/creates the accompanying summary verses. He has power over language: the ability to have something written and to summarize it, therefore controlling it to a certain degree. He also has power over people, in this case a scribe who is commanded to write a tale that Juan Manuel considers appropriate to the intention of the text in a book. Juan Manuel's possession of these powers underscores his almost regal power, highlighting his authority as *auctor* and *defensor* as well as his rhetoric of power.

[15] "Lucanor asks his tutor Patronio for advice on a problem, Patronio tells a story and derives the solution from it, and Juan Manuel then sums up the moral in two lines of bad verse" (Deyermond *Literary History* 138).

[16] The hypothesis that the enigmatic line must refer to something outside (missing from) the text is faulty in my opinion. Scholarship that suggests that it must be so because there is no inherent relationship between the exemplary tales ignores the relationship between the virtues, particularly prudence that will be examined later in this chapter.

[17] Sancho IV, in the *Castigos é documentos* names three powers "que Nuestro Señor Dios te quiso dar á tí é á toda criatura racional; las cuales son: razon, é memoria, é entendimiento, que son tres potencias especiales" (*Castigos* 88). These three in turn lead to three more (Giles places them within the domain of prudence). "Con estas tres spirituales gracias conocerás estas tres que

son muy nescesarias. Las cuales son: conocerse el home et de qué parte viene. La segunda, qué es en sí mesmo. La tercera, qué cosa ha de ser á la fin" (*Castigos* 88).

[18] There is an interesting reversal of this notion in the *Poridat de las poridades*, privileging wisdom and subordinating the soul: "Sepades que la primera cosa que Dios fizo fue una cosa simple spirital et mui conplida cosa, et figuro en ella todas las cosas del mundo, et pusol nonbre seso. Et del salio otra cosa non tan noble que dizen alma, et pusolos Dios con su uirtud en el cuerpo del omne; et pues el cuerpo es commo cipdad, et el seso es commo el rey de la çipdat, et el alma es como el su aguazil quel sirue et quel ordena todas sus cosas" (44).

[19] Giles' entire discussion mirrors the first book of Aristotle's *Nichomachean Ethics*. Sancho IV, in his discussion of prudence also emphasizes the relationship between *prudencia* and *obrar*: "é la prudencia muestra obrar siempre lo mejor, donde paresce que aquellas dos sirven á la prudencia, así como el saber ó el consejar ó el judgar de las cosas sabidas é el consejar sirve al buen obrar é segund razón" (*Castigos* 186).

[20] In the *Metalogicon* of John of Salisbury: "Prudence consists entirely in insight into the truth, together with a certain skill in investigating the latter...Thus it is indubitable that prudence is the root of all the virtues" (74).

[21] Hugh of St. Victor on practical philosophy: "the practical may be called active, likewise ethical, that is, moral, from the fact that morals consist in good action" (*Didascalicon* 62).

[22] One of the elements of prudence is *doctrinanza* which according to Castrojeriz "es sabiduría para ensennar los no sabios e los nescios, en tal manera que por ella el omme primeramente informe a sí mismo e después a los otros... (*Glosa* 80).

[23] The first example of the *Poridat de los poridades* contains a similar structure in which Alexander is advised by Aristotle with the result "fizo comol el mando, et fueron los de persia mejor mandados que ningunas de las otras gentes" (31).

[24] "...et que non vos fiedes en vuestro seso et que vos guardedes que vos non enganne la voluntad, et que vos consejedes con los que entendieredes que son de buen entendimiento et leales et de buena poridat" (*Glosa* 48). This exemplary tale reflects the importance that Castrojeriz places on counselors in his commentary on Giles: ...que siempre tomemos connusco ommes con quienes fablemos e con quienes nos consejemos, ca magüera el omme sea sabio se deve fiar de su entendimiento solo, mas deve oír las sentencias de los otros por dos razones. La una es porque el consejo deve ser de grandes negocios, así como dicho es; e en los grandes negocios no deve el omme creer a su seso, mas deve llamar a otros a su consejo, ca más ven muchos que uno solo; otrosí porque el consejo es de fechos particulares, en que ha menester gran prueba; e cierto es que mayor prueba pueden haver muchos que uno"(*Glosa III* 176). Again in Castrojeriz "...que conviene a todos los reyes de ser sabios, o de tener consigo ommes sabios a cuyos consejos se lleguen e con quien fagan sus cosas (*Glosa* 99). In the *Poridat de las poridades* Aristotle advises: "Alexandre, non fagades cosa pequenna nin grande a menos de uuestro aguazil, que los antigos dizen que en demandar omne conseio cabeça es de la cordura" (*Poridat* 46). In the *Libro de los doze sabios* there are times to solicit advice from anyone and other instances that require the governor to be more circumspect. "Comoquier que tú demandes a todos consejo, por escoger e tomar lo mejor, *lo que tu voluntad determinare en los grandes fechos e peligrosos sea tesoro escondido, que non lo fies salvo de aquéllos que son tuyos verdaderamente*, que muchos ay que juegan al escoger" (*doze sabios* 116 my italics). The *Castigos é documentos* recommends always

soliciting advice before acting. "conviene á los reyes de facer todas las cosas que facen con consejo, é de haber buenos é sábios consejeros. E si ellos non les creyesen de consejo, perescerian todos los consejeros é podria acaescer grand perligro en los fechos del regno, é por ende deben creer á los sábios" (*Castigos* 200).

[25] The importance of this tale is manifested by the in-depth introductory discussion between Count and counselor followed by a lengthy summary by Patronio which mirrors chapter 13 of Giles (*Glosa* 65). These discussions occur in only 6 of the tales, marking them for special consideration. Tales IX, XII, XXIV, XLVII, XLVIII, L.

[26] Von Moos notes the general tendency by John of Salisbury to use exempla in this manner (p. 207-208).

[27] In Boethius II 3 Philosophy says, "The world stays rarely long the same,/So great its instability,/So put your faith in transient luck, And trust in wealth's mortality!/In law eternal it lies decreed/That naught from change is ever freed.' (*Consolation* 61) and Brunetto Latini in the *Tesoro* : "nos devemos ende creer lo que dizen los sabios, que Dios abaxa los muy poderosos & ensalça los humildosos..." (*Tesoro* 165-166) Patronio recognizes fickle fortune as an overpowering influence in medieval life and as one of the inherent dangers of giving advice.

[28] In the *Poridat de las poridades* "Et a tal deuedes buscar que sea uuestro aguazil, et que ame uuestra uida, et que uos obedesca toda uia, et que punne en conplir uuestra uolantad con cuerpo et con auer en quantol mandaredes" (*Poridat* 47). Sancho IV highlights five components of the good counselor: "La primera, que sea honesto en facer cosas guisadas é raigadas en bondat. La segunda, que sea el su cosejo provechoso, en que se faga de las buenas cosas é provechosas, é se esquiven las malas é las dapnosas. La tercera, que sea leal en guardar señor é amigo é vasallo, como lo debe guardar. La cuarta, que sea rahez, porque el consejo puedan dello complir por carraera de lo mas ligero que se non faga por la mas grave. La quinta, que sea libre é non se faga con voluntad de mal talante, sinon con saña é pura voluntad" (*Castigos* 152).

[29] Laurence de Looze attempts a semiotic reading of the first Book in the article "Subversion of Meaning in Part I of *El Conde Lucanor*," *Revista Canadiense de Estudios Hispánicos* 19 (1995): 341-355. His thesis is that due to the unstable nature of the signifier, and despite Juan Manuel's best efforts to control it, the *Conde Lucanor* undermines its own attempts to stabilize meaning allowing the reader, in the final analysis, to interpret the tales as they wish.

[30] Sancho IV, in the *Castigos é documentos* dedicates all of Chapter X "Que fabla de los vasallos cómo deben servir al señor, é mucho mas obedecer é guardar é honrar al su rey" to illustrating proper kingly behavior by looking at historical kings to determine proper present behavior. He offers as an example "Dice mas sant Agostin en el primero libro de la *Cibdat de Dios*, que los reyes antiguos poníanse á muerte por salvar la comunidad. Esto mismo dice sant Agostin en este mismo libro, capítulo XIX, é Valerio en el libro V del rey Codro que, cuando vino á una batalla muy peligrosa que habian los de Atenas con el rey Felipo, é fueron demandar á su Dios cuáles serian vencedores, él díjoles que aquellos cuyo señor moriese en la batalla. Entonces estando las haces paradas, el rey Codro desvistió las sobre señales, é métióse entre los enemigos peleando con ellos muy reciamente porque lo matasen, por tal que podiesen vencer los suyos; é mas quiso que venciesen los suyos, él moriendo, que escapar é que quedasen los suyos vencidos. Et deste rey fizo Vergilio versos desta guisa: Codro, peleador,/mas quiso morir é ser vencedor,/que huir é ser vencido." Et así debe facer todo rey é todo príncipe, morir é darse á los trabajos deste mundo por defender é guardar la comonidat; é los suyos le deben seguir con

corazones encendidos de fuego é con buenas voluntades en le ayudar é morir todos con él por la honra" (*Castigos* 110).

[31] Sancho IV specifies three spiritual graces and three corporal graces that should guide the actions of every powerful man. "Por ende abre los ojos corporales et espirituales, é vee é oye é entiende, et aprende mis castigos é ayúdate de los tres poderíos é gracias que Nuestro Señor Dios te quiso dar á tí é á toda criatura racional; las cuales son: razon, é memoria, é entendimiento, que son tres potencias especiales. Con estas tres spirituales gracias conoscerás estas tres que son muy necesarias. Las cuales son: conocerse el home et de qué parte viene. La segunda, qué es en sí mesmo. La tercera, qué cosa ha de ser á la fin" (*Castigos* 88).

[32] Sancho IV attributes the same qualities to noblemen although he uses the terms *sotiles* and *engeniosos*. According to the King, noblemen are naturally subtle and ingenious. "...é esto les acaesce por dos cosas. La una, por la buena crianza que han, é por la grand guarda que ponen en los sus cuerpos....Lo segundo les contesce de ser sotiles por razon de la compañía, de quien toman buenas maneras é buenas costumbres, é teniendo mientes á ellos, han de ser sotiles en pensar cómo fagan sus obras conveniblemente, porque non sean de reprehender" (*Castigos* 202). That noblemen are subtle and wise can be proven by two "facts." "el alteza é la honra levantan el entendimiento de aquel que la ha á pensar é estudiar cómo la guardará é en qué manera la acrescentará, é cómo por el estudio se gana la sotiliza é la sabidoría.....La segunda razon es esta: que á los nobles se acompañan los sábios, é cualquier que ha compañía con los sábios, conviene que algo tome dellos é sea sábio" (*Castigos* 203).

[33] The *Libro de los doze sabios* underscores the importance of humility or shame in relation to knowing oneself: "Quando te vieres en mayor poderío, estonçe sea en ty mayor omildança, como Dios ensalçe a los omildosos e abaxe los sobervios" (*doze sabios* 116). The *Castigos é documentos* enumerates the evils that happen to him who loses his sense of shame. "El mal home non puede ser acabado en toda maldat á menos de perder de sí vergüenza; é desque la ha perdida non se siente del mal que face; é desque la vergüenza pierde, tiene que faciendo mal vive á su sabor, é es vida astrosa é menguada, é lixosa, é tiénela por buena é por acabada; é tanto le da que ande desnudo como si andoviese bien vestido; é tanto le da que coma mal como si comiese bien; é non se siente de ninguna cosa. ¿Qué te dire mas? tórnale de estado de home á ser bestia" (*Castigos* 96).

[34] Any of the following tales would serve as examples: Tale XIV features St. Dominic and highlights the importance of grace; Tales 15 (Lorenço Suarez), 25 (conde de prouençia), and 27 (Aluar Hannez Minaya) all highlight variations on the importance of *seso*; Tales 25 (conde de prouençia), 40 (seneschal de Carcassone), and L (Saladin) highlight the importance of shame.

[35] The dearth of religious protagonists in the exempla, the fun he pokes at the religious antagonists, and the privileging of the noble estate at the expense of the religious estate in several tales place Juan Manuel squarely within the long standing antifraternal tradition. Juan Manuel stands against a strong centralized power like that proposed by Alfonso XI. This study argues that he would find the centralization of religious power, executed to a large extent through Rome's use of the mendicant orders, equally threatening. The traditional pyramid that passed from pope to cardinal to bishops to parish is subverted (or seen as in danger of subversion) by the itinerant mendicants who engage the secular clergy in a battle for power. Although Juan Manuel showed himself to be partial to the Dominicans, that is not to say that he did not see them as representatives of an encroaching papacy that threatened the noble estate. The Franciscans, on the other hand, may have been seen by Juan Manuel as even more of a threat since they were a more fractious order, splitting into various groups some more radical than others. Among those groups

were the Beguins (the subject of attack in exemplum 42) who subscribed to Joachimism which posited the inauguration of a new era free from authoritative institutions. Joachimism had been around since the end of the twelfth century and its popularity ebbed and flowed in Spain through the sixteenth century. That Juan Manuel may have been familiar with Joachimism finds support in the *Castigos é documentos* in which Joachim de Fiore is mentioned specifically and the issue of his denunciation as a heretic discussed (see Chapter VIII "Que fabla de cómo la creencia del home debe ser verdadera é sana" (*Castigos* 100-101). P. E. Russell in *Spain: A Companion to Spanish Studies* describes the Franciscan cardinal Francisco Ximénez de Cisneros (1436-1517) as sympathetic to "the prophetic dreams which enjoyed wide sympathy among some churchmen...which foretold an imminent *Renovatio mundi* which would both transform the Church and overturn the established political order in the world" (*Companion* 268). Juan Manuel never reveals the specific reason for his antifraternalism, but any encroachment on noble power by lay or religious entity would have met with his most vigorous resistance. For more information on the antifraternal tradition in the Middle Ages see Moorman's *History of the Franciscan Order* (1968) and Szittya's *Antifraternal Tradition in Medieval Literature* (1986).

[36]See *The World of John of Salisbury*, and the essay by Peter Von Moos "The Use of Exempla in the Policraticus" 207 passim.

## Chapter 4: The moral of the story: politics and morality in the exemplary tales

In the collection of exemplary tales, the moral to each of the stories becomes the proper exercise and maintenance of power. Juan Manuel infuses both the structure and the story itself with this politicized version of morality. Structurally, the nobleman blurs the lines between historicized fiction and fictional reality by using both fictional and historical characters (Don Juan Manuel himself) within the narrative. In so doing, he strengthens the veracity of the tales to convince the reader of their worth in social terms as well as their application to contemporary medieval Castilian society.

Medieval Spanish estate society was a carefully organized and orchestrated unit which depended on its members as the body depends on its parts. In order for power relations to be successful from the perspective of dominant ideologies, one needed to impart the appropriate knowledge of how to conduct oneself properly. Don Juan Manuel exhorts, "Si el poder es grand poder, el grand poder ha grand saber" (II 458). Great power requires great knowledge. What is demonstrated in this chapter on the relationships of rhetoric and power in the exemplary tales is that power is never exercised correctly without a presumed basis of knowledge and wisdom grounded in the ideological foundations of the age, (in this case, fourteenth-century society). The fifty exemplary tales in the *Conde Lucanor* illustrate this and reinforce "politically correct" power relationships so that fourteenth-century Castilian society would operate according to a specific plan and could be carefully maintained according to the desires of a small group of historically powerful people like Don Juan Manuel or his fictional representative of power, Count Lucanor. The ideological foundations of the exemplary tales may have a message for readers throughout time, but they are most meaningful and powerful when understood in terms of their culture, society and historical moment.

In the *Conde Lucanor*, no tale is told merely for the sake of telling. The traditional tale chosen always has moral and social implications. There are correspondences between historical and fictional situations and social or political elements that are otherwise dissimilar. By itself, the oral tale has no fidelity to the probabilities of Lucanor's own predicament of doubts. If fidelity is created, it is only due to Patronio's framed elaboration. Patronio's strategy is to transfer the internal coherence of the traditional story pattern to the predicament of Lucanor and make the connection so compelling that the analogy becomes evident and meaningful both to Lucanor as well as to readers or listeners. Each frame is constructed so that it reduces the very artistic elements of the oral tale that might blunt the highlights of its exemplary function. Very few exemplary tales in the collection contain any dialogue of consequence (which would give power to another character) other than Patronio's advice and his telling of the exemplary tale to illustrate this advice. The only persons who "say" anything are Patronio and the omniscient narrator. Even Count Lucanor frames his utterances in the form of questions. Juan Manuel demonstrates an awareness of rhetorical propriety. Since Lucanor wants advice about how to behave, he asks a question. "Aristóteles dice en el VIº libro de las Eticas que todo consejo es una cuestión, ca cualquier que demanda consejo face cuestión...el consejo solamente es cuestión de las obras que el omme ha de facer" (*Glosa* III 173). In addition, an examination of the exemplary tales reveals that Lucanor's petitions for advice fall within the medieval categories specified by Catrojeriz (glossing Giles of Rome).

> Mas aquí conviene de notar que cinco son las deliberaciones de tomar consejo...La primera es del provecho o del no provecho...La segunda es que dubdamos de dos cosas provechosas cuál es más provechosa...La tercera es que dubdamos de alguna cosa si es honesta o no...La cuarta es que dubdamos de dos cosas honestas cuál dellas es más honesta...La quinta es cuando la cosa

> provechosa y la honesta son contrarias, allí dubdamos cuál cosa
> nos conviene de facer o seguir. (*Glosa* III 170)

*It is worth noting that there are five deliberations to take into consideration in order to obtain advice: the first one is whether or not there is profit..., the second one is to discern which one of two profitable situations is most so... the third one is to hesitate about whether one thing is honest or not..., the fourth one is to hesitate about which one of two honest things is most honest..., the fifth one is to determine which one would be best for us to do or follow providing that one thing is profitable and the other is honest.*

Castrojeriz focuses on two crucial elements for which the powerful require advice: profit (advantage) and honor. Lucanor's explanation of a particular social situation leads to his petition for advice which always has to do with issues of profit or honor. The artistic function of the framed version of the traditional story pattern is to penetrate the nobleman's predicament and to bring the very outcome of the difficulty closer to Lucanor's real situation, thus degeneralizing the oral story pattern to such a degree that the framed tale succeeds in actualizing it.

In each exemplary tale, the reader overhears a private conversation between Count Lucanor and Patronio in which Lucanor asks advice on how to respond to a situation presented to him in great secrecy.[1] The private conversation, once overheard, is no longer private, but the fact that it is described as such leads the reader to believe that the information being passed on orally is of greater importance. The gravity of the social relationship in history depends on the ability of the fictional count to keep his business private, out of public earshot. Power also depends on how information is shared and perceived by others as Castrojeríz pointed out.

> *todas las cosas que se ponen en los consejos deven ser muy guardadas e muy enceladas, ca muchas veces se embargan muy grandes fechos porque se descubren los consejos.* E esto paresce por la etimología del vocablo, ca consejo tanto quiere decir como cosa muy bien callada. E esto se deve guardar mucho en los consejos que no sean descubiertos ni revelados, mayormente si son de grandes fechos o de grandes negocios.
> (*Glosa III* 176, my italics)

*Every spoken piece of advice must be secretly and zealously kept. Often, great deeds are impeded because the pieces of advice are discovered. This idea is what the etymology of the words seems to communicate; advice also means something very well kept. So advice must be kept secret especially if they concern important issues such as big profits.*

Advice should be given in private especially when it deals with important issues that affect honor or questions of business that affect profit. In addition, the discussants' social status (a count and his counselor) makes the possibility of overhearing such "privileged" information all the more valuable, doubly valuable since the petition for the advice, and the circumstances by which the petition becomes necessary are both transmitted secretly. Those who wield socio-economic power speak in private of important things. Thus, the text exposes "classified" information. The exemplum receives more credibility with this narrative technique.

In each of the fifty tales Count Lucanor asks for advice before making a decision about personal affairs. Since Lucanor has not taken action, no damage has been done to either honor, estate, or social position, and the reader very quickly deduces that the first lesson on how to wield power properly is always to be prepared and well informed.[2] Proof that this is indeed the case is established when the frame is closed at the end of each episode as the narrator reports that Lucanor heeds the advice he receives and always profits from it.

**Empowering Deceptions: Ends and Means in Tale I**

In the first tale, for example, Lucanor reveals that a man says he wants to sell and give all of his goods to the count. The suspicious Lucanor asks his counselor to advise him. Patronio recognizes the fabrication that has been presented to Count Lucanor and tells him that what is apparently to his benefit is in reality a test of his friendship and therefore dangerous. He demonstrates the danger of the situation through an exemplary tale. The analysis of the story is meant to highlight the structure and serve as a model for the explication all the stories to come.

Patronio tells of a king who, deceived by others, grows suspicious of his right-hand man (*favorito*) and sets out to test him under circumstances similar to those presented to Lucanor in the frame story. The king hints that he is tired of his station and would like to leave it for a hermit-like life. He proposes to leave his wife, child and subjects and puts them in the hands of his *favorito*. When the *favorito* mentions his impending good fortune to his own counselor, a captive Moor, he is warned that he has been deceived and is about to fall into a trap and is in great danger. The *favorito* recognizes the truth of these words, and works to remedy the situation by deceiving the king into believing that he wishes to go with him and continue to serve him wherever he may go. He succeeds in his deception, and the king again believes what was always the case: that his *favorito* is true to him.

In the frame story Patronio summarizes the exemplary tale by telling Lucanor that the situation proposed to him is a test, that he should go and talk to the man who proposes to sell and give him all of his estate to let him know that he only wishes him well, and that he, Lucanor, neither intends to damage the man's honor nor covet any of his possessions. The narrator reports that Lucanor takes Patronio's advice and everything goes well for him. The narrator then inserts the fact that Juan Manuel also found the tale valuable and composed two verses to summarize its worth: *Non vos engannedes, nin creades que, endonado,/ faze ningun omne por otro su danno de grado* (Do not fool yourself nor believe that a man of high social estate will help another at his own expense) and *Por la piadat de Dios et por buen consejo,/sale omne de coyta et cunple su deseo* (A man escapes danger and achieves his goals through God's grace and good advice) (37-38). The first reiterates Patronio's advice while the other eulogizes good advice in general.

There are narrative indicators in the framed story which refer only to Lucanor's social problems. There are also other references within the tale which the informed reader can learn to identify. The king's *favorito* is put to the test as a result of the envy and deceit of others.

*Envidia* and *cobdiçia* are terms that have both religious and social (economic) implications. In religious terms, they are two of the mortal sins.[3] Sin comes from uncontrolled passions, which originate in the will, and envy and covetousness pertain to the passion *tristeza* or sadness. "en dos maneras puede el omme tomar tristeza: o la toma del alma de otro o del bien...si toma tristeza del bien...le pesa del bien que otro ha...e ésta es envidia" (*Glosa* 283). One of the forms of sadness comes at the expense of the wellbeing of another; envy and covetousness fall into that category. Sadness (*tristeza*) can be controlled by the virtues, the possession of which is obligatory in the good governor as has already been discussed. Those who envy the king's *favorito* are wrong to do so and place their souls in grave danger. Having been deceived by courtiers, the king subjects an innocent man (the right-hand man) to a test (another deception) that has (after)life-threatening consequences. The *favorito* is also tempted by the riches and power of the king, and is in danger of losing not only his social position but his place in heaven. Through the rhetoric employed by Patronio, Lucanor and, by extension, readers outside the text are convinced that they must always be alert and protect their property and honor from those who would covet it. In this case, protection includes the use of deception to guard one's position, power, and life.

At the same time envy and covetousness have social implications: what the jealous courtiers want and what tempts the *favorito* is social advancement. This desire too, has grave consequences, and Patronio's framing of the story reinforces the notion that one should be content with his social role. To desire to change that role is wrong because one's social role and responsibilities are based on a divine order, not a human one.

> For God has fixed the seasons' tasks/And each receives its own:/No power is free to disarray/The order God has

> shown./Should then some being precipitate/Aspire to quit its place,/The Lord would not allow success/Its mutiny to grace.
> (*Consolation* 50)

It is not only wrong for the courtiers to desire social advancement, it is also wrong for the king who intimates, albeit it only as a test of his *favorito's* loyalty, that he wishes to leave his social role for another. As the head of the body politic, the king must conduct himself exemplarily and respect the standard of proper behavior. By falling short, he sets a bad example and leads himself and others to perdition. "A enxemplo del rey se compone todo el mundo, e al su mal enxemplo se desordenan e se descomponen todos los ommes" (*Glosa* 248). The king is a model for society: if he is a good model society will be strong, if he is a bad model society falls apart. Again, spiritual good is used to defend social position.

In order to test his *favorito* the king develops a fictional scenario in which he leads the *favorito* to believe that he wishes to leave his throne and look for God. Patronio explains that "entre otras razones muchas que fablare, commence vn pock a dar a entender que se despagavades mucho de la vida deste mundo et que paresce que todo era validate" (II 34). Contempt for worldly possessions is the first step toward a closer relationship with God and as Patronio develops this scenario he has the king become even more specific. The king shall leave all earthly possessions behind for the laudable purpose of doing penance for his sins and earning a place in heaven. If the king's proposal were viewed in purely religious terms and not in social, economic, or political terms it would be sound. According to the Spiritual Franciscans, the king would earn his heavenly reward; however in Dominican teaching the king's actions would be totally improper.

> la Inquisición, dirigida por los dominicos, imputaba a las herejías el propender a la disolución de la sociedad. La imputación parece tan infundada... pero la pobreza absoluta que predicaban los *fraticelli*, la renuncia a la propiedad individual en favor de la comunidad evangélica...equivalía a una condena implícita del orden social establecido. (Lida de Malkiel *Tres notas* 97)

*The Inquisition, directed by the Dominican order, blamed heresies for the termination of society. The accusation seems to be so well grounded ... but the absolute poverty that the fraticelli taught was the rejection of private property in favor of the evangelic community ...amounted to an implicit reprobation of the social status quo.*

Dominican teaching could be applied to the secular social order as well as to the religious, and Juan Manuel found support for his arguments in these principles. Don Juan Manuel was an active supporter of the Dominican order and its orthodoxy. Any movement that rejected the existing social order had to be interpreted as dangerous and required a warning about such disorder within his exemplary tales. An excellent example of this can be found in tale XLII: "De lo que contesçio a vna falsa veguina." Rhetorically, Juan Manuel supports the Dominican philosophy of status quo and rebukes the voices of *contemptu mundi* for those born into the estate of *defensor*.

The way the story is narrated in tale I indicates that the king deceives his *favorito* about his departure while not really contemplating such action. His scenario for penance and redemption is a hoax, but the *favorito* does not know this. Patronio relates how the *favorito* reacts to the news and it is in his telling that the advice to Lucanor's question is formed and delivered:

> Quando el priuado del rey esto le oyo dezir, estranno gelo mucho, deziendol muchas maneras porque lo no deuia fazer. Et entre las otras, dixol que si esto fiziese, que faria muy grant deseruiçio a Dios en dexar tantas gentes commo avia en el su regno que tenia el vien mantenidas en paz et en iustiçia, et que era çierto que luego que el dende se partiese, que avria entrellos muy grant bolliçio et muy grandes contiendas, de que tomaria Dios muy grant deseruiçio et la tierra muy grant dapnno... (35)

*When the king's servant heard the king say such a thing, he thought it was very strange, and told him many reasons not to do it. Among those reasons, he said that should the king do such a thing, he would be doing a great disservice to God. He claimed that there were many people in the kingdom that lived very good, peaceful and just lives; if the king decided to leave his current life, these people would engage in large turmoil and fights. God would be very unpleased with all this and the earth would be in great trouble...*

The idea of the king leaving his kingdom puzzles the *favorito* because the king's plan is improper. The reason the *favorito* gives the king for not pursuing such a course is that, instead of pleasing God and earning himself a place in heaven, the king would be doing God a great disservice by placing his soul in jeopardy rather than in a state of grace. The *favorito*, and even the Moorish counselor, recognize that a decision to affect one's spirituality has material as well as spiritual consequences. In this case such a decision is shown to be ill-conceived because it goes against a divine plan and social requirements. The king's proposal is a hoax to trick the king's *favorito*, but it is also potentially a real social error. Once again the message is that the status quo must be maintained in order to avoid a rupture of the social system, that those who are born into a social station should live their lives in that station thereby earning salvation.

In Juan Manuel's *sentençia* at the end of the exemplary tale the eulogy to good advice becomes the summary of his goal to maintain a static and unchanging society and quell the note of contempt for worldly things that has been sounded by such orders as the Franciscans. "Por la piadat de Dios et por buen consejo,/sale omne de coyta et cunple su deseo" (38). By the grace of God and good advice, one escapes affliction and fulfills God's desire. The refrain does not focus only on good advice but also on the completion of God's desire, the maintenance of the existing societal structure. Man avoids a troubled life through acceptance of his worldly role. In the framed case for Lucanor, a true friend covets neither his neighbor's goods nor his position; he contents himself to working within his own birthright and earning salvation by living his life as prescribed by his estate.

Patronio imposes on his listener Lucanor, and indirectly on the general audience, a social and religious awareness regarding the count's predicament. This is the exemplary function of the framed tale. The reader can extract the social and political attitudes (with their economic implications) of Juan Manuel in these examples through an analysis of the rhetorical art of the texts. The art of Don Juan Manuel produced a historically identifiable contradiction: within the privacy of Lucanor's visit to Patronio, the counselor's oral message of caution and stability to his protégé glosses over the potential contradiction of identifying worldly and spiritual gains.

> Toda la atención se dirige a la orden dominicana para descubrir lo que sus constituciones significan. En realidad, la digresión...se traduce en una defensa de los objetivos que don Juan Manuel persigue; objetivos que necesita para defender su conducta, para explicar su paso turbulento por la tierra.
> (Casalduero *composición* 153)

*All the attention is being placed on the Dominican order to reveal what its doctrines mean. Actually, digression... is translated into a defense of the objectives pursued by don Juan Manuel. He needs these objectives to defend his behavior and to explain his troubled transitory life on earth.*

Gimeno Casalduero discusses Juan Manuel's "doctrine", and argues that he appropriates the scholastic harmonization of the temporal and spiritual for his own ends.

> creo que encontró en Santo Tomás el proyecto de su libro, incluyendo su doctrina y su forma. Era de don Juan la doctrina, no cabe duda, pero en Santo Tomás-gracias a los dominicos-halló los soportes que para sostenerla necesitaba.
> (Casalduero *composición* 155)

*I think that he found his book's project in St. Thomas, including its doctrine and structure. The doctrine was, without a doubt, Don Juan's; however, thanks to the Dominicans, he found the framework he needed to sustain it in St. Thomas.*

With clever means of rhetorical appropriation of an accepted ideology, Juan Manuel transcends the potential contradiction between temporal and spiritual goods by not revealing the possible opposition between means and ends.[4] Simultaneously, within the structured discourse of the framed visit and oral message, the author hides nothing and, on the contrary, allows readers to see everything that might be contradictory in what the tutor tells and the nobleman hears. The frame of the elaborated tale is subtly presented to all readers as if it were the resolved case of contradictory advice. What might appear contradictory during Juan Manuel's age is harmonious in his fiction.

### Nothing is Nothing: Foresight is Power in Tale XXXII

Ironically, Juan Manuel seeks to hide his messages rhetorically yet simultaneously exposes the danger of keeping secrets inappropriately or hiding information from friends. In chapter XXXII, Lucanor again presents a problem and asks for advice. He has been approached in secret by a man who tells him that he has something to offer that would greatly benefit him, but that in order to discover this information Lucanor must not tell anyone, for to do so would place his honor and position in danger. Lucanor places neither honor nor estate in jeopardy by taking immediate action but first prepares himself by asking for advice which ironically reveals to be true beforehand what his counselor, Patronio, is about to tell him. Lucanor does not keep anything secret but instead seeks out Patronio. His counselor relates the story of a Moorish king fooled by three tricksters.

In the exemplary tale, the tricksters tell the King that those who cannot see the clothes that the tricksters profess to be able to weave are bastards, and bastard sons of Moors cannot be inheritors. The king does not fear illegitimacy but mistakenly sees the "magic" clothing as a means of increasing his wealth and position, just as the favorite saw the pretended departure of his king as a means to advance in Tale I.[5] The desire for increased wealth and power at the expense of his subjects motivates the king to house the tricksters and pay them to make the "magic" cloth. The power of the imaginary cloth and the implications of not being able to see it are not secrets, so when the king sends his chamberlain to view the weaving of the cloth, he reports having seen it. Others whom the king sends claim to have seen the cloth also for fear of losing their social status and their goods. The king himself then goes to view the cloth. He, like the servants before him, does not see the cloth, but through fear of losing what he has, decides to keep secret the fact that he does not see what really does not exist.

The description of the cloth becomes more and more elaborate with its fictional weaving until the tricksters present the "cloth" for its cutting into whatever clothing the king wishes. After the "cutting," the king dresses himself in the non-existent cloth and presents himself to his subjects. None of them tell what they see except for a black slave who has nothing to lose by speaking the truth. The slave reveals the truth to all and once it is revealed, all see the king's nakedness for what it is: nakedness.

Patronio re-frames the story by advising Lucanor not to trust the man who urges the count to keep things secret only to trick him. Lucanor heeds Patronio's advice and profits from it.

Juan Manuel contributes another verse to summarize the lesson which reinforces Patronio's advice. "*Quien te conseia encobrir de tus amigos,/sabe que mas te quiere engannar que dos figos* " (270). Whoever advises you to keep secrets from your friends wants to trick you more than two figs. The allusion to the figs may refer to the fall of Adam and Eve who by some accounts ate of the fig tree (Covarrubias 688). Given the existence of two types of figs, *mariscas* and *chías*, one sweet and the other bitter which in appearance were alike, an untrained eye could be deceived into believing that the one was the other and instead of sweetmeats, take a bite of bitter fruit (Covarrubias 688). Through the verse, Juan Manuel shows that in either case, the effect of keeping secrets from friends leads to bitter results.

As in the first framed tale, the apparent signs of exemplary tale XXXII point to the danger of keeping secrets from friends. The exemplary tale's information deals with the social problem facing Count Lucanor. As in the first tale, there are other messages, not so apparent, which are revealed to the readers in a more subtle fashion. The apparent messages of the tale, concerning preparedness, knowledge of friends and the guarding of secrets are the product of a highly contrived convention. The truth of the cloth is its artifice, and the more complete the artifice, through the constant aggrandizing of the nonexistent cloth, the more poignant the point concerning the pitfalls of blindness, deception, gullibility, and succumbing to social pressures.[6]

Social pressure to conform or risk loss of status and wealth leads to learned gullibility in this tale, represented by both the physical inability to see the cloth that does not exist and the verbal/social "cover-up." Juan Manuel uses the traditional dichotomy of appearance and reality in order to dramatize how social hierarchies are threatened. He portrays an estate society where people are born into their estate and they justify their position through their ancestry. Their social position is made manifest through physical appearances.

Historically, however, with the beginning of the increase of the wealthy non-aristocrats, appearances become deceptive and give rise to the distinction between *homes ricos* and *ricos homes*, the latter group endowed with honor and the former without (Maravall *Estudios* 466-467). Sancho IV cites five bad customs proper to this group of *homes ricos*, the fifth being that they consider themselves worthy of being princes or lords. "Lo quinto les acontesce...porque cuidan que las riquezas son de tanta avantaja, que los que las han son dignos de ser príncipes é señores" (*Castigos* 204). In this short tale, Juan Manuel demonstrates through fiction a real historical problem. The nobility, the elite group of *ricos homes*, is threatened from the outside by commerce and opportunism, wit and deception. From the inside it is threatened by the king's own gullibility (symbolically, the foolishness of the nobility, those in a position of responsibility who should have known better).

Patronio frames Lucanor's predicament in terms of the king's nakedness. The fearful king overlooks the reality of this nakedness in the exemplary tale and ends up wearing nothing so that others, refusing through collective fear the reality of illusion, are willing to accept at least outwardly an illusion of reality. The naked king becomes, metaphorically, the man who cannot cover his inner weakness and therefore exposes his inability to govern well; he is a tyrant.

Nakedness is meaningful not only as moral metaphor but also as sociopolitical reality. Patronio's use of contradiction exposes the audience to this metaphor. The king is naked in terms of not being clothed. Neither of the two poles (naked/clothed) is anything in itself; there is a mutual dependency of the two extremes. Patronio describes the king's fear and foolishness not as nakedness per se but as the negation of wearing clothes with which, not withstanding their non-existence, he dresses himself. Subtly, in the verbal structure of the framed story, the accepted, positive norm of being clothed is a double negative because it cannot redress what it exposes: a tyrant. Clothes are described as the norm and they automatically produce what is not nakedness. Nakedness symbolizes pejoratively that which is abnormal. Clothes, then, acquire a social meaning because they refer to the king's nakedness which they both negate and affirm at the same time. "Clothed" in his royalty the king is nevertheless, naked, and thus exposed as a poor ruler.

The tale of the deceived king whose clothes bare his body to his subjects is represented verbally in terms of opposites. Clothed and nakedness have a negative relation; their verbal unity only highlights their hidden, essential disunity. The king ends up wearing nothing because he will not admit that he sees nothing. Fear covers his nudity with non-existent clothes. Foresight for Lucanor is to recognize his potential exposure and, by taking Patronio's advice, "cover" himself. The message to Count Lucanor and to the reader is that foresight is to see that nothing is nothing and that the game of secrecy reveals the vulnerability of not being sure of one's own identity.

**The Measure of Nobility: Giving Truth to the Lie in Tale XXII**

The mirror image of not understanding the nature of oneself is not recognizing the nature of others.[7] In tale XXII "De lo que conteçio al leon et al toro," the initial frame is inaugurated by Count Lucanor's petition for advice on how to act toward a socially and politically powerful friend who, according to an anonymous "they," is planning to do the Count severe harm. Lucanor recognizes the precariousness of his position: if the rumor is true, the nobleman-friend can do Lucanor great harm. However, if Count Lucanor should prepare for a potential

117

treacherous act by his friend who is not considering such activity, the friend may, after observing Lucanor's activity, do the same and therefore render the same outcome as in the first situation. Instead of responding directly to the rumor, Count Lucanor first seeks the advice of his counselor, Patronio, who illustrates the problem and its solution by telling the story of what happened to the bull and the lion.

The tale is given a social dimension in which the herbivores and the carnivores work together to overthrow two leaders. The animals recognize that the bull and the lion rule with the help of the other. They feel that their rule is oppressive, and they discuss the problem to determine a method by which they can escape the perceived tyranny, namely by overthrowing the two rulers. The fox and the sheep are chosen to begin the erosion of the friendship and they, in turn, use the horse and the bear in their scheme to weaken the animal kings.

The animals chosen to begin the undoing of the friendship merit closer examination because their talents, if taken separately, are limited, but when combined they become a powerful force. The fox and sheep are chosen to initiate the unrest due to their roles as counselors to the respective animals. The role of counselor is generally played by those who have shown themselves to be particularly astute, intelligent.[8] This intelligence is special in its breadth in that the role of counselor requires knowledge of social, political, and spiritual topics. What a counselor lacks once advice has been given is the power to initiate action that will insure a successful outcome.

The counselors enlist the aid of the horse and the bear, the most powerful animals of their type. Patronio, in the telling of the tale, highlights their physical power as the reason for the solicitation of their alliance.

> Et el raposo, que era consegero del leon, dixo al osso, que es el mas esforçado et mas fuerte de todas las vestias que comen carne en pos el leon, quel dixiesse que se reçelaba que el toro andaua catando manera para le traer quanto danno pudiesse, et que dias

> avie que gelo avian dicho esto, et commo quier que por aventura
> esto non era verdat, pero que parasse mientes en ello.
> Et esso mismo dixo el carnero, que era consejero del toro,
> al cauallo, que es el mas fuerte animal que a en esta tierra de las
> bestias que pacen yerua. (168)

*And the fox, who was the lion's advisor, told the bear that the strongest and bravest among all carnivorous beasts is the lion. The fox asked the bear to warn the lion about the bull, who was trying to find a way to harm the lion as much as possible. He had been told this days ago and although this could turn out not to be true, he had to pay some attention to it, nonetheless. This is exactly what the ram, who was the bull's advisor, told the horse, which is the strongest animal on earth to graze.*

The counselors enlist the aid of the powerful animals, and thus a marriage of brain and brawn is achieved that will allow the plan to succeed whereas without the unity of thought and action the plan would have been more doubtful of success. The physically powerful animals are entrusted with the first words of discord to be sown in the ears of the lion and bull. They warn their leaders that the other has been saying things that lead him (horse/bear) to believe that he (bull/lion) is looking for a means to overthrow the other. Within the tale, the observations of the powerful animals do not achieve rhetorical credibility on their own, and both the bull and the lion are said to suspect the whispers and whisperers even though the horse and bear are of high rank within their species. It is only when the leaders solicit the advice of their counselors that true doubt begins to enter the relationship.

> Et cada uno dellos fablaron con el raposo et con el carnero, sus
> priuados.
> Et ellos dixieron les que commo quier que por aventura el
> osso et el cauallo les dizian esto por alguna maestria engannosa,
> que con todo esso, que era bien que fuessen parando mientes en los
> dichos et en las obras que faria dalli adelante el leon et el toro, et
> segund que viessen, que assí podrían fazer. (169)

*And each one of them talked to the fox and the ram, their counselors. The fox and the ram told them that since it seemed that the bear and the horse might be plotting against them, therefore, it would be in the best interest of the lion and of the bull to listen and watch them carefully from now on. They should act accordingly to what they see.*

The counselors advise their masters to observe the activities of the other, that their eyes would tell them the truth of the matter, and then they would know how to act. In an interesting juxtaposition of the wedding of physical and mental powers, the bear and horse, endowed with physical prowess warn the lion and bull about words while the fox and sheep, endowed with intelligence imparted by words, warn their leaders about actions. Such criticism is a natural reaction by those endowed with opposite capabilities; those with physical prowess are cautious of those who control others through their words, a skill they do not possess, and those who control others by their words are cautious of others who use physical strength, something they do not have. Warnings to be cautious of both actions and words are given to the bull and the lion, characters which, by virtue of their leadership roles, would be endowed with both powers.

The seed of doubt that is planted by the counselors and their allies and the resultant suspicion become the proof that neither leader trusts the other and lend credence to their fears of attack by the other. The "love" that the two animal leaders once shared becomes hatred with a fight and the ultimate destruction of their rule the inevitable outcomes.[9] The story focuses on the foolishness of the lion and the bull.

> Et assi, porque el leon et el toro non entendieron que por el amor et el ayuda que el vno tomaua del otro, eran ellos onrados et apoderados de todas las otras animalias, et non guardaron el amor aprouechoso que avian entre ssi, et non se sopieron guardar de los malos consejos que les dieron para sallir de su premia et apremiar a ellos, fincaron el leon et el toro tan mal de aquel pleito, que assi commo ellos eran ante apoderados de todos, ansi fueron despues todos apoderados dellos. (169)

*Consequently, because the lion and the bull did not understand that it was due to the love and help they offered each other that they were the most honest and powerful among all other animals. They did not maintain the benefiting love they had for each other and, since they did not protect themselves from the bad advice they were given, they lost all their power and now are ruled by the ones they once ruled.*

Patronio's telling of the story places the blame on the two leaders who did not understand that they owed their honor, power and position to their mutual support and friendship. They did not recognize themselves and so could not recognize the other. Because they did not see their relationship as one of mutual benefit, and because they did not recognize bad advice, where once they ruled others now are they ruled. There is no Modern Age philosophy which condemns oppression here, those who had power foolishly threw it away, and where once they ruled so now they serve. The message is clear: the bull and the lion were poor rulers and did not know how to behave according to their position. For that reason they are too stupid to rule well, and by their own stupidity are they thus overthrown.

Patronio closes the 131, by linking the story of the lion and the bull to the social problem faced by his lord, Count Lucanor. As in the story, Patronio admonishes Lucanor to guard against acting in a manner similar to the lion and the bull. Instead of listening, Patronio urges that Lucanor act, that he tell his friend what has been said about him, and that he punish those who said such things so that no one else will dare try the same trick. If the friend is only one of fair weather, then Patronio advises the count to be tolerant and forgive small errors because the real threat will appear by real action and thus will Lucanor know when a false friend is going to attack him. What Patronio most urges is action rather than words.

> et lo vno faziendol buenas obras et mostranndol buen talante et non tomando sospecha del sin razon, nin creyendo dicho de malos omnes et dando alguna passada a sus yerros; et lo al, monstrandol que assi como cumple a vos la su ayuda, que assi cumple a el la vuestra. Por esta manera durara el amor entre vos, et seredes guardados de non caer en el yerro que cayeron el leon et el toro.
> (170)

*You should show him that you value his help by doing good deeds, showing appreciation, not suspecting him, not believing what evil men tell you about him and forgiving his mistakes. He will show you his appreciation of you the same way. Thus, love will thrive between you both and you will avoid making the same mistake the lion and the bull made.*

By doing good works, showing the friend how much he appreciates him, by forgiving him his mistakes, by recognizing him as a friend, and by not listening to evil men who speak against the friend will the count not make the same mistake as the animal rulers in the tale.[10] Count Lucanor takes this advice and profits from it and the narrator tells the listener that Don Iohan liked the lesson and the story so much that he had it included in the book and wrote a verse to summarize the lesson. "Por falso dicho de omne mintroso/ non pierdas amigo aprovechoso" (170). Valued friendship should not be lost by listening to lies. The admonishment is addressed to those in positions of power since it neither condemns the counselor nor his advice but places responsibility on the shoulders of those who listen to bad advice. The wise ruler recognizes a lie as a lie and a friend as a friend.

**The Power of Knowing Thyself: Shame in Tale L**

*Conocerse* is part and parcel of power for Juan Manuel.[11] Everyone must know his role in society in order to fulfill his duties and, by living as one should, gain salvation. In the case of the nobility, knowing how to govern well comprises their social role.

> Si uno es señor y no se conoce como tal no cumplirá en los deberes de su puesto....Hay, pues, que conocerse a sí mismo, que es conocerse según su estado social, para atenerse a éste y cumplir con los deberes que a ello corresponden. Toda la labor didáctica del Infante Juan Manuel está condicionada por ese conservadurismo social de los estamentos.
> (Maravall *Estudios* 460)

*One who is a lord and does not know himself as such will not fulfill the duties that come with the lord's position... Therefore, one has to know oneself, which is to know oneself according to one's social status, so that one can behave accordingly and fulfill the duties with which that position comes. Prince Juan Manuel's didacticism is restricted to this premise and is geared toward the preservation of the status quo.*

In the case of the Moorish king of tale XXXII, his court and his subjects, none of them truly knew themselves and therefore they were incapable of fulfilling the obligations of their social role. The Moorish king became the butt of a joke which exposed the disastrous consequences of not knowing oneself. In XXII, the bull and lion do not recognize their responsibilities as rulers and are duped and overthrown. Foresight and self-knowledge are inextricably linked: neither one is anything without the other. In order for a nobleman like Lucanor to be prepared to protect and defend his honor and estate, he must first know himself. Without both elements, he cannot exercise power correctly or govern well. "The condition of human nature is just this; man towers above the rest of creation so long as he recognizes his own nature, and when he forgets it, he sinks lower than the beasts. For other living things to be ignorant of themselves, is natural; but for man it is a defect" (*Consolation* 68).

Exemplary tale L treats of Saladín and the wife of one of his vassals. It explores the theme of self-knowledge and serves to close the first book of the *Conde Lucanor*. The analysis of this tale demonstrates once again how ideological foundations concerning social identity influence and determine the narrative structure of the *Conde Lucanor*. In the frame story, a specific social problem does not spark Lucanor's petition for advice, instead, a general desire to protect his estate (*fazienda*) motivates his entreaty. Lucanor asks for something to show him how to act as he should in order to protect that estate. Lucanor demonstrates foresight by being aware and on guard; he lacks the necessary self-knowledge to fulfill his duties as dictated by his estate.

Patronio responds to Lucanor's petition saying that people deceive themselves about who they are and what they know and then tells Count Lucanor directly that even he has deceived himself. Patronio symbolizes the established nobility which educates the new, and his indictment is clear: those who have entered noble ranks think too highly of themselves and need to learn their place. He explains that self-knowledge is gained through the works that one does for God and others. Both are necessary since works done in the name of this world result in the damnation of the doer in the next and, while those who do good works for God choose the better path, they neglect the physical world and God wants good works done in both worlds.

> Et bien cred que non a cosa en el mundo en que omne tanto nin tan de ligero se enganne commo en cognoscer los omnes quales son en si et qual entendimiento an. ...Et para saber qual es en si, asse de mostrar en las obras que faze a Dios et al mundo; ca muchos parescen que fazen buenas obras, et non son buenas: que todo el su bien es para este mundo. Et creet que esta vondat que costara muy cara, ca por este vien que dura vn dia, sufrira mucho mal sin fin. Et otros fazen buenas obras para seruiçio de Dios et non cuydan en lo del mundo; et commo quier que estos escogen la mejor parte et la que nunca les sera tirada nin la perderan; pero los vnos nin los otros non guardan entreamas las carreras, que son lo de Dios et del mundo. (413-414)

*There is not such a thing in the world that fools man so quickly as knowing men and knowing the amount of intelligence men have. In order to find this out, one has to look at the acts for God and for the world. Some people seem to perform good acts, but actually they are not such a good thing as all the good is geared toward this world. He will pay much for this good act, for his good that will last only a day, he will suffer endless harm. Other people do good acts addressed to God and do not care about the rest of the world. These people are playing safe since they will have nothing to lose. Neither the former nor the latter are doing the right thing, since God wants good acts done for him and for the world.*

Patronio's message harks back to the difference between *ricos homes* and *homes ricos* and the Dominican philosophy of orthodoxy. Those who have honor and live within their estate (*ricos homes*) and fulfill the duties imposed upon them by their position will save their souls (be successful) but those who only realize good works for profit (*homes ricos*) will be damned. By extension, then, those who follow the path of contempt for worldly things, like that postulated by the more radical Franciscans, err. Though they are not damned, they will not be exalted. Only those who practice both religious and social orthodoxy do God's will, and will receive their rewards, material and spiritual, in both this world and the next.

According to Patronio, many things determine wisdom. Some people appear to be learned but do not have the common sense to maintain their social position while others have the sense to maintain their position but lack learning.[12]

> Otrosi, para saber qual ha buen entendimiento, ha mester muchas cosas; ca muchos dizen muy buenas palabras et grandes sesos et no fazen sus faziendas tan bien commo les conplia; mas otros traen muy bien sus faziendas et non saben o non quieren o non pueden dezir tres palabras a derechas. (414)

*Therefore, to be able to determine who has good judgment, many things need to be considered. There are many people who say very nice words and have very good minds but fail to perform their duties as well as they should. Also, there are others who handle their duties very well but are unwilling or unable to say three straight words.*

Those who, by the words they use, appear to be educated, but who cannot maintain their households are as foolish as those who keep their estates in order but are otherwise ignorant because, like the Moorish king in XXXII, they do not know themselves, they do not know their place. Likewise there are those who have both learning and common sense but use them for ill purposes. In Patronio's view these ill purposes cause others to suffer because those who do good works for selfish purposes are dangerous.

> Otros fablan muy bien et fazen muy bien sus faziendas, mas son de malas entençiones, et commo quier que obran bien para si, obran malas obras para las gentes. Et destos tales dize la Scriptura que son tales como el loco que tiene la espada en la mano, o commo el mal principe que ha grant poder. (414)

*There are others who speak and fulfill their duties very well, but they hold bad intentions; therefore, the same good they do for themselves, they do wrong to others.*

Patronio again condemns those who wish to improve their social position using the language of Christian orthodoxy. Those rich men who, through financial wealth changed their station did so for selfish purposes and are like madmen with swords or evil princes with great power: they threaten the existing, divine social order with mundane anarchy.

Patronio argues that the degree to which one knows himself can be determined through an evaluation of works done over a long period of time, and an examination of how these works increase and decrease one's estate.

> conviene que non judguedes a ninguno sinon por las obras que fiziere luengamente, et non poco tienpo, et por commo vieredes que mejora o que peora su fazienda, ca en estas dos cosas se paresçe todo lo que desuso es dicho. (414)

*It is in your best interest not to judge anyone for the acts they perform at any one determined point in time, but for those they do over a long period of time and also for how that act increases or decreases his wealth. These two things will determine what has been said before.*

Only those who trace their nobility through ancestors would be able to pass such a test because, for such an evaluation to apply, judgment would have to be rendered after observing an appropriate manner of living over a long period of time. This would exclude the recently titled who were conceded their position by the king for a single act, and who, until the concession of their title, would have had no real *fazienda* to lose or improve.[13] Patronio uses the example of Saladín to provide the answer to Lucanor's question of how to know himself.

Patronio chooses a historical figure for his fiction, one who was greatly admired by people of the time.[14] In the tale, Saladín, the sultan of Babylon, finds himself forced, due to the size of his retinue, to stay in a vassal's home while traveling and while there he falls in love with the vassal's beautiful wife. According to Patronio, Satan, more powerful than any king, blinds Saladín to his responsibilities as sultan and compels him to lust after the wife of another man. In any event, Saladín's love is so deep that he searches out an evil counselor who advises him to send the vassal on a mission so that the king will be able to have what he desires. The wife of his vassal realizes that the love that the king professes is not honorable and asks that he answer one question before having his way with her. Saladín consents so she asks that he tell her what the greatest quality is that a man may have. Saladín, at a loss, cannot immediately respond and goes in search of the answer.

After asking his wise men to no avail, the king disguises himself as a jongleur and with two others goes in search of the answer to the woman's question. Patronio employs the journey or quest metaphor to illustrate Saladín's search for self. The text points to the fact that the king disguises himself as a minstrel during his journey so that he will not be recognized as a king. Patronio reiterates this fact several times. Unlike the ruse conceived by the king in the first exemplary tale, no implication exists here that the king wishes to abandon his social position or responsibilities, although he does so by leaving his kingdom to search for the answer to the question put to him. Instead, the change in clothing is pertinent since as a minstrel he can follow his quest without being recognized either as a social deviant or as an unworthy ruler. Ironically, Saladín does not find the answer in the Pope's court in Rome (religious authority) nor in the palace of the king of France nor in that of any other king (civil authority), and he then chooses to continue the search because, as Patronio says, the truly great man finishes what he has begun.

The king finds his answer in the home of an old, blind, but very wise knight who had served for many years under Saladín. This aged knight reveals that the greatest virtue a man can have is shame (vergüença). It is because of shame that a man dies and through a sense of shame that he does good and avoids evil. According to the knight, shame is chief among all virtues. With this knowledge, Saladín, no longer disguised as a minstrel, returns to his kingdom where his subjects rejoice and celebrate his return. After the celebration he calls for the wife of the vassal who, after hearing the sultan's answer to her original question, poses another. The woman asks the sultan to identify the greatest man in the world. Saladín responds by indicating himself. She begs that he, the greatest man in the world, feel shame for the wrong he wishes to do her and to release her from the promise that she has made. He demonstrates self-knowledge by realizing the error he has committed, and by absolving the woman of her promise, whereby the tale ends with the king, armed with the knowledge of who he is, rewarding the vassal and his wife with honor.[15]

Patronio closes the frame, summarizing the tale by outlining the benefits one accrues with shame and by telling what happens to those who have no shame. Both those with and those without shame perform works (*fazer*). Lucanor began the frame by asking for Patronio's advice so as to maintain his *fazienda*, his personal wealth; *fazer* takes on the specific meaning of maintenance of estate at the close of the frame. Those who perform works because of shame do good and are successful. Those who perform works without shame do ugly and evil things and may be successful; Patronio does not say that those without shame are unsuccessful. Both types may achieve their desired ends but those without shame will eventually be punished. The advice is to know yourself because by knowing yourself you will recognize others for who they are and not who they pretend to be. Such recognition allows for self protection against those who attempt to take what is not theirs.

The frame story reveals the desired ends: amassing and guarding personal wealth. The exemplary tale delineates the means. Shame, dressed as Christian virtue in the tale of Saladín, becomes a guiding tool for behavior and a metaphor for protecting what one has from those without shame, those who, like the three tricksters in XXXII, will take wealth from unwitting victims. Covarrubias uses a similar analogy in his definition of *vergüenças*. He bases the definition on the sixteenth and early seventeenth-century usage of *vergüenza*, but the more modern definition aptly applies to what Juan Manuel has been demonstrating all along in his tales.

> ay algunos desvergonçados que con mucha libertad piden lo que se les antoja a los hombres honrados y vergonçosos, los quales muchas vezes no osan negar lo que estos tales les piden; y es lo mesmo que salir a saltear a un camino, porque aunque lo pidan prestado no tienen ánimo de bolverlo. (Covarrubias 1002)

*There are plenty of shameless people who freely ask honest and decent men for whatever they please. The latter sometimes do not dare deny them what they asked for. Although they claim to borrow it, they have no intention of returning it, and this is the same as robbing somebody.*

Shameless people take wealth under false pretenses without ever intending to return it; they rob those with a sense of shame. Giving to shameless people is allowing yourself to be robbed and those who have shame, but give to the shameless, are foolish: "Avergonçarse en valde, quando han respondido a estos tales pidiendo alguna cosa, *nescitis quid petatis*" (Covarrubias 1002). The Latin response alludes to the biblical story of when the two apostles asked to sit at Christ's right hand. Jesus' response was, "You know not what you ask" (Matthew 20: 20-22). Christ further explains that what the apostles ask is not his to give but belongs to God. In the case of the *Conde Lucanor*, those with shame are ashamed in vain when they respond in an attitude of superiority since what they have is not theirs to give; they do not occupy a position sufficiently powerful to be able to presume greatness, they do not know themselves. While the *Covarrubias* is a sixteenth-century dictionary, the analogy nevertheless applies to the latter part of the Middle Ages as well.

As has already been outlined in the second chapter, the fourteenth-century social system is in a state of evolution and those of noble birth are scrambling to amass more wealth in order to maintain their position over the rising powers of the monarchy. According to the premises of *El Conde Lucanor*, those who have shame recognize themselves and all of the implications of such recognition, and work to maintain a lifestyle befitting their position. Shame is knowing how much you have and protecting what you have from those who would take it from you.

Patronio concludes that the truly foolish are those who have heard this particular tale of Saladín and the other exemplary tales and have not recognized their worth. The truly foolish have been offended by what has been said. Patronio recognizes that there are foolish nobles just as there are shameless ones and identifies some of Lucanor's companions as these fools. A good nobleman knows himself and his estate, prepares himself, and in that way can effectively wield power.

Lucanor finds the lesson to be beneficial, as does the chronicler Juan Manuel, who has it included in the book, and writes a verse to sum up the message. "*La vergüença todos los males parte;/ por vergüença faze omne bien sin arte* (422). "Shame fights evil, as it should,/And makes it easy to do good" (Keller *Book of Count Lucanor* 188). Shame prevents bad things from occurring and to have shame is to know oneself. Self-knowledge (tener vergüenza) in its true sense will prevent one from making the fatal mistake of either desiring to move from one estate to another or allowing others to take what you have, the *males* of the verse. Shame, which is self-knowledge, will allow one to do good unequivocally. To do good it is not necessary to be quick of wit or clever (arte). To do good, and therefore well, is a simple and effective way to protect oneself. A nobleman does well within his estate not with trickery but by knowing himself and protecting his position.

Through clever words and witty stories Don Juan Manuel sends a simple and direct message: to govern well, to exercise power effectively is to increase your estate while keeping what you already have. To do this you must be alert, opportunistic, aware of your social status, and have shame. There remains to examine the three books of proverbs and the fifth book of the *Conde Lucanor* in order to discover if and how this rhetoric of power, introduced in the exemplary tales continues to prevail.

## Notes

[1] The importance of *poridat* and to whom it should be revealed is the subject of Chapter XXIX in the *Castigos é documentos*. "Mientra la poridat tovieres guardada en tí, é la non andodieres sembrando en otras partes, serás tú señor de la poridat, é non te verná dapno della; é desque la hobieres descobierta, será la poridat señora de tí, é tú siempre estarás á sospecha que te verná mal della" (144). By extension, the powerful must have great confidence in their counselors to keep secret what is revealed to them by their lord. "si te amare, guardarte ha é non te descobrirá de aquello que te podria venir dapno, si dello fueses descobierto" (144).

[2] As opposed to Mariano Baquero Goyanes who sees Count Lucanor as "hombre desconcertado, indeciso, agobiado por la incertidumbre, mal aconsejado por gentes indeterminadas" (VII Centenario 33).

[3] "Los pecados criminales son siete: sobervia, *envidia*, yra, luxuria, *cobdiçia*, descreencia, avariçia...de envidia viene mal querençia, decibimiento, plazer de mal de su amigo, maldezir & abaxar el bien...de cobdiçia nasçe cativa alegria, & feedunbre, mucho fablar, vanas casas fablar, salimiento de entendimiento, beudez, prodegalidat, desmesura, desonestad, desverguença" (*Tesoro* 174-175). See also the second chapter of the *Libro de los sabios* "De lo que los sabios dizen en lo de la cobdiçia" (74-75), or Chapters 23 & 24 in the *Castigos é documentos*, "De cuánt mala cosa es la cobdicia, é cuántos males nascen della" and "Que fabla de cuán mala cosa es la envidia en algunos logares, é cuán buena en otros logares" (139-141).

[4] That there is a potential contradiction between temporal and spiritual goods is manifested in Giles. In the first part of the text, he devotes thirteen chapters to the happiness (bienandanza) of the prince. Six of those chapters tell where happiness will not be found: carnal delight, temporal riches, worldly honor, fame, vainglory, civil power, health, beauty, or physical power. (*Glosa* 328). The same can be found in John of Salisbury, although his overriding philosophy seems to be moderation in all things. Brunetto Latini also addresses the temporal goods, dividing them into those of the body and those of Fortune. He highlights the very fine line between proper and improper enjoyment of them. "et tales ay que se deleytan mucho & se esfuerçan mas en ellos que los otros, et acaesçe ende muchas vezes mas mal que bien, & mas de verguença que de onrra" (*Tesoro* 165). Boethius condemns them all. "If you try to hoard money, you will have to take it by force. If you want to be resplendent in the dignities of high office, you will have to grovel before the man who bestows it: in your desire to outdo others in high honour you will have to cheapen and humiliate yourself by begging. If you want power, you will have to expose yourself to the plots of your subjects and run dangerous risks. If fame is what you seek, you will find yourself on a hard road, drawn this way and that until you are worn with care. Decide to lead a life of pleasure, and there will be no one who will not reject you with scorn as the slave of that most worthless and brittle master, the human body" (*Consolation* 91).

[5] The king in this story fits the classic description of a tyrant as articulated by Castrojeriz, glossing Giles. "en esto se departe el verdadero rey del tirano, ca el verdadero rey ama el bien del común principalmente e salvando el bien común salva el suyo propio; mas el tirano face todo lo contrario, ca principalmente ama el su bien propio e si ama el bien común o el bien del reyno no lo ama sino por razón de su bien propio" (*Glosa* 246).

[6] Recall the citation from Giles that says that as the king behaves, so behave others, or in the *Castigos é documentos*: "*Cuando la cabeza duele, todos los miembros se sienten*" (*Castigos* 93). In this case, all the servants of the king report having seen the cloth as did the king. The king's desire for increased wealth backfires and becomes his desire to not lose what he already has.

"no ha leyes que así puedan apremiar a los ommes a bien facer como la buena vida del buen príncipe, ca el malo que suelta así da soltura a todos los otros e el pueblo menudo va en pos de su sennor" (*Glosa* 248). The king's tyranny is due to the absence of virtue, particularly prudence, which would show him how to use temporal goods properly. "todo pecado está en mal usar de las cosas temporales e en mal usar de aquello que deve usar bien" (*Glosa* 249).

[7] *Policraticus* Book III "One with certain knowledge has knowledge of himself, which cannot happen if one does not estimate one's own strength or if one is ignorant of others" (John of Salisbury 16).

[8] In Giles, counselors must be good, virtuous, true friends as well as astute and intelligent. The combination of these attributes should lead the counselor to counsel truthfully and avoid lies and falsehoods, something noticeably missing in these counselors (*Glosa* III 180).

[9] Their passions are out of balance. *Amor* and *mal querençia* operate properly when in harmony, but when one is more dominant than the other, the passionate individual falls into sin.

[10] This is a true measure of nobility. The prince is an ideal in which resides the best of the best. In Giles, "conviene de notar que magüera que el rey o el príncipe o cualquier governador deva en los consejos oír las sentencias de los otros, empero él deve ser más magnífico...e más justo...e más piadoso...e más largo...ca el corazón del rey deve ser más manífico e más acordado con la voluntad de Dios e más gracioso e más largo que los corazones de sus súbditos" (*Glosa* 3 175).

[11] See Gilson's *Spirit of Mediaeval Philosophy* for a discussion of the importance of self-knowledge in medieval Christian philosophy, especially pp. 209-228.

[12] Latini in the *Tesoro* divides understanding in a similar although expanded manner: "Et razonamientos son en quatro maneras: ca los unos son conplidos de grand seso & de buena razon, et esta es la flor del mundo; los otros son vazios de seso & de buena razon, & esta es la muy grand mal andança; los otros son menguados de seso, mas son bien razonados, [& esta es la muy grande malandança]; los otros son bien conplidos de seso, mas son callantios por mengua de saber & este a mester ayuda" (177).

[13] The *Libro de los doze sabios* emphasizes the importance of determining the good works that one has done before rewarding him. "Que una de las prinçipales graçias que cunple aver en los señores...ser largo de coraçón e de obra, pero que non se deve mover ligeramente a fazer merçed fasta ser çierto del bien que cada uno fizo. E en esto deve ser el rey o príncipe o regidor pesquiridor, porque muchas vezes acaéçele ser fechas relaçiones ynfyntosas, e fazer bien a quien non lo mereçe e non al que lo mereçe" (87).

[14] Saladín was Yusuf Salah al-din who ruled Egypt and succeeded the *fatimíes* for the caliphate. He participated in the battles against the crusades for Palestine and ruled between 1160 and 1194. The Keller and Keating English edition, *The Book of Count Lucanor and Patronio* (Lexington: U P of Kentucky, 1977), notes the more general medieval fascination with the sultan.

[15] In three of the four tales analyzed, three honorless characters speak out to correct the misbehavior of governors. In the first tale the counselor to the king's favorite is a slave who, upon hearing what the favorite took to be his good fortune, "començo lo a maltraer muy fieramente, et dixol que fuese çierto que era en muy grant peligro del cuerpo et de toda su fazienda" (36). The

slave treats his master in a particularly harsh manner. In spite of the slave's insight into the problem such behavior might earn him severe punishment.

In Chapter XXXII, the black stablehand addresses his king directly: "Sennor, a mi non me enpeçe que me tengades por fijo de aquel padre que yo digo, nin de otro, et por ende, digo vos que yo so çiego, o vos desnuyo ydes" (269). The stablehand accosts the king in a very informal and impudent manner and the King upbraids him, not for his impudence, but for revealing the truth.

Saladín, when faced with the truth, must concede that he does not know the greatest virtue a man can have, and when he discerns the answer, a woman must instruct him about honor and nobility: "Et sennor, pues vos esto conosçedes, et sodes el mejor omne del mundo, pido vos por merçed que querades en vos la mejor cosa del mundo, que es la vergüença, et que ayades vergüença de lo que me dezides (420). In effect, the woman shames Saladín into recognizing his error and into behaving as a good and proper king.

In all three cases, commoners recognize the errors of their sovereigns, people without personal honor and whose access to the nobiliary codes and requirements for behavior is limited. Rhetorically this has a double effect. Since estates are well defined and the roles that individuals should play within their estate well known, it is apparent to everyone, including the laborers, that these noblemen are not acting in a noble manner, are not living up to their estate, and they need correction. The significance of the advice to correct erroneous behavior, which comes from commoners, is that the noble must recognize that he is not living up to his estate. The reminder from commoners assigns more gravity to the lack of honorable action by these noblemen. Since none of these characters has honor, Patronio focuses on their corrective action as well as their character, placing the emphasis on the message rather than the source of the message. Neither the slave nor the black nor the woman has honor to lose and therefore they risk nothing by correcting their sovereign. They gain everything by having their lord avoid committing an error. Each lives and behaves harmoniously within his/her estate.

## Chapter 5: From Storytelling to Proverbial Lore

Just as Patronio first educates his charge with popular exemplary tales of fictionalized experiences, in Books II, III, and IV, he resorts to stylized snippets of popular experience, what he calls *proverbios*, and invites Count Lucanor to teach himself. The collections of *sentenciae* employ a more learned form than the exempla with a broader base of experience for a more refined and noble listener. The purpose is to induce the noble listener to look within himself for the lessons needed to exercise and maintain power, to protect his honor, estate, and household so that he may attain salvation.

Analysis in this chapter focuses on Juan Manuel's rhetoric of power contained in proverbs. An analysis of *texture*, in which the construction of the proverb and its parts is examined; *text*, in which the proverb is examined as a complete utterance; and *context*, in which the proverb is analyzed in the light of the social situation in which it is presented, demonstrates that the three books of proverbs continue to emphasize the message of the collection of exemplary tales: that understanding comes through the performance of "works" which is the proper exercise of power. The proverbs continue that theme while presenting the messages on another rhetorical plane. The rhetoric and messages of Patronio are couched in pithy statements endowed with great truth value and authority that function at more obscure levels than the "plainly spoken" exemplary tales.

### The function of obscurity and rhetorical construction

Throughout the various extant works of Juan Manuel many references can be found to how he or his characters believe books should be written. One of the best examples is in the Prologue to the *Crónica abreviada* in which the issue of clarity in writing is addressed in terms of readership:

> Segunt que dice Iohan Damasçeno [en] el libro de *Las propiedades de las cosas*, por que los omes sson enbueltos en esta carnalidat espessa, non pueden entender las cosas muy sotiles que sson para mostrar las cosas que son fechas sy non por algunas maneras corporales, asi como por yngenios o por semejanças. E pues esto fizo Iohan Damasçeno en todos los omnes, mucho mas deue entender en los que non son letrados. E por esta razon, los que fazen o mandan fazer algunos libros, mayor mente en romançe, que es sennal que se fazen para los legos que non son muy letrados, non los deuen fazer de razones nin por palabras tan ssotiles que los que las oyeren, non las entiendan, o por que tomen dubda en lo que oyen. (I 574)

*According to St. John Damascus in his book The properties of things, men are covered by flesh and can not understand very difficult ideas used to explain the way things are done unless they are related to earthly matters, like the ones explained through analogy and examples. Therefore, St. John Damascus determined that from all man, the ones who are not educated should be able to understand it the most. When a book is written or commanded to be written for the laymen, especially in a romance language, it should not contain difficult concepts or words. This is so because these people are not very well educated and it needs to be ensured that when they listen to these words and concepts they will understand them and not doubt them.*

In one of his few references to authorities, Juan Manuel cites Saint John Damascus to develop his argument that writing should be within the reach of its hearer, and particularly in those texts written in *romance*. Man is inherently incapable of understanding difficult concepts because he is tied to this physical world.[1] The only way in which subtle things can be made accessible is through consonance, the relationship of subtle things to corporeal things of this world. The use of the vernacular indicates, according to this prologue, that the intended readership is comprised of those who cannot understand great subtlety, and subtlety therefore should be avoided. In fact, Juan Manuel establishes a hierarchy of human beings. There are those who can understand a little subtlety ("non son muy letrados") and those who cannot understand subtle things at all ("non son letrados"). *Romance* is used for those who are not very educated, but are still capable of understanding some subtlety. This is not to say that Juan Manuel sees no value in anything other than "plain speaking" exemplary tales or similitudes. The opposite, in fact, is true. In the same prologue the nobleman goes on to say that the *Cronica* does contain *cosas sotiles* that will require close reading.

> non quiso poner i palabras nin razones muy sotiles; *pero quiso que lo fuesen ya quanto* por que, segunt dizen los sabios, quanto omne mas trabaja por aver la cosa, mas la terna despues que la ha. E otrosy por que dizen quel saber deue ser cercado de tales muros que non puedan entrar alla los neçios. (I 573, my italics)

> *I did not want to use very difficult words or ideas; I did not want it to be that easy either because, according to the wise men, the more a man works to attain something the more he will appreciate it once achieved. Also, because it is said that such precious knowledge should be kept away from fools.*

Repeating two medieval commonplaces, Juan Manuel says that lessons too easily understood are not appreciated, and that important knowledge should be kept out of the hands of fools.

The issues of rhetorical propriety that Juan Manuel addresses in the *Cronica abreviada* are mirrored in the *Libro de los estados*.

> Et por ende estas cosas en que los que non pudiesen entender podrian tomar alguna dubda por mengua de los sus entendimientos, estas tales cosas quiero las yo poner por letras tan escuras, *que los que non fueren muy sotiles non las puedan entender. Et cuando viniere alguno que aya entendimiento para lo leer, so çierto que avra entendimiento para lo entender, et placer le a por lo que fallara escripto, et aprovechar se a dello;. Et el que lo non entendiere, non podra caer en dubda por lo que veyere, pues non lo pudiere leer por escuridat de las letras.* (I 429, my italics)

> *Hence, there are ideas that can be misunderstood by people who can not comprehend due to their lack of intelligence. Such ideas I wish to make obscure so that they will remain incomprehensible to those who lack intelligence. Should anybody with a brain able to read it come along, he will have the brain to understand it also. He will find pleasure in the reading and will take advantage of it. He who fails to understand it will not be in danger of misinterpreting as he will be unable to read it due to the difficulty of the writing.*

The character Julio differentiates between levels of understanding and tells his charge that the way to control the diffusion of a message is to obscure the form in which it is recorded. Those who are endowed with knowledge of subtle ways will work to understand the message and appreciate the knowledge they gain through its understanding. That same understanding will elude those who are not endowed with such abilities, but at the same time, the obscure form in which the text is written will protect them from falling into any doubt about what they read. The implications are clear. While some things should be accessible to all, other ideas, important ideas, must be written in such a way that the information not fall into the wrong hands; obscurity is used like a secret code, accessible to those possessing the tools to decipher the code.

In the case of *El Conde Lucanor* this obscurity of style will be manifested from the easily understood summary verses at the end of each exemplary tale in the first part through the three collections of pithy sayings, each collection becoming more and more obscure so that only those endowed with the greatest wit and intelligence will be able to understand the entire book. Those with lesser degrees of intelligence will be left with part of the lesson but never its entirety. Through the hierarchical arrangement of understanding (obscure, obscurer, obscurest writings), Juan Manuel proposes to extend the hierarchy by which to measure nobility proposed in the collection of exemplary tales. (Recall the emphasis on knowing oneself, thereby knowing others, especially in tale L).

Juan Manuel feels obligated to justify his use of *sentençias* in the second part of the *Conde Lucanor*, and reminds the reader that in the first part of the book he wrote just as he intended: he wrote in a manner easily understood. He attributes this style of writing to his lack of formal education, that he, like the readers or listeners, cannot understand subtlety in writing, and it is this self-deprecation, a rhetorical trope, which will put Juan Manuel's listeners in a favorable state of mind. Far from being ignorant Juan Manuel is very clever. He writes from a position of extreme modesty so that he may win the good will of his listeners; he is a man with only the best intentions. This posturing provides him with rhetorical credibility, and also sets up his justification for the second and succeeding parts in which he employs a variation on the modesty *topos*.

In the *Razonamiento* (prologue to part II), Juan Manuel introduces the reader to Don Jayme of Xérica and claims that Don Jayme wants the author to write in a more obscure manner. Juan Manuel says that what he is about to write he does out of the love he has for Don Jayme, another rhetorical topos related to the modesty formula.[2] Juan Manuel recalls the problem of making lessons palatable to his readers. In the collection of exemplary tales, this was accomplished in part by his use of language and entertaining tales. In the succeeding parts the nobleman deals with the more difficult lessons by introducing the reader to Jayme of Xérica and blaming him for what is to come.

> dire yo, con la merçed de Dios, lo que dixiere por palabras que los que fueran de tan buen entendimiento commo don Jayme, que las entiendan muy bien, et los que non las entendieren non pongan la culpa a mi, ca yo no lo queria fazer sinon commo fiz los otros libros, mas pongan la a don Jayme, que me lo fizo assi fazer, et a ellos, por que lo non pueden o non quieren entender. (440-441)

*I will say, by God's mercy, the ideas I express in my writings will be easily comprehended by those with good judgment, such as don Jayme. Those who can not understand them should not blame me. Blame don Jayme, as I wanted to write this book in the same manner I wrote the others; but he had me write it this way knowing there would be those who could not or would not understand. They should blame themselves also if they can not or will not understand it.*

Juan Manuel writes the succeeding Parts II, III, and IV in a more obscure style than that of the first Part, and he does so at the request of his good friend Don Jayme. Juan Manuel establishes the code for reading: although the topics to which Juan Manuel will direct his writing are not subtle in and of themselves, the manner in which they are told is obscure. If the reader cannot understand them, they are to blame Don Jayme for obliging Don Juan Manuel to write in a manner of which he does not approve or blame themselves for their inability or unwillingness to understand what is contained in the succeeding sections.

The idea of blaming Jayme of Xerica is a straw man argument, the clever application of a rhetorical trope because for all his position and power, Don Jayme is not capable of forcing Juan Manuel, a nobleman on a par with royalty, to write in one or another manner.[3] The reader familiar with the two historical figures would be aware of this and would then be forced to focus on the second group: themselves. Juan Manuel tells the reader that *noble* men can understand what he is about to write, and if they cannot they must blame themselves for their ignorance. Once again the nobleman shows his awareness of rhetorical propriety. Brunetto Latini, discussing rhetorical propriety in the construction of a prologue to a text that deals with unpleasant things suggests that one of the ways to win your readers is to displace the negative onto somebody else who is "loved" by the listeners, claim sympathy with the reader and blame what is to come on this "other".[4] This is precisely what Juan Manuel does in the *Razonamiento* to the second and succeeding parts.

In each of the second, third and fourth parts of the book, the character Patronio refers to the previous sections and discusses how they progress from the clear to the obscure.

> trabaje de vos dezir algunas cosas mas de las que vos avia dicho en los enxienplos...et pues en la segunda parte ha çient proverbios et algunos fueron ya quanto oscuros et los mas, assaz declarados; et en esta terçera parte puse çinquenta proverbios, et son mas oscuros que los primeros çinquenta enxienplos, nin los çient proverbios.
> (461)

*I attempted to add ideas to those you already mentioned in the examples...the second part contains one hundred proverbs more, some of which were labeled as the most difficult; in the third part I added another fifty proverbs, more difficult than the first fifty examples or the hundred proverbs.*

Patronio describes the tales as easily understood and says of the proverbs through the second and third parts of the book that some are easy to understand and others more difficult. He tells Count Lucanor that whoever understands everything that has been told him to this point will be able to successfully save his soul, protect his estate and his honor. The Count responds that he wants more knowledge and so Patronio, to conclude the hierarchy, tells the count that that which he is to reveal is so obscure that Lucanor will have to sharpen his ability to understand in order to determine their meaning. "Et si mas me affincaredes, auer vos he a fablar en tal manera que vos conuerna de aguzar el entendimiento para las entender"

(462). Count Lucanor has reached the limits of the knowledge held by his *ayo* that is expressible in (relatively) easily understood language. Only those with the most developed wit and knowledge will be able to learn the lessons contained in the fourth section of the text due to the obscurity of language that Patronio must employ.

While the origins of the *sententiae* in Juan Manuel's *Conde Lucanor* themselves are obscure, it is safe to say that proverbs, maxims, and aphorisms have been recorded through oral or written means of transmission by almost every clan, group, or people of the world. Luis Iscla Rovira names experience as the mother of proverbs, although an observation based on experience is not enough to create one. One essential element of any proverb is popularized wisdom stylized in a polished form.

> It is hardly conceivable, however, that it was the ordinary people who gave a proverb its perfect form. There must have been among them anonymous poets who, seeing the raw beauty of the material, took it upon themselves to polish the saying to perfection. Spanish proverbs prior to Cervantes are much more polished with regard to rhyme and meter than later proverbs in which the meter has disappeared and only rhyme has remained. (Rovira 5)

While proverbs may be based on common experience they have been refined and stylized by the learned elite. It is this idea of the *letrado* versus *non letrado* in the creation of pithy sayings that distinguishes proverbs or *sententiae* from the Spanish *refrán*.

> El manejo de la gran masa de material proverbial español de la Edad Media ha sugerido por sí mismo la conveniencia de esta distinción (aislar los refranes populares de las sententiae de origen erudito): si bien los autores y sus personajes de ficción usan ambas clases de proverbios y les conceden el mismo honor, es notable el diverso efecto que en su estilo producen uno y otro tipo. La máxima erudita evoca el tono grave de la meditación libresca; el dicho popular capta la nota de frescura inherente en la observación espontánea del pueblo. El propio español de la Edad Media sentía

> hondamente esta diferencia: después de experimentar considerablemente con una docena y pico de nombres, deja el término romance proverbio, ampliamente adoptado, para la sabiduria sentenciosa, y se decide por refrán para designar el dicho popular. (O'Kane 14-15)

*The handling of the numerous Middle Age Spanish proverbs has triggered the convenience of this distinction (the separation between popular sayings from proverbs): although authors use both indistinguishably, they grant them the same prestige, it is remarkable the different effect in style that each independently cause. Proverbs connote the serious tone of educated meditation; sayings capture the spontaneity in everyday observations of lay people. Even the Middle Age Spanish language struggles with this difference and experiments with different labels to express these nuances. The term romance proverb survived and is widely adopted to label the knowledge encrypted in the proverbs, the term saying comes to label the popular knowledge.*

Proverb is the term that is given to sententious statements of erudite origin, graver in tone and less colorful. The refrán is a colorful saying of popular origin. Ernst Curtius, recalling the early Middle Ages, places the origins of the learned pithy sayings in the mouths of the *auctores*, crediting Quintilian with the term *sententiae*.[5]

> Let them learn, too, to take to pieces the verses of the poets, and then to express them in different words; and afterward to represent them, somewhat boldly, in a paraphrase, in which it is allowable to abbreviate or embellish certain parts, provided that the sense of the poet be preserved. He who shall successfully perform this exercise, which is difficult even for accomplished professors, will be able to learn anything. (Quintilian 69)

These short summations of earthly experience were used to teach, within the study of grammar, the art of speaking. *Sentenciae* were to be written by the student along with the context from which they originated (Quintilian 69). They were also used to teach through the invention of types of parlor games in which, much like the alphabetical arrangements of exempla, words from one proverb were used to begin another and so on for the purpose of challenging the student's knowledge.

In Spain *sententiae* maintain their didactic function, and appear interspersed with *exempla* in collections of exemplary tales like the *Disciplina*

*Clericalis* or, as in the case of the *Bocados de oro*, collections of *sententiae* with some exempla mixed in. The chief difference between *exempla* and *sententiae* according to Alan Deyermond is their origin.

> Most of the wisdom literature is derived directly or indirectly from Arabic, and most of the Spanish texts are related to one another, either by descent from common sources or by direct influence....In most of these works, the sententiae-which either originate in the Arabic tradition or have been filtered through it-are not attributed to particular wise men by name....Very few of the sententiae contained in thirteenth-century wisdom literature are biblical, although many of them could be turned to an edifying purpose in sermons. (Deyermond *Literary History* 99-100)

While Deyermond's assertion about the origins of exempla and sententiae is suspect, the lack of attribution to the *auctores* with regard to the *sententiae* is interesting. The *sententiae* found in Juan Manuel's works are not attributed to any authority and are not biblical in origin. In the case of the *Conde Lucanor*, Juan Manuel chooses to use *sentençias* and *proverbios*, and to follow contemporary practices in the construction of his text, mixing exemplary tales and *sententiae*. The didactic function of the *sententiae* in fourteenth-century Castile does not vary significantly from their function in Greek and Roman texts that date back to the Classical period.

### *Sentenciae* and experience in Book One

The genesis of all *sententiae* is experience. It is also true that *sententiae* give meaning to experience through form. In the first part of the *Conde Lucanor,* Juan Manuel gives meaning to the experiences in the exemplary tales and their frames through the concluding verses. Count Lucanor experiences a social situation and requires more information in order to act upon the circumstances correctly. Patronio provides an illustration of parallel experience which leads the count to act upon his circumstances, and at the same time gives him more experience in the difficult job of learning how to govern correctly. The narrator records that Don Iohan found the lesson pleasing and important enough to include in the book as well as to recall the lesson he garnered from the tale in the form of a *sententia*. Through form, these *sententi*ae give meaning to the experiences exposed in the tale. By writing a summary verse associated with a social function, Don Juan Manuel emphasizes its importance by encouraging the placement of the message in the reader's memory, facilitating both the ability to recall the tale (frame and all) as well as the lesson through *memoria ad res*. He likewise encourages the adoption of the described behavior by means of the same exercise. The nobleman tells the reader that he considers the tale to be worthy of inclusion in his text and it inspires him to action. A consequence of acting on Don Iohan's memorial cues is that the *sententiae* signal membership in a particular group, in this case, both a national and social group: the Castilian nobility.[6] It is the experience of the tale that leads to the "creation" of an appropriate proverb, and the proverb in turn imparts meaning by recalling the experience of the tale. While the frame, the tale, and the proverb can be separated for ease of discussion, they cannot be separated in terms of context and how they impart meaning.

By virtue of their historical tradition and those historical figures that employed them, the use of the *sententiae* reinforces the idea that understanding comes through works. This process is repeated for each of the fifty episodes of Part I, and it forms part of Juan Manuel's plan for the rhetorical manipulation of his readers. Lucanor's action on Patronio's advice, his profit from that action, Juan Manuel's judgment of the exemplary tales as good and worthy of inscription in the book, and his summation of the lesson in sententious verse address the issue of reception within the overall textual framework. Within the encounter between lord and counselor, Patronio's lesson always has moral, spiritual, and economic value. None of the fifty exemplary tales leaves room for doubt or gives pause to consider what has been told. "El conde se fallo por bien aconsejado del consejo de Patronio, su consejero, et fizo lo commo el le consejara, et fallose ende bien"

(37). Readers are told that Count Lucanor instantly recognized the advice as good, acted upon it, and profited from it. The use of past tense is fundamental. Patronio's advice is infallible because its proper reception has led to appropriate action. Everything is presented in the past tense as a *fait accompli* with positive results. The narrator records that Don Juan Manuel, an actual nobleman of fourteenth-century Castile, believes the lesson to be beneficial and also records his interpretation of the lesson of the story in proverb form. "Et entendiendo Don Iohan que estos exienplos eran muy buenos, fizo los escribir en este libro, et fizo estos viessos en que se pone la sentençia de los enxienplos" (37). While Lucanor benefits from the tale told by Patronio, Juan Manuel learns from the exempla (frame **and** tale).

The nobleman considers the entire tale of Lucanor and Patronio worthy of inclusion in the collection and emphasizes its value by recording a *viesso* to summarize its lesson. The inclusion of the sententious verse recalls the lesson and forces the listener to recreate the context in which it was told; thus, reinforcing the lesson. It also brings to play within the fiction the credibility of historical figures of classical antiquity. The blurring of the fiction/reality line by reporting the reaction of a character whose namesake is a true historical figure (Don Iohan) reiterates and reemphasizes the infallibility not only of the lesson, but also of an immediate response to good advice. Juan Manuel gives the advice universality and weight by composing or citing a verse that summarizes the lesson of the exemplary tale. The fact that the *sentençia* recorded by Juan Manuel may be of dubious historical origin does not affect the impact of the use of a learned tradition on the reader, because readers are led to believe, on the basis of form, that Juan Manuel draws on a long, prestigious, historical tradition of *sententiae*.

The formula is important in terms of the construction of the verse and its universality. Patronio takes each tale and moulds it to fit a frame. He actualizes it by giving it a specific meaning in a specific (social) context. Patronio takes a generic form and makes it mean or signify socially and historically for his advisee. The character Juan Manuel actualizes the story and makes it signify as well, but on an even larger scale since he shapes his verses not solely on the basis of the exemplary tale, but rather on both the larger frame which includes the count and his counselor and the interior tale told by the counselor in response to the petition of Count Lucanor.

The *sententiae* within the text have their origin in an extrapolation from an enjoyable experience. Juan Manuel enjoys his reading experience and is motivated to summarize what he has learned by writing a sententious verse. Likewise, this verse has its genesis in a life experience which is focused on universal norms. According to the narrator, Don Juan Manuel likes the story that has been told, decides that it should be included in the book and then inscribes a proverb to summarize the meaning of each tale. The proverb links private (secret), fictional experience to public, real (historical) experience. The initial statement, that an historical character both likes the tale and decides to have it included in the book *El Conde Lucanor,* establishes the credibility of the fiction and its didactic purpose for the immediate historical reader. It also establishes a type of ethos between the reader and Don Juan Manuel. He, like they, likes the story, finds it pleasant, entertaining and instructive enough to inspire the recording of learned *sententiae*. He is amused, as are they, and is properly inspired. Juan Manuel records these *sententiae* to summarize the meaning of the story so that once again the reader outside the text faces the interpretation of the proposed problem and the urgent significance of the fictional tale.

In the case of Juan Manuel's interpretation in sententious verse, his interpretation or analysis may or may not reflect the apparent lesson already articulated by Patronio. At the end of the first tale in Chapter I, the narrator concludes:

> Et entendiendo don Iohan que estos exienplos eran muy buenos, fizo los escribir en este libro, et fizo estos viesos en que se pone la sentençia de los exienplos. Et los viessos dizen assi:

> *Non vos engannedes, nin creades que, endonado,*
> *faze ningún omne por otro su danno de grado.*

Et otros dizen assi:

> *Por la piadat de Dios et por buen consejo,*
> *sale omne de coyta et cunple su deseo.* (60)

*Don Iohan understood the quality of these examples and had them written in a book. He also wrote these verses, which provide the moral of the examples. The verses go as follow:*

> *Do not let yourself be fooled, nor believe that, if given the chance*
> *Any man will harm himself for the benefit of another.*

*Other verses go as follows:*

> *Through God's mercy and good advice,*
> *a man flees trouble and makes his wishes come true.*

Each proverb written by Don Juan Manuel synthesizes what has just been experienced through reading into two memorable tidbits for popular and learned consumption. In this case, the first verse reiterates the counsel of Patronio that Lucanor faces a test because no one does himself harm for the benefit of another (*faze ningún omne por otro su daño de grado*). The first verse gives common sense advice and also summarizes Patronio's tale. The second verse highlights a new interpretation of the tale by praising good advice, an element of the tale but not the specific focus given the tale by Patronio although exemplified in their relationship. This second verse at the end of the first tale is significant in that the nobleman, to whom the tale seemed worthy of inclusion in his text, models true learning from a fourteenth-century point of view. Don Iohan has not only heard the tale, he has truly understood it because, in the memorial culture of the later Middle Ages, one demonstrated learning by making the text one's own. In other words, by writing not only one verse but two, Juan Manuel shows the depth of his learning. He has taken the tale, frame and all, and extends his knowledge or understanding of the lesson manifested through the creation of two verses that summarize the one lesson. The writing of two verses also goes to prove the assertion that Juan Manuel is trying to create a position for himself as *auctor* and imbue his text with *auctoritas*. "An 'author' acquires 'authority' only by virtue of having his works retained *'sententialiter'* in the memories of subsequent generations" (Carruthers 190). (This is clearly a function of Jayme of Xérica in the prologue to the second part). While the passage of time in the text is not that of "subsequent generations" in the literal sense, it is so in the figurative sense that Don Iohan writes his verses after hearing the tale...his verse is a second generation response to the first generation "telling" by the character Patronio. The point is that the adaptive process through Don Iohan's interpretive verses serves to "authorize" the text or to encourage the authorization process.

## *Sentenciae* and experience in the succeeding books

The second part of the *Conde Lucanor* Patronio continues to teach Lucanor, but instead of Lucanor's presentation of social circumstances which in turn motivate an illustrative parallel on the part of Patronio, there is a long uninterrupted recitation of one hundred proverbs on the part of Patronio without the motivation of a petition by Count Lucanor that Patronio teach him more. Unlike the first book, the *sententiae* are not placed in a particular association to a story. Meaning in the second book, and of *sententiae* in general, is generated by context, and in order to decipher the function of the second and succeeding books the focus must be placed on the creation of context.

In an attempt to define folklore, of which proverbs form a part, Alan Dundes proposes three levels of analysis for the purpose of identifying a work as folkloric: texture, text and context (22).[7] Texture is the language employed in a given genre. Textural features of proverbs, for example, may be rhyme and alliteration like that employed in the verses that summarize the exemplary tales.[8] The second level of analysis is that of the text, a recitation of a proverb, for example. Research on the books of proverbs in *El Conde Lucanor* has focused on these two levels.

## Proverbial texture and its function

At the level of texture, the three books of maxims in the *Conde Lucanor* clearly demonstrate Juan Manuel's familiarity with contemporary rhetorical theory. Juan Manuel rewrites many of the proverbs and maxims that he employs in the three books of proverbs, and employs such rhetorical figures as *zeugma* among many others.[9] Matthew of Vendôme in the *Art of Versification* defines *zeugma* as "making a single verb serve as the predicate of different clauses" (*Art* 27). As an example of *zeugma*:

> Guiamiento de la naue, vençimiento de lid, melezinamiento de enfermo, senbramiento de qual quier semiente, ayuntamiento de nouios non se pueden fazer sin seso de omne et voluntat et gracia speçial de Dios. (II 450)

*Things such as piloting a ship, winning a battle, curing a sick person, sowing a seed and matchmaking can not be undertaken by men who lack intelligence, and the will and grace of God.*

From the specialized activity (piloting a ship) to the mundane (sowing the seed) Juan Manuel attributes every temporal action, in a sort of extended metonymy, to the knowledge of Man, as well as the will and grace of God. The verb that serves as the predicate for each clause is *poder* (*fazer*). *Poder* expresses the ability to do (or not do) something, a form of power, and is even more closely linked to power in that the noun "power" in Spanish is also *poder*. The reader's eyes are guided to the "empowering" verb and find that in order for such activities to occur, Man must use his knowledge in their employ. Man's knowledge is privileged in position to God's will and grace with the effect that Man's power to act is most emphasized. This is not to suggest that Juan Manuel or the maxim are positioning Man over God; it is to recognize that God's will is inscrutable and his grace is given according to his will, neither over which Man has any power. The maxim underlines the importance of acting and exercising power, informed by knowledge and supported by God's blessing.[10] Similar advice is seen in the following example:

> Por fuertes animos, por mengua de auer, por vsar mucho mugeres, et bino et malos plazeres, por ser tortiçero et cruel, por auer muchos contrarios et pocos amigos se pierden los sennorios e la vida. (II 465)

*Power can be lost by exercising a lack of self-control, by lacking profit, by womanizing, by drinking and surrendering to earthly pleasures, by being cruel and unfair, and by having many enemies and few friends.*

Man is most certainly capable of acting, but the exercise of power has consequences. Where an individual may act properly and profit from his acts, in this second example, actions that are abusive of either self or others cause loss. Desires must be controlled, so too the passions in the proper exercise of power; control without which both temporal and spiritual wealth are forfeit.

Juan Manuel employs other tropes, figures and colors in the three collections as well: *polysyndeton* in which parallel phrases are joined with a number of coordinating conjunctions, "Todas las cosas an fin et duran poco et se manitenen con grand trabajo et se dexan con grand dolor et non finca otra cosa para sienpre sinon lo que se faze sola mente por amor de Dios" (444); *paronomasia* in which words appearing at the beginning or ending of the same line have a similar sound, "Grant marabilla sera, si bien se falla, el que fia su fecho et faze mucho bien al que erro et se partio sin grand razon del con qui avia mayor debdo" (454); *contentio,* where contrasting ideas are in adjacent phrases, "Todas las cosas paresçen bien et son buenas, et paresçen mal et son malas, et paresçen bien et son malas, et paresçen mal et son buenas" (445); *homoeoteleuton,* in which a group of words end in the same sound, "Por riqueza, nin pobreza, nin buena andança, nin contraria, no deue omne parar se del amor de Dios" (446); *exclamatio,* an exclamation, "¡Commo es aventurado qui sabe soffrir los espantos et non se quexa para fazer su danno!" (447); *paranomeon,* the repetition of the initial syllable of immediately adjacent word, "El rey rey reyna" (448); *membrum orationis*, which emphasizes an idea by expressing it in a series of parallel phrases, usually without conjunctions, "Lo caro es caro, cuesta caro, guardasse caro, acabalo caro; lo rehez es rehez, cuesta rehez, guardase rehez, acabalo rehez; lo caro es rehez, lo rehez es caro" (454); and *apostrophe,* an expression of grief or indignation, to name but a few.

The apostrophe in the first collection of proverbs is important because of the incongruity of its presence and length. Rhetorically, the function of an apostrophe is to amplify a topic and is supposed to be a passage that slows the tempo, giving the reader pause to consider what is being said. Thematically in this case it recalls Patronio's discussion of *verguença* in tale L, and anticipates his discussion of the nature of Man in the fifth Book. It is decidedly negative in describing Man and does so by depending on the juxtaposition of contrary notions to make the point that Man is truly a foolish being. "lo quel dize non se entiende, nin entiende lo quel dizen...non quiere perdonar et quiere quel perdonen; es escarnidor, e el es el escarnido" (443).

The collections of proverbs depend on the use of adjectives, what Vendôme calls *epithets* or *rhetorical colors* which show attributes of a noun. These epithets are attributed to both things and people; a look at the series of maxims in the second book underscores this observation: "En *las cosas* que...," "El mas conplido de los omnes *es el* que...," "De mal seso *es el* que...," "Non es de buen seso *el que*...," "De mal seso *es el* que..." (442). The notion of "Truth," for example, is modified, specified, to yield "Ay verdat buena, et ay verdat mala" (448). Patronio in this case distinguishes between types of truth. When a king is "de buen seso et de buen consejo et sabio [et] sin maliçia, es bien del pueblo; et el contrario" (450). The good king is one who is wise, wisely counseled, and not malicious. The tyrant lacks these characteristics. As the two cited *sentenciae* demonstrate, modifiers are used to establish oppositions that create a *sic et non* in which meaning is described as much by what the subject is not as by the subject itself. This technique permits Patronio to synthesize his ideas into the short and pithy pieces he presents. Sometimes the reader has to supply the opposite reading, sometimes Patronio provides it for him. "El mas conplido de los omnes es el que cognosce la verdat et la guarda," defines the complete man as one who knows and keeps the truth. The reader, by extension, learns that the least complete man does not recognize or keep truth. "Non es de buen seso el que se tiene por pagado de dar o dezir buenos sesos, mas es lo el que los dize et los faze," provides both sides of the coin for the reader: he who is satisfied to say wise things is not really wise; the wise man both says wise things and acts on them. *Brevitas,* the use of *sententiae* to synthesize ideas into short but pithy statements, is the first level of obscurity to which Juan Manuel refers in the prologue to Part II.

Introducing another level of obscurity, many of the maxims in Books II, III, and IV, operate on the repetition of the same lexical element. "Fuerça no fuerça a fuerça; fuerça se desfaz con fuerça, a vezes mejor sin fuerça. Non se dize bien 'Fuerça a vezes presta la fuerça'. Do se puede escusar, non es de prouar fuerça" (459). "Force does not force force; force undoes itself with force, at times it is better to do without force. The saying 'Force helps force at times' is wrong. Where something can be forgiven or avoided, that is not the time to use force." The repetition of the term "force" is paired with its use as various parts of speech causing the reader to perform an exercise that serves to actualize the sentencia (Diz 140). This exercise includes considering the various permutations of the word "force" to arrive at a statement that makes sense to the reader, and given the variety of possibilities, more than one satisfactory sententious statement may be derived from the one written. In this case Patronio presents the issue of the exercise of power and the subtleties of its use. One reading of the maxim argues that power is most effectively wielded through gentle persuasion; that the most powerful force is restraint. Another reading suggests that when faced with overwhelming force, he who knows how to exercise power also knows when to give in to unbeatable odds. A deeper level of obscurity is, then, a broadening of the realm of a word or phrase which obliges the reader to consider various possibilities of meaning before deciding on one or another.

Another level of obscurity in the books of maxims depends on *hyperbaton* like that of the fifth book in which the word order of eleven of the proverbs is mixed up: "De mengua seso es muy grande por los agenos grandes tener los yerros pequennos por los suyos" (463). The use of *hyperbaton*, a third level of obscurity, requires the reader to be able to reconstruct the proper proverb either through playing with the word order until something emerges that makes sense, or through a familiarity with the original, correctly worded *sententia*. The corrected proverb yields "Muy grande mengua de seso es tener los agenos yerros por grandes et los suyos por pequennos." In this particular case, the use of *hyperbaton* obliges the reader to go beyond the exegetical exercises in Books II and III to include the additional exercise of having to order the parts of the *sententia*, making the sentence mean logically before deriving meaning from a consideration of what the proverb actually "says". The effort itself of rearranging the words of the proverb proves the truth of the proverb: It is foolish to consider other's mistakes as larger than your own. Patronio's mixed-up maxim reminds the reader of the importance of humility to the truly powerful as well as to those of lesser consequence: sometimes the playing field does not allow for great difference. In each of the cases presented, meaning is derived from analysis of the texture, the language used in each of the *sentenciae*.

**The proverb as text**

Text is another area of analysis in which the complete proverb or sentencia is studied. Textual analysis can include examining the individual proverbs in the light of those that precede or follow based on rhetorical notions of amplification, interpretation and digression (Ayerbe-Chaux "libro de proverbios" 8). Through such analysis, what has commonly been seen as a hodge-podge of not-necessarily-related *sentenciae* becomes more coherent and gives meaning to what has otherwise been considered by some scholars (Sturcken, Goyri, Deyermond, Macpherson) an inferior example of Juan Manuel's art. This approach sees the

152

individual proverb as related to and gaining meaning from others around it. In the fourth Book for example, the proverb "Grand vengança para menester luengo tienpo encobrir la madureza seso es" reads " Gran madureza [de] seso es menester para encobrir luengo tienpo la vengança" (465).[11] What may refer to the control of the passions or a distinction between a good governor and a tyrant receives additional shades of meaning in the light of the following proverb, "Assi es locura si el de muy grand seso se quier mostrar por non lo seer, commo es poco seso si el cuerdo se muestra cuerdo algunas vezes" (465). "It is therefore foolishness if the very wise man wishes to show himself wise by acting the fool, just as it is sometimes foolish if the wise man show himself to be wise." The second proverb amplifies the various possible meanings by refining them, establishing additional parameters for proper behavior or further specifying the definition of a good governor or a tyrant. Adjacent proverbs may parody, expand, limit, or (re)define the previously stated idea. Textually, then, the proverb is profitably analyzed in this case in its relation to the one before and/or after it.[12]

### The proverbs and their context

The third level of analysis is that of context, an exploration of the social situation in which, for purposes of this study, the *sententiae* are presented. It is important to establish context because, as in the case of the fifty exemplary tales, without context there is no fidelity of meaning or interpretation. The proverb "Meior seria andar solo que mal acompannado" (444), as a contextless utterance (in the sense of being uninformed by either the first book or the prologue to the second book) may refer to an evaluative judgment of the past, a commentary on the present, or it may prescribe action for the future. It may refer to marriage, sin, social stations, rumor, the advantages of teamwork, etc.

One of the contexts available to the reader coming to the text from the outside is the cultural context which imbued *sentenciae* with the weight of truth. Such truth was comprised of not only Scriptural truth that came from association

153

with the sapiential books (Proverbs, Wisdom, Ecclesiasticus, etc.), but also the truth that was associated with the secular authorities (Vergil, Ovid, Quintilian) which came down from Antiquity. The writings of the secular authorities were harmonized with religious authorities by the medieval schoolmen.

Concomitant with the notion of truth in the *sentenciae* is that of the polyvalence of meanings that could be gleaned from texts as mentioned above, and in this particular case, the proverbs narrated by Patronio.[13] Patronio is aware of the many possible readings of the proverbs, and his first proverb reinforces this notion: "En las cosas que ha muchas sentençias, non se puede dar regla general" (442); those things that contain many ideas or bits of wisdom cannot be easily defined. This is not to say that any reading of the text was valid, but that a reading that was informed by existing codes of behavior and belief could be said to be accurate. Certainly a reader coming to the text without having read the first part or the *Razonamiento* of the second part would be able to find meaning in the collections of proverbs. However, the *Conde Lucanor* has an established mode of discourse that is reiterated in each of the prologues to the various sections of the text. That is one of the functions of the prologue: to provide guidance to the proper interpretation of the text. In the collection of tales, meaning is controlled not only through the prologue, but also the frame that surrounds each of the exemplary tales. In the succeeding parts the frame is reduced, releasing control of the text to the reader. That is the obscurity to which Patronio refers: the reader is left to decipher the *sentenciae* in a search for truth.

In the context of *El Conde Lucanor*, each proverb is informed by the various lessons of the first book both through the continued dialogue between Patronio and Lucanor as well as through the *Razonamiento* recorded by Don Juan Manuel, in which one listens to or acts upon the words of another. These lessons are organized around the cardinal virtues, privileging Prudence, with special emphasis placed on advice (consejar), and action (obrar). In other words, the *sententiae* oblige the hearer to recreate the context already established in what has come before. The exemplary tales are easy to understand because frame, tale and sententious verse are all placed in this context. The collections of proverbs are more difficult because the reader must provide the context based upon what he has already read. The lessons are similar, but the manner in which they are learned and taught is more complex. This is what Patronio means when he tells Lucanor, "...fablar vos he daqui adelante essa misma manera, mas non por essa manera que en el otro libro ante deste" (279). Patronio will teach Lucanor how to exercise power properly, be prudent, to protect honor, estate and soul, but not through the same literary style as in the first book.

For the reader of the text the message is the same. In order to understand what is written, in order to prove one's worth as a nobleman, the reader must create the context that corresponds to the *proverbio*. Juan Manuel provided the context for the first fifty-one *sententiae* (in the first book), and he now leaves it to the reader to follow his model, drawing upon their experiences, their memories, and applying them to the verse thereby recasting their experiences and memories in a new light and learning from, realistically, themselves.

Within the text, Patronio tells Count Lucanor that the prudent man is one who knows himself and is cautious before acting in every case in Part I. This becomes one context into which the proverb may be placed, and it is reiterated frequently in the collections of *sentenciae*.[13] "-La mayor desconosçençia es quien non conosçe a ssi, pues ¿como conozcra a otri?"(448). Every sententious remark that refers to man, wisdom, or the lack of wisdom, speaks to self-knowledge. Of the 180 proverbs (by Patronio's count) included in the three collections, some 125 address the issue of knowing oneself. Of the remaining proverbs, most treat of works (obrar): "Meior es perder faziendo derecho, que ganar por fazer tuerto: ca el derecho ayuda al derecho" (446). "El yerro es yerro; del yerro nasçe yerro; del pequeno yerro nasçe grand yerro; por vn yerro viene otro yerro; si bien biene del yerro, sienpre torna en yerro; nunca del yerro puede venir non yerro" (458). "Mas tienpos aprouecha paral continuado deleyte, que a la fazienda pensamiento e alegria" (465). A good nobleman knows himself and his social estate. He works to maintain it, for it is through his proper actions that he will be able to protect honor and estate, and thereby attain the salvation of his soul.

Patronio recites *sententiae* to Count Lucanor not because of their ambiguity, but because of their authority and their ability to prescribe action. Evidence that prescription is a function of proverbs is found in Neal R. Norrick's study *How Proverbs Mean*.

> Hearers tend to react to proverb utterances as they would to directives from authoritative sources. The weight of traditional or majority opinion inculcates utterances of proverbs with authority. A simple statement of fact or belief like *An ounce of prevention is worth a pound of cure* seems to bear a directive force equal to that of a true imperative like *Look before you leap;...* (Norrick 28)

A proverb has the effect of a direct command and so the collections of proverbs in *El Conde Lucanor* become prescriptive lists of obligatory activities to be followed by those who need to learn to use their power, to maintain their social roles, and thus perpetuate the existing status quo.

The fact that these authoritative remarks come from an older and wiser man in the character of Patronio as well as the historical figure Don Juan Manuel is also no accident. Norrick's study again provides insight into the structure of the exchange between *ayo* and lord.

> due to their didactic, authoritative character, proverbs tend to place the speaker in a one-up position vis-à-vis his hearer. In citing a proverb, the speaker signals an interactional meaning that he wants to or at least is willing to assume the role of teacher/advisor for his hearer....So a speaker shows with a proverbial utterance that he has the right...to council his hearer, and thereby that the relationship is either one between equals or one in which the speaker is one-up.
> (Norrick 29)

Within the context of the dialogue between Patronio and Lucanor, Patronio demonstrates his superior wisdom, and therefore his right to educate his charge.

Through Patronio, Don Juan Manuel does the same thing: his use of *sententiae* tacitly imbues him with superior knowledge and places him in the role of teacher to the uninitiated. The reader grants this superior position to Patronio within the text, and Juan Manuel in the larger historical context.

## Notes

[1] The notion that Man's ability to understand is limited to things of this earth is central to the works of Pseudo-Dionysius. For an overview of Dionysian literary theory, see Minnis and Scott, Medieval *Literary Theory*, Chapter V, pp. 165-196.

[2] "The modesty formula is often connected with the statement that one dares write only because a friend or a patron or a superior has expressed such a request or wish or command." Ernst Robert Curtius, *European Literature and the Latin Middle Ages*. Princeton University Press, Princeton, 1973. p. 85.

[3] Devoto makes the same observation in his *Introducción*, "si Don Juan Manuel no hubiese tenido gana de emplearla, todos los ruegos de Don Jaime hubieran sido inútiles, artísticamente por lo menos" (Devoto 466). Reinaldo Ayerbe-Chaux in his article "El libro de los proverbios del conde Lucanor y de Patronio," takes Juan Manuel's announcement of Jayme of Xérica's petition in the *Razonamiento* as the starting point for his argument that the *Conde Lucanor* was revised to include the books of proverbs and the Fifth Part at a later date. Ayerbe's hypothesis is that Juan Manuel combined the *Conde Lucanor* with the *Libro de los sabios*, which would explain its absence from the extant manueline corpus.

[4] Sy por aventura tu materia desplaze, convienete encobrir tu prologo en tal manera que si es cuerpo de ome o otra cosa que desplega o que non ama, tu encubres & nonbraras un ome o otra cosa quel plega et que ame...deves dar a entender que non quieres aquello que ome cuyda que tu quieres, o que tu non defiendes lo que querries defender...et tu deves asi fazer, & entrar tu poco a poco a tañer tu entençion, et dezir que todo aquello que plaze a ellos plaze a ty, & lo que a ellos desplaze non plaze a ty. Et quando avras apaziguado aquel con quien fablas, diras que aqueste fecho non es tuyo nin aca nin alla, que quier dezir que tu non feziste el mal, mas que otro lo fizo. (*Tesoro* 190)

[5] "But the auctores are not only sources of technical information, they are also a treasury of worldly wisdom and general philosophy. In the antique poets there were hundreds and thousands of lines which put a psychological experience or a rule of life in the briefest form. Aristotle discussed such apophthegms in his *Rhetoric*. Quintilian called them 'sententiae' because they resembled the decisions of public bodies." Ernst Robert Curtius, European Literature and the Latin Middle Ages. Princeton University Press, Princeton, 1973. p. 58.

[6] cf. Neal R. Norrick. *How Proverbs Mean*. Mouton Publishers: Berlin, 1985. p. 25.

[7] These three levels have been appropriated for use in this study; their definition and application is an expansion of Dundes' use of them. In other words, Dundes uses texture, text and context in closely defined terms in order to define folklore. This study is not concerned with determining whether or not the proverbs are folkloric, but how the proverbs in Parts II, III, and IV may be studied to elucidate how they mean in the text.

[8] Latini, in Chapter 10 of the third book of the *Tesoro*, a *vademecum* on rhetoric, discusses textural features, highlighting rhyme and meter: "Ca el que quiere bien rimar, convienele contar los puntos & sus dichos, en tal manera que los viesos sean acordados en cuento & que los unos non ayan mas que los otros. Et convienele mesurar las dos postrimeras silabas del viesso, en manera que todas las silabas postrimeras sean semejantes...Et conviene que contrapassen los açentos & las bozes, asi que las rimas se acuerden en su açentos...Et commo quier

que tu fabla sea por rima o por prosa, guarda que tus dichos non sean magros nin secos, mas sean llenos de derecho & de seso & de sentençia" (*Tesoro* 182-183).

[9] Devoto records correspondences between Juan Manuel's text and others of the same period (pp 469-477), most notably the *Bocados de oro*. To the extent that what exist are correspondences and not verbatim copies of the proverbs, I argue that Juan Manuel re-wrote those that he uses thus showing his background in rhetoric.

[10] Matthew cites both *zeugma* and *hypozeuxis* as appropriate methods of beginning. Juan Manuel does not use *zeugma* as such in that he provides lists of maxims in the three collections of proverbs.

[11] In contrast to this proverb is the advice given in the *Libro de los doze sabios*, a mirror for princes commissioned by Juan Manuel's grandfather, Fernando III, a text most probably known to Juan Manuel. "Quando vieres creçer el daño, non esperes el tienpo de la vengança, que muchas vezes queda la manzilla e non el logar" (*doze sabios* 115).

[12] This type of analysis runs the risk of forcing a reading of a proverb or series of proverbs by establishing a relationship between two *sentenciae* where none may exist. John of Salisbury in the *Policraticus* uses a "stream of consciousness" presentation that makes it difficult, if not impossible to understand why one proverb or exempla follows another.

[13] Van Moos quotes William of Conches as saying: "several meanings to one passage are to be approved of, because one may consider any object from various points of view.... Variety of meanings is desirable and even pleasing, since it indicates the semantic potential of a text" (238).

[14] The notion that one must be cautious and flexible is also reiterated in the editor's explication of Sem Tob's *Proverbios Morales*. "El hombre tiene que enfrentarse con los acontecimientos con toda precaución y sagacidad, porque la idiosincrasia tanto del hombre mismo como del acontecimiento de cada ocasión, determinarán la forma y condición de acontecimientos futuros. No puede formularse regla general alguna para el trato con otros hombres, ya que cada situación plantea su propia lógica de la inestabilidad. Es preciso conocer mejor a los hombres que a las cosas y las propias reacciones deben ser espontáneas" (*Proverbios* 50-51). This observation mirrors what Patronio declares in the second part of the *Conde Lucanor*: "De las cosas que an muchas sentençias no se puede dar regla general" (II 442). Every man and every situation is different and cannot be reduced to a single rule, hence the large number of tales and proverbs.

## Chapter 6: Juan Manuel's Rhetoric of Power: the Fifth Book

Whereas in the first, second, third, and fourth books the examples and proverbs are presented as lists of good advice, the fifth Book presents a tightly reasoned narrative that begins with a short prologue in which Patronio summarizes what has come before and introduces Lucanor to what is to come. The prologue is followed by an outline of Patronio's topic of salvation of the soul. He then interrupts his argument with a digression on the sacraments. This is rhetorically proper and serves to highlight the importance of his material.[1] Patronio demonstrates or shows where his argument is going through division, which also reminds the reader of where he has been. Each of his points is presented and proved through his arguments. His proofs are confirmed through an enthymeme, example or maxim. Patronio also argues against any counter position in order to further strengthen his argument. He draws a conclusion, recounts his arguments and concludes by affirming the fact that he has done as he intended. Juan Manuel's rhetoric of power is complete.

In the fifth book only Patronio speaks. He addresses himself to Count Lucanor without a petition from Lucanor that Patronio teach him. This final section, according to the counselor Patronio, is the most important of all the others that comprise his *libro* because it deals specifically with the salvation of the soul. The ultimate goal of those who wield power is simultaneously to save their souls.

In the *Castigos é documentos*, Sancho IV says much the same thing while specifying that spiritual goods are superior to those of this earth. Spiritual gains give impetus to the governor's desire to save himself.

> si quesiesen pensar los reys que otros bienes hay en el mundo que son mayores é mejores que las riquezas nin las honras,

> despreciarlas-y-an é non las ternian en tanto. E estos son bienes de virtudes é de sabidoría, que son bienes del alma, los cuales son mejores sin comparación que los bienes del cuerpo; ca dan mayor alegría é mayor placentería al que los ha que los bienes del cuerpo. E cuanto el alma es mejor que el cuerpo, tanto estos bienes son mejores que las riquezas nin que los otros bienes del cuerpo.
>
> (*Castigos* 204)

*Kings may believe that there are goods on earth that are grander and far better than wealth and honor, which are not usually appreciated nor taken in great regard. These goods are wisdom and virtue and they belong to the souls. These goods are grander without comparison to the goods associated with the body. The former provide more happiness and pleasure than the latter. The same way the soul is better than the body, its goods are better than wealth and the goods of the body.*

Virtues and wisdom are goods that pertain to the soul. Since the soul is better than the body, the worth of these goods of the soul far outweigh those of the body. They bring greater happiness and are far more satisfying than temporal goods to him who possesses them. This outline of spiritual goods comes in a chapter in which Sancho IV tells his son that one of the elements that separates the nobleman from the rich man is the pride the rich have because they believe that with their wealth they possess all the goods they need. Sancho in the *Castigos*, and Patronio in the *Conde Lucanor* argue that because the soul is eternal and the body mortal, salvation of the soul and the concomitant goods of the soul are of primary importance. Salvation is seen as a reward for virtuous life on earth. While it is theoretically available to all, the further one is away from the religious and secular tips of the social pyramid, the more difficult it is to achieve (recall Juan Manuel's temporal and spiritual stratification in the *Libro de los estados*). The most virtuous of those occupying the secular estates are those who govern. However, they can also be the least virtuous: tyrants. Governors, like all men, do what they ought because, in Aristotelian terms (and recalling Giles' *De regimine*), it brings them happiness. Temporal happiness, the goods of the earth, for example, is not enough to merit the trials and tribulations of governing others. Those who govern well merit something more, specifically, salvation of their souls.[2] This notion serves to close the circle begun in the prologue to the first book where Juan Manuel says that his intention is to offer a book that will help others to save their souls and help their bodies: "que se aprouechen del a seruicio de Dios et para saluamiento de sus almas et aprouechamiento de sus cuerpos; asi commo el sabe que yo, don Iohan, lo digo a essa entencion" (28). This clearly stated intention and its re-elaboration in the fifth book serves to tie the five books together as a whole. They are united by Juan Manuel's intention to edify and more specifically, to help those in powerful positions earn the rewards that come with the effective use of power.

**Rewards and the Rhetoric of Power**

According to Patronio, in order to save one's soul the individual must do good works and avoid bad works. In order to avoid bad works, good works must be done. The redundancy is important for a better understanding not only of the fifth Book, but also of the entire *Conde Lucanor*.[3] Good works, according to Patronio are comprised of four elements: life within the law of salvation; faith; the performance of good works; and the avoidance of bad works. The Apostle's Creed is used to define the law of salvation. Faith is the belief in the truth of the elements of the Creed. With these perfunctory definitions established, Patronio says that what he really wants to talk about are the remaining two elements. His dismissal of the first two elements is telling: because Don Juan Manuel has delved into them in detail in the *Libro de los estados*, Patronio will not need to do so here. Patronio notes that Juan Manuel dealt with the latter two issues in depth as well in the same text. Since some readers might not be familiar with the *Estados*, however, and because the issues are of paramount importance, he will tell how good works should be done and evil works shunned in order to earn Heaven and avoid Hell. Patronio in a remarkable act of "self-referentiality" sluffs the elaboration of the first two of his divisions off onto another text so that he can elaborate the remaining two. By skirting the explicitly religious issues of the law of salvation and the importance of faith, he privileges the remaining two elements of a decidedly more ambiguous nature.

In order to understand why Patronio may choose to skirt a discussion of the law of salvation and the importance of faith, and their relationship to the performance of good works one must return to the stated intention of the book. Included in the notion of *intention* is the ability to effect change, the ability to do something by oneself, to act. Juan Manuel's stated intention is that the nobleman, through the *Conde Lucanor* text, wants to move the reader to exercise power in such a way so as to save his soul and protect his honor, estate, and physical condition. The function of rhetoric is to move the auditor to understand and act. The individual, in this case Patronio within the text and Juan Manuel both inside and outside it, cannot effect change with regard to the law of salvation or faith; Juan Manuel and his mouthpiece Patronio can effect change with regard to the performance of good works and the avoidance of evil works.

Also implicit to the notion of *intention* is the concern with means rather than specifically an end itself. Rhetoric is used as a means (to move to act) to an end, for example the adoption of a certain belief or custom. It can be argued that since the law of salvation and faith cannot be affected by the intention of the text, they are ends and therefore lie outside the scope of the text. Patronio passes by the topics because they lie outside the parameters of the *Conde Lucanor*; he focuses instead on good and evil works as means to the ends (honor, wealth, power, physical wellbeing and salvation of the soul) described in the intention of the text.

**Good, Bad, and the Function of Contraries**

The relationship between good works and bad works as stated by Patronio invites a review of the function of contraries in the later Middle Ages. It has already been noted that ethics and poetry as perceived in the later Middle Ages treat of behavior, and behavior is action as distinguished from cognition. Poetry exhorts the reader to act rather than simply to know (in the *Conde Lucanor*, readers are to *aprouecharse*). Explicit to ethics is the notion of "good." Poetry moves the reader toward the good, to be made good, to act properly. Praise and blame illustrate proper behavior according to medieval conceptions of poetry. These two qualities are normative: what is praiseworthy is good, worthy of emulation. That which is blamed is not good and should be avoided.[4] Goodness can be perceived through these contraries, and both elements in poetry can move the reader to the good. In the Middle Ages something is known not only by a description of its qualities or properties, but it is also known through what it is not, its opposite, a notion found in the oft-quoted *Sic et Non* of Peter Abelard. In the case of *El Conde Lucanor, buenas obras* can be known by their own qualities or through *malas obras*, their very opposite. The function of poetry in the later Middle Ages is to have the reader achieve a mode of existence related to the good. Juan Manuel's stated intention is the achievement of this mode of existence, and it is reiterated throughout *El Conde Lucanor* by the counselor Patronio. Poetry that either praises or blames or does both fulfills this function.

Averroes, in his commentary on Aristotle, illustrates the popular concept that all poetic utterance is either praise or blame.[5] The purpose of poetry is to move men to do one thing or dissuade them from doing another, and this necessarily involves virtue (praise) or vice (blame) because "every action and every trait of character is concerned only with one of these two" (Minnis *Medieval Theory* 291). Averroes explains that both praise and blame have the same purpose:

> And since, without exception, all comparison and representation occur through showing what is becoming or unbecoming or base, clearly this can have no other purpose than the pursuit of what is becoming and the rejection of what is base.
> (*Medieval Theory* 291)

What Averroes says is that the end of poetry is the same regardless of the means, that both *ars laudandi* and *vituperandi* serve to exhort readers to virtuous action. To do this, poets employ images, comparison, and representation (*assimilatio*), because men are made in the likeness of others. He concludes that *assimilatio* should contain both praise and blame.

If praise and blame are the end of poetry, then assimilatio is its form. Judson Allen summarizes the array of meanings associated with *assimilatio*:

> assimilatio involves indirect reference, it is verified by the imagination, it expresses the metaphysical form or ratio of that species of language whose end is praise and blame, it uses similitudes and even fictions, and it is different from 'sermo demonstrativus.' (*Ethical Poetic* 186)

Clearly *assimilatio* is difficult to define in its complexity; it comprehends comparison, representation, similitude, example and the like, all of which are employed in the *Conde Lucanor*. What is apparent is the elevation of exemplification with the purpose of moving the audience to virtue and to reject vice.

*Assimilatio* is related to decorum in that poets may praise, blame or do both, and to do so they employ different styles. Averroes provides a detailed description of tragedy or the poetry of praise. He divides poetry into six parts: fictional descriptions, customs, conscious formalism of language, beliefs, persuasiveness that is based on descriptions, and expressive power. The most important parts are customs and beliefs with the former subdivided to include both actions and manners while the latter is described as the power of representing a thing as "thus-and-so or not thus-and-so" (*Ethical Poetic* 24).

Averroes divides all poetic language into two parts, the one *assimilatio* and the other *assimilantur*. *Assimilatio* is made by description, formalism of language and expressive power while that which is "likened" or *assimilantur* is composed of customs, beliefs and the fit encouragement of belief. As already discussed, *assimilatio* is the manner of representation in poetry and according to Averroes:

> all representation either refers through the representation of its contrary and afterward it is changed to its proper intention (and this is the mode that is called among them 'indirection'), or it is representation of the thing itself without making any mention of its contrary and this is what they call signification.
> *(Ethical Poetic* 24)

Poetic language, through *assimilatio*, points to customs, beliefs or the fit encouragement of belief by representing one or the other or all three as what they are not as well as what they are. Contraries are used in poetic representation to inspire an audience to proper behavior where that behavior is concerned with adopting the proper actions, manners, and beliefs. Various poetic decorums may be employed (the use of indirection or signification, for example) to reach their laudatory ends (correct behavior).

Judson Allen, in *The Friar as Critic*, arrives at the conclusion that differing poetic decorums do not obscure the message and elaborates his point in a footnote. He provides the links between Averroes and the existing literary poetic.

> It does not really matter here whether the story be courtly or pious. The fact that the doctrine of charity was a crucial and central truth for medieval literate culture does not eliminate the possibility of other conventions, other decorums. The sensibility is the same whether the meaning is the love of God or the love of lady...Ultimately, in a sacramental universe, and as Dante proved, the distinction doesn't matter. The love of the one is the love of the All who is One.
> *(Friar* 59)

Allen, echoing D.W. Robertson, discusses the problem of medieval interpretation of literary works and finds that interpretation is the doctrine of charity as well. Augustine articulates this doctrine of charity in *On Christian Doctrine* and states that "whatever appears in the divine Word that does not literally pertain to virtuous behavior or to the truth of faith you must take to be figurative...Scripture teaches nothing but charity" (Augustine 88). This notion is akin to Averroes' discussion of representation and the use of contraries. Allen traces the doctrine of charity from its Scriptural base to its entrance into medieval literary culture where it comfortably resides in the fourteenth century. As a part of the literary culture of the later Middle Ages, charity would exercise a strong influence over the interpretation of a work - not in the modern sense that requires a rigorous, empirical interpretation, but in a relaxed sense that would allow myriad interpretations, any of which would be valid if they agreed with the notion that if the text does not literally treat of virtue it does so figuratively. In the case of the *Conde Lucanor*, this notion serves to explain the two different decorums used by Juan Manuel in the presentation of his text. Written clearly or obscurely, interpretation of the five books necessarily points to virtuous behavior which in the case of the *Conde Lucanor* is decidedly socio-political, and therefore primarily concerned with prudence.

All of the elements of poetry elaborated above are employed by Juan Manuel in his text to move the reader to do good. He employs both praise and blame in the exempla as well as in the proverbs (he also does the same in the fifth Book) to move his readers to act prudently, specifically to be astute in their exercise of power. The nobleman privileges exemplification in the creation of his text (*assimilatio*) and that which he compares (*assimilantur*) revolves around proper customs (proper behavior of a nobleman, for example), beliefs (i.e., human society as the reflection of divine social organization), and the fit encouragement of belief (the sacramental nature of *caballería*, for example). Juan Manuel never necessarily studied the poetics of Averroes, but he was very aware of contemporary rhetorical concepts, and his text is a constant reminder of that fact.

## Doing Good Works: The Sacramental Nature of Nobility

Patronio interrupts the flow of his discourse to digress and prove the truth of the Sacraments. He says that he is going to do this because, while Juan Manuel has done so in the *Libro de los estados*, his manner was more obscure than that proposed in the present text. The subject of his digression is no accident in light of the subject matter of the fifth Book. The reader of *El Conde Lucanor* may or may not already be familiar with Juan Manuel's notion of the sacramental nature of nobility. What cannot be ignored is the relationship between the sacraments and his topic in the fifth Book: the performance of works. The sacraments are specific works that are done to attain salvation. Patronio chooses to highlight two: the Eucharist (specifically transubstantiation) and Baptism.

Beginning with the Eucharist, Patronio says that it is important to prove its veracity as a sacrament because it is the most important to believe. Its relation to the thesis of the text is readily apparent as Patronio reminds the reader that Juan Manuel, in the *Libro de los estados* shows Man as composed of body and soul, the former temporal and the latter spiritual in nature. In order for Man to receive his reward or damnation these two elements together must be taken into consideration.

> que lo crio compuesto de alma et de cuerpo, que es cosa corporal et cosa spiritual, et que es conpuesto de cosa duradera et cosa que se ha de corronper; et estas son el alma et el cuerpo, et que para estas aver amas gloria o pena, conuinia que Dios fuesse Dios et omne.
> (473-474)

*I believe man to be made of flesh and soul, the former being corporal and corrupting and the latter spiritual and everlasting. Jesus Christ was both God and man so that both his flesh and soul would experience suffering and enjoy glory.*

God made Man comprised of soul and body, the former everlasting spirit and the latter corruptible flesh. Jesus Christ was born God and Man for the purpose of making it possible that both body and soul enjoy glory or suffer damnation. Reward or damnation of the individual then must take both body and soul into consideration. It is not enough that the governor receive earthly rewards, they only satisfy the body. Likewise, the governor cannot only receive salvation; it would only satisfy the soul. Patronio clarifies this latter statement later in Book Five, reinforcing suggestions to the same effect in the first Book (example III), and in the collections of proverbs (For example, "Quien quiere que su casa este firme, guarde los çiemientos, los pilares et el techo" (449); "Por fuertes animos, *por mengua de auer*, por vsar mucho mugeres, et bino et malos plazeres, por ser tortiçero et cruel, por auer muchos contrarios et pocos amigos se pierden los sennorios e la vida" (465 my italics).

According to Patronio, the fall of Adam condemned Man to eternal damnation, unable to save themselves from the power of the devil. Christ as God and man chose to sacrifice his human body so as to redeem Man and provide him access to Heaven. He also chose to leave Man his true body ("cuerpo verdadero assi conplido commo lo el era"), through which Christians are saved. That is the function of the transubstantiation of the bread and wine during the Last Supper. This discussion sharpens the focus on acts with the juxtaposition of Adam's sin and Christ's sacrifice: they are illustrations of absolutes, the most grievous act committed by Adam, and the greatest act, the sacrifice of Christ. They provide the reader with models of behavior that Patronio wishes to define and elaborate, and both point in the direction that Don Juan Manuel, through Patronio and his rhetoric of power, wants the reader to take: to do good works and avoid evil works in order to win both their earthly and heavenly rewards.

The elaboration of good and evil acts is continued with Patronio's lecture on baptism. He defines original sin as the standard sin of birth due to the inherently pleasant, hence sinful, nature of sexual intercourse.

> por ende todos los que nasçieron et nasçeran por engendramiento de omne et de muger nunca fue nin sera ninguno escusado de nasçer en el pecado deste deleyte. Et a este pecado llama la Scriptura 'pecado original', que quiere dezir, segund nuestro

> lenguaje, 'pecado del nasçimiento'; et por [que] ningund omne que este en pecado non puede yr a Parayso... (476-477)

*Consequently, anybody who was or will be born from a man and a woman will unavoidably be born in sin. The holy scriptures call this sin "the original sin", which means, according to our language, birth sin; no man who has sin can go to paradise.*

Since everyone comes into being through sexual intercourse they are stained with original sin, the sin of birth, and cannot go to Heaven until they are cleansed of the sin. According to Patronio, circumcision fulfilled this cleansing function, and for that reason Christ was himself circumcised. He was also baptized. Circumcision was not available for women therefore condemning them to Hell because they could not be cleansed of original sin. Baptism makes it possible for women as well as men to be shriven of original sin and thus earn Heaven.

As with the discussion of transubstantiation, the focus of Patronio's elaboration of baptism is on contrary acts: the natural and pleasant (sinful) act of sexual intercourse, and the cleansing acts of circumcision and baptism. The performance of these "good" acts that benefit the spirit bring with them concomitant "goods" that benefit the body: "Otrosi, le ayudan a los bienes deste mundo para aver salud et onra et riqueza et las otras bien andanças del mundo" (480). Good works done by men in a state of penance bring them not only salvation, but health, honor, riches and other worldly happiness.[6] Patronio confirms the mutual dependence between spirit and body alluded to earlier in the Fifth Book. Performance of spiritual acts will lead to earthly benefit as well as salvation of the soul. In the next sentence Patronio tells Lucanor for whom these benefits are possible.

Transubstantiation and baptism as well as their contraries are acts of and signal membership in a particular community. The practice or lack of these acts serves to identify an individual or group which imply knowledge of others and therefore of self (*conocerse*). Since the cited acts pertain to the Christian community one would conclude that participation in these acts would be available to all thus guaranteeing the possibility of eternal happiness to every member of the Christian community. This, in fact, may have been only theoretically true. In the context of what Juan Manuel wrote about the various social groups and their respective possibilities for salvation, Patronio proposes a simile that serves to highlight to whom salvation was most readily or easily accessible: "Et estando en este bien aventurado estado, las obras que omne ha de fazer para aver la gloria de Parayso son assi commo limosna et ayuno et oraçion et romeria et todas obras de misericordia" (480). The good works performed by men in a state of penance in order to earn salvation are like giving alms, fasting, praying, going on pilgrimages, and doing all types of charitable works. An important fundamental power of the good governor was his generosity (*franqueza*) to God and his subjects. Such a power would have been prohibitively difficult to exercise by those of the laboring classes. This distinction between classes is highlighted in text after text of the period. Juan Manuel, through the old knight in the *Libro del cauallero et del escudero*, establishes the relationship between good sense (*seso* or "understanding", an attribute of the good governor), and generosity in his definition of *caualleria*.

> el buen seso le es muy mester, ca el seso le amostrara...que es lo que el cauallero deue guardar a Dios et a su sennor et a las gentes, et que onra le deuen fazer a el, et otrosi la que el deue fazer a si mismo. Otrosi le demostrara que es lo que deue dar et que es lo que deue tener. Et, fijo, uos deuedes saber que por el dar et por el tener razonan las gentes al omne por franco o por escaso... (I 47)

*Good judgment is very much needed as it will tell the knight ... what to give to God, to his lord and to the people, what he should keep to himself and how he should be honored. It will also show him what to give away and what to keep. People will label men as generous or stingy depending on what they have and what they give away.*

Good sense or prudence, a necessary attribute of the good nobleman, will show the nobleman what to give, to whom, and what to keep for himself. Giles of Rome highlights the nobleman's responsibility of giving and doing for others. In particular, his definition of *magnificence* is pertinent to this analysis and thus merits an extensive citation.

> magnificencia quiere decir omme que quiere facer grandes obras e despiende mucho en ellas...E ha de ser esa virtud en cuatro cosas...a Dios, e a la comunidad, e a algunas personas especiales, e a sí mismo.
>
> Ca el magnífico a todas estas cosas ha de tener mientes e principalmente a Dios, ca, si ha poder, deve expender muy grandemente en las cosas divinales, faciendo grandes iglesias e onrrados sacrificios, e así de las otras cosas que pertenescen a Dios....Lo segundo, el magnífico deve facer grandes expensas, si ha poder, cerca toda la comunidad, ca los bienes comunes son divinales...Lo tercero, deve el magnífico expender largamente cerca algunas personas especiales...Lo cuarto, deve el magnífico facer grandes expensas cerca su persona propia, e esto en tres cosas: lo primero, en aquellas cosas que duran por toda la vida del omme, así como son casas o villas o castillos...deve facer grandes expensas en aquellas cosas que contescen, así como son bodas o caballerías...deve ser largo en convidar e facer onrras e convites e vestir onrradamente. (*Glosa* 165)

*Magnificence refers to the man who wishes to do good acts and depends very much on them... Magnificence must be shown in four situations... toward God, toward the community, toward some special people and toward himself. The magnanimous nobleman must have God in mind first and foremost. Therefore, he should spend his money on divine things such as building great churches, making honest sacrifices and other acts along this line. Second, he should do good acts to the community as the good acts you do to the community you also do to God. Third, he should spend money on special people... Fourth, he should spend money on himself, especially in matters regarding three main topics: first, on things that last for a lifetime, like houses or castles... he should also do good acts on events such as weddings or on a cavalry... he should be generous in treating others, honoring others and in throwing parties, he should always dress properly.*

According to Giles, the virtuous nobleman should be magnanimous in four situations: with God, with the community, with others and with himself. This virtuous behavior is an obligation of the nobleman and is only limited by the degree of power/wealth wielded by the individual (*si ha poder*). The importance placed on this type of behavior and Patronio's simile equating all "good" acts to the magnanimous acts emphasizes the fact that the performance of these acts and the benefits that accrue pertain primarily to the noble estate. Here rhetoric serves Patronio to expose the nature of true power and to persuade others about the power of Magnanimity.

A good, virtuous, magnanimous act is comprised of three elements according to Patronio: that it be a good work, that it be done with good intentions, and that it be done by choice. Conversely, the individual, in order to avoid the pain of Hell should avoid doing a bad act, also comprised of three elements: that it be a bad act, that it be done with bad intentions, and that it be done by choice. The qualifications are important. In the case of good works, Patronio says that they must be done on God's behalf because anything done for the personal gain of the individual corrupts the good work: personal gains at the expense of another (God or community) are a marker for identifying tyrants. To support this argument rhetorically, Patronio refers to tale XL in the first Book, about the seneschal of Carcassone.

The tale, about a seneschal who arranges his affairs prior to his death not for the purpose of serving God, but for increasing his worldly fame after his death, serves to remind readers of the dangers of doing good works for self-gain. It is the classic case of "fame" in life which can endanger "glory" in the afterlife. The frame into which the tale is placed, however, changes the focus. Lucanor asks Patronio for advice on doing a good work, an issue of magnanimity involving money that would help to save his soul. Patronio retells the traditional tale and summarizes it by providing five qualities that should guide the performance of good works: that the gift be of a significant amount; that the giver be in a penitent state; that the amount be enough that the giver "feel" it; that it be done while the giver is alive; and that it be done for God rather than for personal fame. The first and the last characteristics have already been re-introduced in the fifth Book. Realizing the difficulty of meeting these five requirements in the performance of every work, Patronio explains that these are the ideal, that good works should not be avoided because they do not fulfill the five requirements. In summarizing the exemplary tale, Patronio argues that every good work is "good" to some degree.

> ca çierto es que en qual quier manera que omne faga bien, que sienpre es bien; ca las buenas obras prestan al omne a salir de pecado et venir a penitençia et a la salut del cuerpo, et a que sea rico et onrado, et que aya buena fama de las gentes, et para todos los vienes tenporales. Et assi, todo bien que omne faga a qual quier entencion sienpre es bueno... (318)

*The truth is that any way a man can do a good act is good. Good acts help man leave sin, lead him into a penitent state, helps him achieve body health, in order to become rich, honest, well-liked by people and to achieve temporal goods. Thus, any good act performed by a man led by good intentions is always good...*

Every good work is good; they lead the doer from sin toward a penitent state, provide for bodily health, wealth, honor, fame, and significantly all other temporal goods. Patronio invites the reader to recall the tale in order to emphasize that it is enough that a good work be good to have its desired (salvational) effect. This is reflected in Patronio's definition of a bad work.

The three qualities of a bad work, that it be bad, done with bad intention, and that it be done by choice, are mitigated by the same reasoning as that provided for the definition of good works. Any bad work that does not fulfill all three requirements is not all bad, and may in fact, be good. To illustrate how this is possible, Patronio includes an exemplary tale about a young nobleman who killed his father and his lord.

The tale is told of a youth, placed in the service of a lord as a squire by his father. The youth proved himself so worthy that he quickly became a knight in the service of this same lord. This lord has a falling out with another who is the lord served by the young knight's father. In the battle, the father of the young knight knocks the knight's lord to the ground and prepares to kill him. The young knight yells at his father to desist and races out to protect his lord. The knight's father does not yield so the knight swings a mighty blow that kills his father. It is such a tremendous blow that it also kills the knight's lord. The young knight offers himself up for judgment by other lords in the area. They refuse to condemn him because, although his was a bad work, it was not done with bad intention or deliberately. They instead honor and reward him as a loyal knight ("ante lo preciaron mucho et le fezieron mucho bien"). Patronio's summary synthesizes the lessons of the two works to privilege the issue of intention in the performance of works through his use of a Latin proverb: "Quicquid agant homines intençio judicat omnes" (483).

What stands out in Patronio's definition of good and bad works is their ambiguous nature whereby good works are (almost) always good and bad works are (in most cases) good. The reader is led to conclude that if the doer's intention is that the act be done for God it is inherently good, and the doer will be rewarded with both temporal and spiritual benefits. Endowed with social, financial, and even spiritual power, the nobility perform works that are done for the honor and glory of God; as a consequence of their devotion to God, nobles are likewise rewarded with more wealth, better health, increased estate and honor. If the nobleman is prudent, his temporal and spiritual lives are assured. Here rhetoric succeeds in connecting the general Christian principle of "good work" to the welfare of the nobility, a welfare that at the same time depends on power.

Patronio re-emphasizes the importance of prudence and its relation to self-knowledge in the next section of the fifth Book. He tells Count Lucanor that what is to come is of great importance to the prudent man. "...fablar vos he vn poco en dos cosas por que entendades que todo ome que buen entendimiento oviesse deuia fazer esto que yo digo" (483-484). The two items upon which Patronio wishes to elaborate are self-knowledge and knowledge of the world through which man must pass.

The topic of self-knowledge is examined through a discussion of negatives. Patronio says that he is going to present a picture of Man through a description of what Man lacks and his vile elements. The first vile element has to do with sexual intercourse.[7] Reiterating the inherently sinful nature of sexual intercourse, Patronio extends the negative description to the problems faced by the fetus in its development. Due to the placement of the fetus in the woman's womb, the fetus is doomed to suffer trials and tribulations before ever being born.

Herein lie the relations between human physiology and the concept of original sin.

If the child makes it to term and emerges successfully into the world, it is again destined to suffer primarily because it has no understanding. According to Patronio God provides the child with three signs that allow the child to articulate the suffering that a newborn must suffer on his way to death: he cries, he trembles and he clenches his fists. Patronio interprets these to mean that the child is destined to live with pain and suffering, for that reason he cries. He will live in a fearful state all of his life and leave this life in fear, for that reason he trembles. He will covet more than he can ever have, and will never feel himself complete, for that reason he clenches his fists.

Patronio's reading of these signs continues through to old age and death. He says that even the rich die like all others, once again drawing on a Latin proverb to synthesize his point.

> Et si muere pobre o lazrado, de amigos et de contrarios es despreçiado; et si muere rico et onrado, toman sus amigos grand quebranto, et sus contrarios gran plazer, que es tan mal commo el quebranto de sus amigos. Et demas, al rico contesçe commo dixo el poeta: "Dives diviçias", etc., que quiere decir; "Que el rico ayunta las riquezas con grand trabaio, et possee las con grand temor [et] dexalas con grand dolor". (487)

*And should he die poor and miserable, he will be belittled by friends and enemies alike; should he die rich and honest, his friends will suffer and his enemies will rejoice. His enemies' joy is as bad as his friends' suffering. Also, the poet says that this is what happens to the wealthy: "Dives diviçias" etc. which means: "the wealthy gathers his wealth with great effort, owns it with great fear and leaves it with great pain"*

Death comes to rich and poor alike, the poor in ignominy and the wealthy in a mixed state of sorrow and joy. The wealthy, according to the proverb live their lives as Patronio has described it, through trials, pain and suffering. Animals, according to the counselor, have a much easier time of it.

Patronio concludes his first point through a short comparison between man and animals. Animals are born with clothing; man, on the other hand, must look to things outside himself to cover himself and keep him warm. Animals govern themselves, and innately know what is best for themselves; men must look to others for guidance and government. Man, according to Patronio, is in no position to think very highly of himself. His reading of the signs is a constant forewarning to the powerful: life is a dangerous, treacherous, unreliable journey and the only way to deal with it is to be forearmed, to know the nature of oneself, and thus live one's life virtuously, prudently, and hope for eternal life after death.

Danger, treachery, and unreliability are also descriptors of the world. Developing his second point, Patronio divides knowledge of the world into three: the nature of the world, how men spend their time in the world, and their reward for doing so. Taking a page from typical grammatical exegesis, Patronio defines *mundo* etymologically. According to the counselor it comes from *movement* (*mouimiento*) and from *change* (*mudamiento*) since the world is constantly moving and undergoing change. All of creation falls under this umbrella definition of *mundo*. This definition of *world* complements Patronio's explication of Man's life, and is homogenous with the thesis of the text in which the world is seen as a dangerous place where transitory fortune and the passions rule at the expense of prudence and reason. It is only through a prudent, virtuous life that Man can make it through to old age, death, and then everlasting life.

Patronio's second division, the ways that men live in this world, underlines the continuum between a life ruled by passions and one ruled by pure reason. Recalling the lessons of the exemplary tales, Patronio finds that there are three ways of living: one ruled by the passions, one ruled by prudence, balancing works leading to salvation with maintenance of honor and estate, and one in which the things of this world are rejected in favor of good works for the sole purpose of saving one's soul. Patronio condemns the first, exalts the second, and highlights the impracticality of the third while recognizing its superiority.

> los que passan en este mundo teniendose en el por estrannos et no[n] ponen su talante en al sinon en las cosas por que mejor

puedan saluar las almas, sin dubda estos escogen la meior carrera....mas porque si todos lo fiziessen seria desfazimiento del mundo, et nuestro Sennor non quiere del todo que el mundo sea de los omnes desanparado, por ende non [se] puede escusar que muchos omnes no passan en el mundo por estas tres maneras dichas. (490)

*Those who go through life thinking themselves strangers on this earth and performing solely those good acts that will save their souls do certainly chose the easiest path ... however, if all of us chose the same path the world would come to an end. Our lord does not wish the world to be entirely forgotten by men. Therefore, these three ways in which many men choose to go through life can not be tolerated.*

There is room in the world for those who consider themselves strangers on earth, travelers on their way to Paradise who do only those worldly works that get them to their destination. But God himself wants the world to be maintained, and those who live their lives taking care of earthly concerns as well as attempting to do what is necessary to earn salvation do God's will. Rhetorically, Patronio once again privileges the role of the noble estate on earth: they maintain the earth in God's place and according to his will. By doing so they will be rewarded on this earth and in Heaven. There is no room in Heaven for those to live according to the whims of their passions.

Patronio closes the text with a final reference to an exemplary tale contained in the first Book (XLV) in which the protagonist, in the "Faustian" tradition, sells his soul to the devil in exchange for worldly wealth thus emphasizing the danger of an imprudent life ruled by the passions, and with that concludes that he has done as he intended: provided Count Lucanor with the means to save his soul, body, honor, wealth and estate.

The fifth Book is the most complete in rhetorical terms. It is a polished document that is predominantly deliberative in that it persuades and dissuades the reader from actions that have future consequences, but uses epideictic premises of praise and blame, and applies them to the deliberative by tying praise and blame of present situations to future actions.[8] It applies the exemplary tales modeled in the first Book, and uses them to underscore particular arguments.[9] It does the same with maxims like those in the second through fourth books, using them as testimony to the truth of a particular argument.

The fifth Book of the *Conde Lucanor* harmonizes with the political and moral ideology expressed in the previous four books. It exalts nobility by exalting virtuous behavior that pertains to the noble estate. Juan Manuel is portrayed as an exemplary nobleman, and what is more, as an *auctor*, especially through Patronio's references to Juan Manuel's other works and the *Libro de los estados* in particular. The noble codes of behavior are privileged most notably through the "digression" in which Patronio chooses to prove the veracity of the sacraments, relating noble works to the sacramental.

The fifth Book itself is an example of a good work. The proper rhetorical structure of the treatise presents exemplary discourse about exemplary behavior. The writing of the text is itself an exemplary act, and serves to underscore Juan Manuel's exemplarity as a nobleman. The fifth Book is structured so as to facilitate understanding (the importance of which has already been established), and highlight proper, exemplary behavior for the nobleman wishing to emulate the ideal.

In terms of power relations, the book highlights the position occupied by the nobility vis a vis God. While acknowledging that a superior position exists for those who practice *contemptu mundi*, it also points out that those who do so must necessarily be few because God himself wishes Man to take care of his creation that is the earth. To that extent, the nobility are privileged over the latter group in that they most completely do God's will, and are rewarded for it. These rewards are comprised of physical, temporal rewards benefiting their efforts, as well as their eternal reward in Heaven. Juan Manuel, through Patronio, presents a highly polished rhetoric of power that reflects the author's nobiliary notions of a divinely ordered society in which the nobility are obligated to rule, and in order to do so properly, in order to save their souls, must maintain their honor, wealth, and estate.

## Notes

¹Latini writes: "La segunda manera del cuento es quando ome se departe de su propria materia & traspassa a otra cosa estraña de su prinçipal fecho, por denostar el cuerpo o la cosa, o por cresçer el mal o el bien de aquello, o por [moustrer que] cosas [son] semejantes entrellos...Esta manera de fablar usan mucho los razonadores para provar mucho mejor lo que quieren del cuerpo & de las cosas" (*Tesoro* 196-197).

²See Aquinas' *De regimine* for more background. In Chapter Seven Aquinas recognizes the need for reward for the governor. "the task of a king may seem too burdensome unless some advantage to himself should result from it" (Aquinas *De Regimine* 62). In Chapter Eight he argues that the king should look to God for his rewards just as a servant looks to his master. God's rewards are varied. "God sometimes rewards kings for their service by temporal goods. But such rewards are common to both the good and the wicked....Therefore, if God recompenses wicked kings...by giving them such great rewards as to yield them victory over their foes, to subject kingdoms to their sway and to grant them spoils to rifle, what will he do for good kings who rule the people of God and assail his enemies from a holy motive? He promises them not an earthly reward indeed but an everlasting one and in none other than in Himself" (Aquinas *De Regimine* 67-68).

³The *Libro de los doze sabios*, commenting on the qualities of a good king, offers what would be an excellent synthesis of Juan Manuel's thesis in the fifth book of the *Conde Lucanor*: "Sy piensas e conoçes quien eres e has a ser, non puedes fazer mal fecho. E conoçerás a Dios e a ty mesmo, e juzgarás sabiamente, e non serán reprehendidos tus fechos, e tu alma yrá a manos de Aquél que la fizo, e la crió" (*doze sabios* 110-111).

⁴Aristotle's *Ethics* Book Rho 2: "Thus every evil man is in ignorance of what he should do and what he should abstain from doing, and it is through such error that men become unjust and in general bad" (37).

⁵The first part of Matthew of Vendôme's *The Art of Versification* is dedicated to the proper ways of describing others which is assigning the proper attributes to the object of the description. The purpose of description in Vendôme is to praise or blame.

⁶The *Libro de los doze sabios* establishes a similar relationship between the religious and the secular that is consonant with what Juan Manuel writes: "Teme e ama e obedeçe e sirve a Dios sobre todas las cosas, e junta con Él tu voluntad e obra, e abrán buena fin todos tus fechos, e tu regimiento, e acabarás toda tu entençión, e tus conquistas serán todas a tu voluntad, e verás reynas e reys de tu linage, e serás bienaventurado, e será amunchiguada la ley de Dios, si sigues e guardas el consejo de los sabios" (*doze sabios* 112).

⁷Castrojeriz, glossing Giles' discussion on the avoidance of carnal delectation, summarizes the argument for the need to avoid lust and fornicación by referring to two specific examples. "que Cornelio Scipión cuando fué enviado a Espanna a colpe que fué llegado a la hueste de los romanos, mandó e fizo pregonar que todas aquellas cosas que podían ser a delectación carnal que fuesen echadas del real, donde luego fueron echadas dende dos mil malas mugeres, *por que sabía muy bien aquel sabio caudillo que la placentería carnal facen al omme flaco e sin virtud e enflaquescer en todas las virtudes del cuerpo e del alma*. Donde dice San Jerónimo en la Epístola XXXIV.[a], que los muy sabios e muy santos fueron engannados por las

mugeres, do dice que ¿cuál fué más sabio que Salomón e cuál más santo que David e cuál más fuerte que Sansón? E todos estos fueron engannados por mugeres. E por todos estos males se deven guardar mucho los reyes dellas" (*Glosa* 34 my italics). Devoto in his *Introducción* highlights other texts of the period that refer specifically to the place of birth, and the fact that both baby and urine, for example, pass through the same tract (Devoto 478).

[8]The *Libro del tesoro*, for example, contains a book of rhetorical precepts modeled on Aristotle and Tully. Latini divides rhetoric according to Aristotle's three types: demonstrative, juridical and epideictic. "Et por ende diz Aristotil que la materia desta arte es sobre tres cosas solamente, que son mostramiento, consejo, judgamiento. Et a esto mesmo se acuerda Tullio, & diz que mostramiento es quando los razonadores alaban & denuestan onbre o otra cosa generalmente, o alguno señaladamente....e esta question non ha lugar si non en las cosas passadas & presentes...Consejo es quando los razonadores consejan sobre alguna cosa que es propuesta delante dellos o generalmente o particularmente, para mostrarles quales son mas aprovechables o quales non....Et esta question non ha lugar si non en las cosas que an a venir" (*Tesoro* 179).

[9]In Latini: "una fermosa palabra o una semejança o un enxienplo que sea semejante a la materia confirma todos sus dichos & fazlos fermosos & creybles" (*Tesoro* 179).

## Chapter 7: Conclusion

The purpose of this short study has been to identify and discuss the ideological foundations of exemplary tales and proverbs in order to begin to understand the evolution of power - its maintenance, transformation, shifts, use and abuse - by exploring the rhetoric of power in Don Juan Manuel's well known text, *El Conde Lucanor*. Juan Manuel employs a range of strategies of expression and persuasion (prologues, exemplary tales, proverbs and a rhetorical treatise), as well as expressive devices (frames, scripts, rhetorical colors) that are all concerned with moving the reader or listener to act in a desirable manner. The text itself is a model of the type of behavior that the author intends for the reader or listener to adopt. This behavior is concerned with the "proper" use of power, the ability to act or initiate action. The ability to act implies social privilege, and it is to the socially privileged nobility that the text is specifically directed. Analysis in this study has concentrated and focused on *El Conde Lucanor* which serves as a useful model for future studies on Juan Manuel's literary corpus as well as other medieval texts employing exempla and proverbs like the *Libro de buen amor*, the *Bocados de oro*, *Libro de los gatos*, *Disciplina Clericalis*, *Calila e Dimna*, and the *Caballero Zifar* to mention only a few. I limited this study to one of many books that fall within the "regiment of princes" genre or that contain exemplary tales, proverbs, and the like, which contain exemplary elements that are found in those same books. I chose Don Juan Manuel's work though, because, by virtue of the five Books that comprise the *Conde Lucanor*, the text is an excellent model for the study not only of exemplary tales, but of prologues, refrains, proverbs, and treatises, and their use to solve or attempt to solve historical problems, which in this case involve the proper implementation and maintenance of power relations.

The *Conde Lucanor* is comprised of five books: Book One is a collection of fifty exemplary tales, Books Two, Three, and Four are collections of proverbs, and in Book Five, Patronio elaborates a rhetoric of good works that is at the same time a synthesis and polished articulation of Juan Manuel's rhetoric of power. In the first book a nobleman confronts a series of socio-political problems and asks his counselor for advice on how to solve the problems. The counselor poses an exemplary tale as a parallel to the problem and through the tale elaborates his advice on how to deal with the situation. In every case the nobleman heeds the counselor's advice and profits from it. In the succeeding three books the nobleman continues to ask for more advice although without a specific framing conundrum as in the first Book. Patronio recites lists of proverbs that are general mandates for the proper exercise of power. In the final book, Patronio presents a *summa* on power and its proper use that employs rhetorical elements of the previous four books. He uses exemplary tales and proverbs as confirmations and proofs of the importance of the correct use of power, which in the final book is lifted to a sacramental plane. Like the previous four books, the fifth extols virtuous behavior through the acquisition of understanding and self-knowledge that leads inherently to virtuous action, an element of the virtue prudence.

Four components of prudence and their relation to the rhetoric of power are explored in the study: advice, action, prognostication and memory. Using Giles of Rome's *De Regimine Principum* to highlight the above components (a text that Juan Manuel himself cited), I have tried to show how Juan Manuel relied on the virtue of prudence as a fundamental component of the correct use of power and as an organizing principle of the text.

Advice and action are privileged in describing prudence, the virtue seen as a mediator that shows the other virtues what must be done. The prudent man has sufficient understanding to be able to teach or show others what should be done, as well as to put his own advice into practice. The *Conde Lucanor* is a manifestation of such action. Through his prologues to the various books, Juan

Manuel guides the reader to a correct understanding of what he intends to accomplish. He also actively re-enters the text in the book of exemplary tales to write summary verses extolling the advice of the tale, and as *auctor* in the fifth Book, where Patronio cites another of his works as exemplary in proving the veracity of the sacraments. The counselor Patronio advises his lord, Count Lucanor, through the telling of tales, reciting of proverbs and declamation of a treatise. Count Lucanor asks for advice and acts on it. In every case, each character demonstrates correct understanding and prudence by giving correct advice and putting that advice into action.

Also important to the notion of prudence are prognostication and memory. The truly prudent are able to recognize the consequences of actions, thereby understanding future possibilities as well. Paradoxically, this ability to see into the future is accomplished by remembering the past. Exemplary characters from the past, both good and bad, signal through their past actions what can happen in the future and the prudent governor uses his memory to recall the lessons of the past and applies them to the future. The exemplary tales and the proverbs (by virtue of their historical function), in the *Conde Lucanor* provide memorial cues to both Count Lucanor in the fiction and the reader outside of the story so that, armed with past lessons, they might avoid future consequences that may prove dangerous to their honor, estate or soul.

Memory and learning are perceived as the same in the late Middle Ages and Juan Manuel organizes his text in such a way so as to facilitate its entry into the reader's memory. He does this by dividing the text into parts, using exemplary tales, refrains, maxims, proverbs and the like. It is important to understand the function of memory in the organization of the text because it explains many facets of Juan Manuel's text that to date have been the subject of conjecture.

While the ideological foundations of the popular and institutionalized rhetoric of power can be analyzed in each of the books of the *Conde Lucanor*, my intention has been to provide a model to suggest how scholars might go about analyzing the other texts that comprise Juan Manuel's literary corpus as well as other late medieval "regiments of princes." All of the texts elaborate potential power relationships for the purpose of governing correctly, and serve as proof of the lessons contained in the *Conde Lucanor*.

*El Conde Lucanor* imparts the fusing of knowledge and action in order to achieve success: one must learn to govern oneself or others well; neither knowledge nor action is sufficient without the other: "Non es de buen seso el que se tiene por pagado de dar o dezir buenos sesos, mas eslo el que los dize et los faze" (280). Giving good advice or repeating bits of wisdom do not make the speaker wise; the wise man is one who acts on the wisdom he speaks. In each of the tales, proverbs, and the final Book, the reader is never allowed to forget that the satisfying words employed in the telling of tale, proverb or Book have an important stabilizing social function when translated into action. Juan Manuel includes pleasant language and entertaining stories in his book, but in the introduction he also advises the reader that the function of his text is not reducible to mere entertainment. He has carefully chosen his words, stories, and proverbs for the purpose of educating those nobles who need to learn to govern themselves and others properly so that society, as it existed at that time, might continue unchanged and unchallenged.

To divorce the framed books of the *Conde Lucanor* from themselves and their historical age constitutes a danger which has been suggested throughout this study. The ideological foundations of these books have a message for readers throughout time, but they are meaningless unless readers view and understand them in terms of the other books, as well as the culture, society and historical age in which they were produced.

The medieval Spanish estate society was a carefully organized and orchestrated unit which depended on its members as the body does its parts. Each member had a role that was defined in terms of soul, estate and honor, and that could neither be rejected nor changed but, rather, depended on each constituent to live within their estate and act accordingly. Proper government of society was determined by this harmony of action within one's estate, and in order for the power relationships to work correctly, or successfully from the perspective of dominant ideologies, one needed to impart the appropriate knowledge of how to act.

The maintenance of power becomes the moral to each of Patronio's *consejos*, whether tale, proverb or rhetoric, and Juan Manuel infuses both the structure and the advice (tale, proverb and Book) itself with this politicized version of morality. Structurally, Juan Manuel blurs the lines between historicized fiction and fictional reality by using both fictional and historical characters within the narrative. He thus strengthens the truth of the advice in order to convince the reader of their worth in social terms as well as their application to contemporary medieval Castilian society. The ideological foundations of Castilian society are thus highlighted indirectly through fictionalized comments by the narrator, a fictional dialogue between two outstanding representatives of Castilian society, and an historically recognized member of the political hierarchy, Don Juan Manuel. The two principle characters, Patronio and Lucanor, are carefully exposed throughout the narratives so that readers see that Patronio is a good counselor who never errs in his advice regardless of the circumstances while Lucanor is a prudent Count who never acts rashly, never puts his estate in jeopardy, always follows Patronio's advice, and profits from it.

The methodology that I employed, the methodological tools that I used, are eclectic taken as a collection. Both contemporary and medieval literary and rhetorical theories were essential in the process of decoding the text, its structure and meaning. This historical and contemporary approach re-situates Juan Manuel studies in a European context and proves that the work was not produced in isolation, but influenced by theories that were debated and discussed in the universities all over the continent. Attention to the entire text as an articulation of a rhetoric of power re-locates the text in the Spanish canon, not just as a collection of exemplary tales and proverbs, but as a tightly constructed and reasoned rhetoric of power that is most complete, most artistic, when read as a whole rather than in pieces. Through systematic analysis of the rhetoric of power I have answered some nagging critical questions about the text such as the functions of the verses included at the end of each tale, the importance of the remaining four books not only artistically but their function as well, the queries concerning structural issues including the probable function of the "et la historia deste enxiemplo"; and I provided a model of how the late medieval rhetoric of power functions.

My investigation of the historical function of the medieval rhetoric of power in the *Conde Lucanor* provides a substantial reason to discard still-prevalent notions about the superior value of the first book at the expense of the remaining four. It makes sense to replace that uncritical notion with a new appreciation of Juan Manuel's text that includes exemplary tales, proverbs and treatise as a unified whole that is most profitably read as such. We can no longer accept that Juan Manuel's art lies predominantly in the retelling of the exemplary tales themselves, ignoring or devaluing the final verses. A new appreciation of not only the verses that the nobleman includes at the end of the tales, but also the importance of considering the "enigmatic" last line is warranted. Chapter five disproves the notion that the books of proverbs are, especially in the case of the fifth book "puerile" or "silly" as some critics have suggested. The maxims are important components of Juan Manuel's rhetoric of power. My investigations into the historical context of author and text expand scholarship on ideological notions as held by Juan Manuel about the role of nobility in society, the secularization of power, the clergy (especially the mendicant orders) in general and the Church specifically. I provide models for readings of medieval texts as products of a concern with memory, expanding the ramifications of the "didactic" label that is so often hung on medieval texts. I provide models of analysis for the production of authority, and the relation between form and meaning in the construction of a medieval text.

The contributions of this study are clear: the secularization of religious ideals by Juan Manuel in the text, his argument for the sacramental nature of nobility, the attempt by the author to have himself considered as *auctor* and the *Conde Lucanor* as *auctoritas*, and the description of the ethics of power, expand the dimensions of future studies on rhetoric and power. They do the same for Juan Manuel studies in general and the *Conde Lucanor* in particular.

What now loom ahead are comparative studies that will focus on the rhetoric of power from national, temporal and genre points of view. No one has yet investigated the evolution of the rhetoric of power through the Middle Ages. This needs to be done to substantiate the notion that the articulation of the rhetoric of power is indeed an ever-changing process that can fruitfully be studied before during and after the fourteenth century. The process of analysis is begun in this study.

## A MODEL FOR FUTURE STUDIES

This work is necessarily incomplete in that it relies on one book of Juan Manuel's literary corpus. Seven books by the nobleman remain as well as many others by Juan Manuel's contemporaries writing in the same or similar vein. The next logical step in the development of the ideological foundations of exemplary discourse through the study of the rhetoric of power is to apply the present analysis to these other books to discover how Juan Manuel or any of the other authors uses his/their texts to impart popular conceptions of power relationships. According to the *Libro de los doze sabios*:

> E razonable es que el que non ha poderío non ha lugar de cunplir justiçia, nin de regir nin fazer ninguna cosa de las que a regimiento de reyno pertenecen, que puesto que sea de sangre real, sy poderío non ha, non podrá regir los poderosos nin los flacos tan solamente.
> 
> (*doze sabios* 75)

> It is commonsense that a person who enjoys no power has no means of making other people comply with justice. That person cannot command nor do anything which does not pertain to the ruling of the kingdom. Despite the fact that the king is royalty, should he not have power, he would be unable to govern either the powerful or even the powerless.

It is not enough that governors be governors, they must be powerful and use their power to rule. Without the ability to implement and control power relations a king is not a king, royal blood notwithstanding. The *doze sabios*, for example, exists in five manuscripts dating from the fourteenth to the sixteenth centuries, a fact that shows its recurring popularity on the peninsula. What is there about the text that encourages its re-presentation throughout the cited time period? The analysis of other extant texts would not only substantiate the arguments of the present study, but more importantly, would clue modern readers into ideological foundations which permeated many popular spheres of the time through tales, proverbs, treatises, and general advice on the one hand, and institutionalized social thought on the other. The didactic works of Juan Manuel and many others of the Middle Ages such as *Calila y Dimna, Caballero Zifar, Disciplina Clericalis,* and the *Libro de los doze sabios* are a few examples with which scholars might begin to test the theoretical perspectives on rhetoric and power presented in this study.

The perspectives of this work would also serve analysis of later collections of exemplary tales well. Cervantes' *Novelas ejemplares*, for example, contains a prologue in which the author refers to himself in the light of his previous and successful work, the *Quijote*, thus authorizing the present work in the light of the previous one. The work is further authorized with the attached *Fe de erratas, Tasa, Aprobaciones,* and *Privilegios*. In the prologue the author employs the Aristotelian *causae* in order to prepare his readers for what is to come. Juan Manuel's prologue or that of Juan Ruiz in his sermonic opening to the *Libro de buen amor* and that of the *Novelas ejemplares* couldn't be more similar. Cervantes describes his materials, the structure of the work, himself as author and Don Pedro Fernández de Castro as efficient causes, and the objective of his writing. He takes pains (excuse the pun) to point out that while the text may induce improper desires or thoughts in the reader, it is not at all his intention ("antes me cortara la mano con que las escribí, que sacarlas en público"). Cervantes highlights morals to stories such as in *Rinconete y Cortadillo*. The satirical *Coloquio de los perros* emphasizes flawed power relationships in which governors (butcher, shepherds *et al*) are morally inferior to the servant (Berganza). Although Cervantes brags of presenting works never before seen (excepting the notion of using past examples to influence future behavior), they are notably called *ejemplos* whose purpose is to teach proper behavior.

Recently exemplary tales have seen a renaissance in popularity. William Bennett, for one, has been very successful through the publication of his *Book of Moral Virtues, The Moral Compass, The Children's Book of Virtues*, and *Our Sacred Honor: Words of Advice from the Founders in Stories, Letters, Poems and Speeches*. Bennett, like Juan Manuel takes old and familiar tales, outfits them with a frame and moral and re-presents them as examples of proper behavior in a society that is, in his opinion, suffering a crisis of morality. According to Bennett, authority figures have lost control and no longer know how to govern well, whether they be parents, or politicians. This study provides tools for the fruitful analysis of the ideological foundations of Bennett's exemplary tales and their telling.

The body of texts need not be limited to exemplary literature. Sermons constitute a body of oral or written literature which would provide ample material for the study of the ideological foundations of tales and the rhetoric of power. In history, one might consider the recorded sermons of Jesus Christ as found in the *Bible* or those of any modern-day televangelist. In literature, one might begin with the sermons in *Guzmán de Alfarache*, a picaresque novel. The picaresque novel would serve as a particularly interesting study of the rhetoric of power narrated from the perspective of the reformed rogue. The very foundation of the picaresque is predicated upon the misadventures of lower class fools who try to improve their lot by passing themselves off as of more noble birth such as in

Quevedo's *Buscón*. Picaresques are written by ex-rogues who tell of their foolish attempts to improve their station, and the impossibility of such improvement implore a rhetoric of power: the ex-rogue himself proves that one must live within his estate and not attempt to change the status quo.

Other texts, specifically the "arbitrista" literature of the late sixteenth and early seventeenth century on how to govern and how to restore the empire, would be served by such an analysis. The "memorials" by Sancho de Moncada or González de Cellorigo would be excellent test cases. In the eighteenth and nineteenth centuries Larra's *Artículos de costumbres* or Cadalso's *Cartas Marruecas* articulate, through critical examination, the state of Spanish being. In the twentieth century such a critical examination continues in the literature of the members of the Generation of '98 through the works of Cela and Matute, for example. Values and culture can be examined in such works as Unamuno's *Niebla*, or Cela's *Mazurca para dos muertos*. The latter in particular could be discussed in terms of the recorded speeches of Francisco Franco. Such an investigation might reveal how power relationships were articulated during the Spanish Civil War.

Theater from Lope de Vega to José Ruibal shows similarities with such texts as *El Conde Lucanor*. The "comedias" are filled with examples of the effects of not living within one's estate. Recall the exposure of a tyrant in *Fuenteovejuna,* or the implications of the abuse of honor in *El burlador de Sevilla* for example. In the twentieth century, theater like the underground drama of Ruibal, bad government is again the topic as in *El hombre y la mosca.* In theater, an analysis of the rhetoric of power would include visual and aural interpretation, potentially the most effective, and therefore most powerful methods of elaborating power relationships and convincing an audience of the (im)propriety of living in one way or another.

In terms of modern examples, television and movies, video games and cartoons, as well as the entire print medium, are now capable of manipulating all of our senses for rhetorical effect. The new perspective is more verisimilar, and given the appropriate frame or focus, the image and its communication would speak clearly and ever so subtly to the ideological foundations of twentieth-century society. Not only do magazines, newspapers, and the like contain pictures, but they are capable of using holographic images which place the image in three dimensional perspective. They can also add scents in order to manipulate the reader as well as sound effects (talking books, greeting cards or the www). Movies, television, and more and more frequently computers, thanks to their screen size, are already larger than life and make use of special effects that can simulate the trembling of an earthquake or place the spectator in the middle of a battlefield with explosions occurring in front and behind. Special effects create in fiction that which one can only imagine. The technological advances have made rhetorical devices more effective by manipulating more of the senses and by extending the realm of the imagination thereby making them more powerful. Power is now a global concern, and in the case of television, the viewer can be transported to any point on Earth or even in space to witness what before could only be imagined or, if known, described. Analysis of how each artist or set of technicians chooses to portray ideological foundations of power provides a clue to how any particular society handles the ideas, notions, successes and failures of their time.

The rhetorical capabilities of contemporary media and their ability to affect power or questions of government are well known by the media themselves. Their language is filled with euphemisms that indicate an awareness of their suasory power: "disinformation", "damage control," "censorship," "hype," the notion of being "politically correct." Any of the police actions of the past decades and their presentation to the public, for example, would be a telling study of the contemporary rhetoric of power and its ideological foundations. Concepts such as "patriotism" and "support of the troops" or "collateral damage", "the war on terrorism," "friendly fire," "freedom fighters," "the coalition," "WMD" and "insurgents" explain how the United States sells the idea of war to its citizens and the world. Even the amount of time spent covering support for a war as opposed to dissent needs to be analyzed to reveal important ideologies of twentieth- and twenty-first century government. A broader, more interdisciplinary study might compare the war-time conflicts of the twentieth century and develop a model of the rhetoric of power used in war to answer the question: Has the "sale" of war changed over the centuries or are similar ideologies used repeatedly? The movie "Wag the Dog" might serve as an example.

What Don Juan Manuel wrote in 1335 in an entertaining collection of exemplary tales as *El Conde Lucanor* exposed certain ideological foundations that continue to exist and can be examined yet today. To play with what Michel Foucault calls "interpretive analytics," in order to understand what readers take seriously, one needs to look at what entertains them. In order to understand what is meant by war and government, scholars need to examine what is considered to be peace or anarchy. In order to understand good government, corruption must be studied. That is the function of an analysis of the ideological foundations of the rhetoric of power.

# BIBLIOGRAPHY

**Editions**

Juan Manuel. El Conde Lucanor. José Manuel Blecua, ed. Madrid: Clásicos Castalia, 1985.
___. El conde Lucanor. Carlos Alvar and Pilar Palanco eds. Barcelona: Editorial Planeta, 1984.
___. El Conde Lucanor. José Manuel Fradejas Rueda, ed. Bilbao: Plaza & Janés, 1984.
___. Libro del Conde Lucanor. Reinaldo Ayerbe-Chaux, ed. Madrid: Editorial Alhambra, 1983.
___. Obras Completas. José Manuel Blecua, ed. Madrid: Gredos, 1983.
___. Juan Manuel: A Selection. Ian Macpherson, ed. London: Tamesis Texts, 1980.
___. El Conde Lucanor. Alfonso I. Sotelo, ed. Madrid: Cátedra, 1976.
___. El Conde Lucanor. Angel González Palencia, ed. Zaragoza: Editorial Ebro, 1969.
___. Obras de don Juan Manuel. José María Castro y Calvo y Martín de Riquer, eds. Barcelona: Consejo superior de investigaciones científicas, 1955.
___. El libro del caballero et del escudero, in Gayangos, don Pascual de. Escritores en prosa anteriores al siglo XV. Madrid: Ediciones Atlas, 1952.
___. El libro de los estados, in Gayangos, don Pascual de. Escritores en prosa anteriores al siglo XV. Madrid: Ediciones Atlas, 1952.
___. Libro Infinido y Tractado de la Asunción. José Manuel Blecua, ed. Granada: Universidad de Granada, 1952.
___. El Conde Lucanor. F.J. Sánchez Cantón, ed. Madrid: Editorial "Saturnino Calleja" S.A., 1920.
___. El libro de Patronio o El conde Lucanor. Eugenio Krapf, ed. Vigo: Librería de Eugenio Krapf, 1902.
___. El libro de los enxiemplos del conde Lucanor et de Patronio. Hermann Knust, ed. Leipzig: Dr. Seele and Company, 1900.

**Translations**

Juan Manuel. El Conde Lucanor: A Collection of Mediaeval Spanish Short Stories. John England, trans. Warminster: Aris & Phillips Ltd., 1987.
___. The Book of Count Lucanor and Patronio. John E. Keller, and L. Clark Keating, trans. Lexington: U P of Kentucky, 1977.

___. Count Lucanor: or, The fifty pleasant tales of Patronio. James York, M.D, trans. London: George Routledge & Sons, Ltd., 1924.

**Dictionaries**

Diccionario de la lengua española. Madrid: Real Academia Española, 1992. 21st edition.
Covarrubias, Sebastián de. Tesoro de la lengua castellana o española. Martín de Riquer, ed. Barcelona: Alta Fulla, 1989.
Van Scoy, Herbert Allen. A Dictionary of Old Spanish Terms Defined in the Works of Alfonso X. Ivy A. Corfis, ed. Madison: Hispanic Seminary of Medieval Studies, 1986.
Diccionario de Autoridades. Madrid: Gredos, 1969.
Diccionario ideológico de la lengua española. Barcelona: Editorial Gustavo Gili S.A., 1959.

**Criticism**

Abad, Francisco. "Lugar de don Juan Manuel en la historia de la lengua," in Don Juan Manuel: VII centenario. Murcia: Universidad de Murcia y la Academia Alfonso X el Sabio, 1982. 9-16.
Alborg, Juan Luis. "Capítulo VII. Don Juan Manuel y el canciller Ayala. Otras manifestaciones literarias" in Historia de la literature española. Madrid: Gredos, 1980 (2nd ed., 4th printing). 280-297.
Alvar, Carlos. "Ay cinquenta enxiemplos." Bulletin Hispanique 86 (1984): 136 141.
Araluce Cuenca, José R. El libro de los estados: Don Juan Manuel y la sociedad de su tiempo. Madrid: Porrúa, 1976.
Ayerbe-Chaux, Reinaldo. El Conde Lucanor: materia tradicional y originalidad creadora. Madrid: Purrúa Turanzas, 1975.
___. "El libro de los proverbios del conde Lucanor y de Patronio" in Studies in Honor of Gustavo Correa. Charles B. Faulhaber, Richard P. Kinkade, T.A. Perry, eds. Potomac, Maryland: Scripta humanistica, 1986.
___. "Don Juan Manuel y la corona de Aragón, la realidad política y el ideal de los tratados," in Don Juan Manuel: VII centenario. Murcia: Universidad de Murcia y la Academia Alfonso X el Sabio, 1982. 17-26.
Baquero Goyanes, Mariano. "Perspectivismo en el Conde Lucanor," in Don Juan Manuel: VII centenario. Murcia: Universidad de Murcia y la Academia Alfonso X el Sabio, 1982. 27-50.
Barcia, Pedro Luis. Análisis de El Conde Lucanor. Buenos Aires: Centro Editor de América Latina, 1968 (Enciclopedia Literaria, 27).
Biglieri, Aníbal. Hacia una poética del relato didáctico: ocho estudios sobre El Conde Lucanor. Chapel Hill: U of North Carolina P, 1989.

Blecua, Alberto. La tansmisión textual de *El Conde Lucanor*. Barcelona: Bellaterra, 1982.

Burgoyne, Johnathan. "Ideology in Action: The Consequences of Paradox in *El Conde Lucanor*, Part 1." Corónica 30:1 (2001): 37-65

Burke, James F. "Counterfeit and the Curse of Mediacy in the *Libro de buen amor* and the *Conde Lucanor*." In Discourses of Authority in Medieval and Renaissance Literature. Kevin Brownlee and Walter Stephens, eds. Hanover: UP of New England, 1989. 203-215.

___. "Frame and Structure in the *Conde Lucanor*." Revista Canadiense de Estudios Hispanicos 8 (1984): 263-274.

Castro y Calvo, José María. El arte de gobernar en las obras de Don Juan Manuel. Barcelona: Consejo Superior de Investigaciones Científicas, 1945.

Catalán, Diego. "Don Juan Manuel ante el modelo alfonsí: El testimonio de la *Cronica abreviada*" in Juan Manuel Studies. Ian Macpherson, ed. London: Tamesis, 1977. 17-52.

Darbord, Bernard. "Acerca de las técnicas de expresión alegórica en la obra de don Juan Manuel," in Don Juan Manuel: VII centenario. Murcia: Universidad de Murcia y la Academia Alfonso X el Sabio, 1982. 51-62.

De Looze, Laurence. "Subversion of Meaning in Part I of *El Conde Lucanor*." Revista Canadiense de Estudios Hispánicos 19 (1995). 341-355.

___. "*El Conde Lucanor*, Part V, and the Goals of the Manueline Text." Corónica 28:2 (2000). 129-154.

___. "The "Nonsensical" Proverbs of Juan Manuel's *El Conde Lucanor*, Part IV: A Reassessment." Revista Canadiense de Estudios Hispánicos 25:2 (2001). 199-221.

Devoto, Daniel. Introducción al estudio de Don Juan Manuel y en particular de *El conde Lucanor*: una bibliografía. Madrid: Castalia, 1972.

___. "La introducción al estudio de la obra de don Juan Manuel doce años después," in Don Juan Manuel: VII centenario. Murcia: Universidad de Murcia y la Academia Alfonso X el Sabio, 1982. 63-74.

Deyermond, Alan. "Cuentos orales y estructura formal en el *Libro de las tres razones*," in Don Juan Manuel: VII centenario. Murcia: Universidad de Murcia y la Academia Alfonso X el Sabio, 1982. 75-88.

Díaz Arena, Angel. "Intento de análisis estrucutural del exemplo XVII del *Conde Lucanor*," in Don Juan Manuel: VII centenario. Murcia: Universidad de Murcia y la Academia Alfonso X el Sabio, 1982. 89-102.

Diz, Marta Ana. Patronio y Lucanor: La lectura inteligente "*en el tiempo que es turbio.*" Potomac: Scripta Humanistica, 1984.

Don Juan Manuel VII Centenario. Murcia: Universidad de Murcia, 1982.

Dunn, Peter N. "The Structures of Didacticism: Private Myths and Public Fictions" in Juan Manuel Studies. Ian Macpherson, ed. London: Tamesis, 1977. 53-67.

England, John. "*¿Et non el día del lodo?*: The Structure of the Short Story in *El Conde Lucanor*" in Juan Manuel Studies. Ian Macpherson, ed. London: Tamesis, 1977. 69-86.

___. "Exemplo 51 of *El Conde Lucanor*: The Problem of Authorship." Bulletin of Hispanic Studies 51 (1974): 16-27.

Flory, David A. "A Suggested Emendation of *El Conde Lucanor*, Parts I and III" in Juan Manuel Studies. Ian Machperson, ed. London: Tamesis, 1977. 87-100.

Gayangos, don Pascual de. Escritores en prosa anteriores al siglo XV. Madrid: Ediciones Atlas, 1952.

Giménez Soler, Andrés. Don Juan Manuel: biografía y estudio crítico. Zaragoza: Tip. La Académica, 1932.

Gimeno Casalduero, Joaquín. "*El Conde Lucanor*: composición y significado" (1975), in La creación literaria de la Edad Media y del Renacimiento, Madrid: Porrúa Turanzas, 1977. 19-34.

___. "El *Libro de los Estados* de don Juan Manuel: composición y significado," in Don Juan Manuel: VII centenario. Murcia: Universidad de Murcia y la Academia Alfonso X el Sabio, 1982. 149-162.

Gómez Redondo, Fernando. "El diálogo en *El Conde Lucanor*", in Manojuelo de estudios literarios ofrecidos a José Manuel Blecua Teijeiro (Publicaciones de la Nueva Revista de Enseñanzas Medias), Madrid: Ministerio de Educación y Ciencia, 1983. 45-58.

Grabowska, James A. "The Rhetoric of Power in Juan Manuel's *El Conde Lucanor*." South Central Review 11 (1994): 45-61.

Green, Otis H. Spain and the Western Tradition: The Castilian Mind in Literature from *El Cid* to Calderón. v.II Madison: U of Wisconsin P, 1964.

Jaffe, Catherine M. "'Las vestias que van cargadas de oro': The Reader and 'Exemplo L' of Juan Manuel's *El Conde Lucanor*." Revista de Estudios Hispánicos 21 (1987): 1-12.

Keller, John E. "'*Enxiemplo de un cavallero que fue ocasionado et mató a su señor y a su padres*': Don Juan's 54th ejemplo" in Hispanic Studies in Honor of Joseph H. Silverman. Joseph V. Ricapito, ed. Newark, Delaware: Juan de la Cuesta, 1988. 37-44.

___. "A Re-Examination of Don Juan Manuel's Narrative Techniques: 'La muger Brava" in Collectanea Hispanic: Folklore and Brief Narrative Studies. Dennis P. Seniff, ed. Newark, Delaware: Juan de la Cuesta, 1987. 93-103.

___. "Don Juan Manuel's *El Conde Lucanor* Contains Fifty-Three Stories and No Fewer." Romance Notes 24 (1983): 59-64.

Lida de Malkiel, María Rosa. "Tres notas sobre don Juan Manuel" in Estudios de literatura española y compared. Buenos Aires: Editorial universitaria de Buenos Aires, 1966.

López Estrada, Francisco. Introducción a la literatura medieval española. Madrid: Gredos, 1979 (4th ed., revised).

MacPherson, Ian. "*Dios y el mundo* - the Didacticism of *El Conde Lucanor*." Romance Philology 24 (1974): 26-38.

——, ed. Juan Manuel Studies. London: Támesis, 1977.

Martín, José Luis. "Don Juan Manuel fundador del convento de San Juan y San Pablo de Peñafiel," in Don Juan Manuel: VII centenario. Murcia: Universidad de Murcia y la Academia Alfonso X el Sabio, 1982. 177-186.

McSpadden, George Elbert. The Spanish Prologue Before 1700. Stanford University, Ph.D., 1947.

Menéndez Pelayo, Marcelino. Orígenes de la novela. Madrid: Consejo Superior de investigaciones científicas, 1962 (2nd ed., vol. 1).

Molina Molina, Angel Luis. "Los dominios de don Juan Manuel," in Don Juan Manuel: VII centenario. Murcia: Universidad de Murcia y la Academia Alfonso X el Sabio, 1982. 215-226.

Munuera, Celia Wallhead. "Three Tales from *El Conde Lucanor* and their Arabic Counterparts" in Juan Manuel Studies. Ian Macpherson, ed. London: Tamesis, 1977. 101-118.

Muñoz Cortés, Manuel. "Intensificación y perspectivismo lingüístico en la elaboración de un ejemplo en *El Conde Lucanor*, in Estudios literarios dedicados al profesor M. Baquero Goyanes. Murcia: 1974. 529-585.

Orduna, Germán. "El exemplo en la obra literaria de don Juan Manuel" in Juan Manuel Studies. Ian Macpherson, ed. London: Tamesis, 1977. 119-142.

___. "La autobiografía literaria de don Juan Manuel," in Don Juan Manuel: VII centenario. Murcia: Universidad de Murcia y la Academia Alfonso X el Sabio, 1982. 245-258.

Palafox, Eloísa. "Las fábulas del poder: una lectura de *El Conde Lucanor*," in Discursos y Representaciones en la Edad Media. México: Universidad Nacional Autónoma de México, 1999. 259-270.

Perry, T. A. "Juan Manuel's 'Ystoria deste exienplo'." Romance Notes 27 (1986): 89-93.

Piccus, Jules. "The Meaning of 'Estoria' in Juan Manuel's *El Conde Lucanor*." Hispania 61 (1978): 459-465.

Pretel Marín, Aurelio. Don Juan Manuel: señor de la llanura. Albacete: Instituto de estudios albacetenses, 1982.

___. "Aproximación al estudio de la sociedad en la Mancha albacetense bajo el señorío de don Juan Manuel," in Don Juan Manuel: VII centenario. Murcia: Universidad de Murcia y la Academia Alfonso X el Sabio, 1982. 287-311.

Rubio García, Luis. "La muerte de don Juan Manuel," in Don Juan Manuel: VII centenario. Murcia: Universidad de Murcia y la Academia Alfonso X el Sabio, 1982. 325-336.

Ruiz, María Cecilia. Literatura y política: el *Libro de los estados* y el *Libro de las armas* de don Juan Manuel. Potomac, Maryland: Scripta Humanistica (57), 1989.

Scholberg, Kenneth R. "Figurative Language in Juan Manuel" in Juan Manuel Studies. Ian Macpherson, ed. London: Tamesis, 1977, 143-156.

Stéfano, Luciana de. "Don Juan Manuel y el pensamiento medieval", in Don Juan Manuel. VII Centenario. Murcia: Universidad de Murcia y la Academia Alfonso X el Sabio, 1982. 337-351.

___. La sociedad estamental de la baja edad media española a la luz de la literatura de la época. Caracas: Universidad Central de Venezuela, Facultad de humanidades y educación instituto de filología "Andres Bello," 1966.

Sturcken, H. Tracy. Don Juan Manuel. Twayne Publishers, Inc.: New York, 1974.

Sturm, Harlan. "*El Conde Lucanor*: The Search for the Individual" in Juan Manuel Studies. Ian Macpherson, ed. London: Tamesis, 1977. 157-168.

Tate, R. B. "The Infante Don Juan of Aragon and Don Juan Manuel" in Juan Manuel Studies. Ian Macpherson, ed. London: Tamesis, 1977. 169-180.

Valdeón Baruque, Julio. "Las tensiones sociales en Castilla", in Juan Manuel Studies. Ian Macpherson, ed. London: Tamesis, 1977. 181-192.

___. "Castilla, días de miseria." historia 16, 75 (1982): 44-51.

___. "Don Juan Manuel y Peñafiel," in Don Juan Manuel: VII centenario. Murcia: Universidad de Murcia y la Academia Alfonso X el Sabio, 1982. 385-395.

Zimmerman, Samuel A. Arabic Influence in the Tales of *El Conde Lucanor*. unpublished dissertation University of Florida, 1969.

## Select Bibliography for the Study of Rhetoric and Power in the *Conde Lucanor*

Alfonso X. Las Siete Partidas. Tomo II. Partidas segunda y tercera. Madrid: Ediciones Atlas, 1972.

Alfonso, Pedro. The Scholar's Guide. The Pontifical Institute of Mediaeval Studies: Toronto, 1969.

Allen, Judson Boyce. The Ethical Poetic of the Later Middle Ages. Toronto: U of Toronto P, 1982.

___. The Friar as Critic. Nashville: Vanderbilt U P, 1971.

Allen, Peter. The Art of Love. Philadelphia: U of Pennsylvania P, 1992.

Aquinas, St. Thomas. On the Governance of Rulers (De Regimine Principum). Gerald B. Phelan, trans. London: Institute of Mediaeval Studies, 1938.

___. Commentary on the Nichomachean Ethics. 2 vols. C. I. Litzinger, O.P., trans. Chicago: Henry Regnery Company, 1964.

Aquino, Santo Tomás de. El Gobierno Monárquico (bilingual edition). León Carbonero y Sol, ed. Sevilla: D.A. Izquierdo, 1861.

Aristotle. On Rhetoric: A Theory of Civic Discourse. George A. Kennedy, trans. Oxford: Oxford U P, 1991.

___. Nicomachean Ethics. Hippocrates G. Apostle, trans. Boston: D. Reidel Publishing Company, 1975.

Auerbach, Erich. Literary Language and Its Public in Late Latin Antiquity and in the Middle Ages. New York: Pantheon Books, 1965.

___. Mimesis: The Representation of Reality in Western Literature. Willard Trask, trans. Garden City, New York: Doubleday Anchor Books, 1957.
Bailey, F. G. The Tactical Uses of Passion. Ithaca: Cornell U P, 1983.
Barilli, Renato. Rhetoric. Minneapolis: U of Minnesota P, 1989.
Beneyto Pérez, Juan, ed. Glosa Castellana al Regimiento de Príncipes de Egidio Romano. vols. I, II, III. Madrid: Instituto de estudios politicos, 1947.
Bettelheim, Bruno. The Uses of Enchantment (The Meaning and Importance of Fairy Tales). New York: Alfred A. Knopf, 1976.
Black, Edwin. Rhetorical Criticism, A Study in Method. New York: The Macmillan Company, 1965.
Boethius. The Consolation of Philosophy. London: Penguin Books, 1969.
Booth, Wayne C. A Rhetoric of Irony. Chicago: U of Chicago P, 1974.
Briscoe, Marianne G. and Barbara H. Jaye. Artes Praedicandi and Artes Orandi. Typologie des sources du moyen âge occidental. L. Genicot, Director. Brepols Turnhout-Belgium: Institut d'Etudes Médiévales, 1992.
Brownlee, Marina S., Kevin Brownlee and Stephen G. Nichols, eds. The New Medievalism. Baltimore: Johns Hopkins UP, 1991.
___. "Hermeneutics of Reading in the *Corbacho*" in Medieval Texts and the Contemporary Reader. Laurie A. Finke and Martin B. Sichtman, eds. Ithaca: Cornell U P, 1987. 216-233.
Bryant, Donald C., ed. Papers in Rhetoric and Poetic. Iowa City: U of Iowa P, 1965.
Burke, Kenneth. A Grammar of Motives. Berkeley: U of California P, 1945.
Burke, Peter. "Oblique Approaches to the History of Popular Culture," in Approaches to Popular Culture, C.W.E. Bigsby, ed. Bowling Green, 1977. 69-106.
Burns, Robert I. Emperor of Culture: Alfonso X the Learned of Castile and His Thirteenth-Century Renaissance. Philadelphia: U of Pennsylvania P, 1990.
Cameron, Averil. Christianity and the Rhetoric of Empire: The Development of Christian Discourse. Berkeley: U of California P, 1991.
Caplan, Harry. Of Eloquence. Ithaca: Cornell U P, 1970.
Carruthers, Mary. The Book of Memory. Cambridge: Cambridge U P, 1990.
Castro, Américo. The Structure of Spanish History. Edmund L. King, trans. Princeton: Princeton U P, 1954.
Cicero. On Oratory and Orators. J.S. Watson, trans. Carbondale: Southern Illinois UP, 1970.
___. Rhetorica Ad Herennium. Harry Caplan, trans. Cambridge: Harvard UP, 1977.
Coleman, Janet. English Literature in History 1350-1400, Medieval Readers and Writers. London: Hutchinson, 1981.
Curtius, Ernst Robert. Essays on European Literature. Princeton: Princeton U P, 1973.
___. European Literature and the Latin Middle Ages. Willard R. Trask, trans. Princeton: Princeton U P: 1953.

Dagenais, John D. The Ethics of Reading in Manuscript Culture: Glossing the *Libro de Buen Amor*. Princeton: Princeton U P, 1994.
Dahlberg, Charles. The Literature of Unlikeness. Hanover: U P of New England, 1988.
Deyermond, A. D. Edad Media. Barcelona: Editorial Crítica, 1980.
___. A Literary History of Spain: The Middle Ages. London: Ernest Benn Limited, 1971.
Duby, Georges, ed. History of Private Life: Revelations of the Medieval World. Cambridge: The Belknap Press, 1988.
Dundes, Alan. Interpreting Folklore. Bloomington: Indiana U P, 1980.
___. Analytic Essays in Folklore. The Hague: Mouton Publishers, 1975.
___. Essays in Folkloristics. Meerut, India: Folklore Institute, 1978.
Eco, Umberto. Art and Beauty in the Middle Ages. New Haven: Yale U P, 1986.
Faulhaber, Charles. Latin Rhetorical Theory in Thirteenth and Fourteenth Century Castile. Berkley: U of California P, 1972.
Fischer, David Hackett. Historians' Fallacies: Toward a Logic of Historical Thought. New York: Harper and Row, 1970.
Foucault, Michel. The Order of Things. Pantheon Books: New York, 1973.
___. Power/Knowledge. New York: Pantheon Books, 1980.
___. "What is an Author?" in Richter, David H., ed. The Critical Tradition Classic Texts and Contemporary Trends, New York: St. Martin's Press, 1989.
___. "Afterward." in Dreyfus, Hubert L. and Paul Rabinow. Michel Foucault: Beyond Structuralism and Hermeneutics. Chicago: U of Chicago P, 1982.
Frantzen, Allen J., ed. Speaking Two Languages: Traditional Disciplines and Contemporary Theory in Medieval Studies. Albany: State U of New York P, 1991.
Frye, Northrup. Anatomy of Criticism. Princeton: Princeton U P, 1990.
___. Myth and Metaphor: Selected Essays 1974-1988. Robert D. Denham, ed. Charlottesville: U P of Virginia, 1990.
Gellrich, Jesse M. The Idea of the Book in the Middle Ages. Ithaca: Cornell U P, 1985.
Giles of Rome. On Ecclesiastical Power. R.W. Dyson, ed. Suffolk: The Boydell Press, 1986.
Gilson, Etienne. The Spirit of Mediæval Philosophy. New York: Charles Scribner's Sons, 1940.
Gimeno Casalduero, Joaquín. La Creación Literaria de la Edad Media y del Renacimiento: Su forma y su significado. Madrid: Ediciones José Porrúa Turanzas, 1977.
___. Estructura y diseño en la Literatura Castellana Medieval. Madrid: Ediciones José Porrúa Turanzas, 1975.
Goffman, Erving. Frame Analysis: An Essay on the Organization of Experience. New York: Harper and Row, 1974.

Hampton, Timothy. Writing from History: The Rhetoric of Exemplarity in Renaissance Literature. Ithaca: Cornell U P, 1990.

Hardison, O.B. Jr., Alex Preminger, Kevin Kerrane, and Leon Golden, eds. Medieval Literary Criticism Translations and Interpretations. New York: Frederick Ungar Publishing Co., 1974.

Henninger, Mark G. SJ. Relations: Medieval Theories 1250-1325. Clarendon Press: Oxford, 1989.

Horace. Horace on the Art of Poetry. Edward Henry Blakeney, Ed. London: Scholartis Press, 1928.

Huizinga, Johan. The Waning of the Middle Ages. Garden City, NY: Doubleday Anchor Books, 1954.

___. Men and Ideas: History, the Middle Ages, the Renaissance. Princeton: Princeton U P, 1959.

John of Salisbury. Policraticus: of the Frivolities of Courtiers and the Footprints of Philosophers. Cary J. Nederman, ed., and trans. Cambridge: Cambridge UP, 1990.

___. The Metalogicon of John of Salisbury: A Twelfth-Century Defense of the Verbal and Logical Arts of the Trivium. Daniel D. McGarry, trans. Berkeley: U of California P, 1962.

Johannesen, Richard L., Rennard Strickland, and Ralph T. Eubanks, eds. Language is Sermonic: Richard M. Weaver on the Nature of Rhetoric. Baton Rouge: Louisiana State U P, 1970.

Kantoriwicz, E. H. The King's Two Bodies: A Study in Medieval Political Theology. Princeton: Princeton U P, 1957.

Kedar, Leah, ed. Power Through Discourse. Norwood, New Jersey: Abelex, 1987.

Keller, John E. "The *libro de los exenplos por a.b.c.*" in Collectanea Hispánica: Folklore and Brief Narrative Studies. Dennis P. Seniff, ed. Newark, Delaware: Juan de la Cuesta, 1987. 49-60.

and Richard P. Kinkade. Iconography in Medieval Spanish Literature. Lexington: U P of Kentucky, 1984.

Kelly, Douglas. The Arts of Poetry and Prose. Typologie des Sources du Moyen Age Occidental (Fascicule 59). Brepols Belgium: Institut D'Etudes Medievales, 1991.

Latini, Brunetto. Libro del tesoro. Spurgeon Baldwin, ed. Madison: Hispanic Seminary of Medieval Studies, 1989.

Lausberg, Heinrich. Manual de retórica literaria. Madrid: Editorial Gredos, 1966.

Le Goff, Jacques. The Medieval Imagination. Chicago: U of Chicago P, 1988.

Lida de Malkiel, María Rosa. El cuento popular y otros ensayos. Buenos Aires: Editorial Losada, 1976.

___. La Idea de la Fama en la Edad Media Castellana. México: Fondo de Cultura Económica, 1952.

Linehan, Peter. The Spanish Church and the Papacy in the Thirteenth Century. Cambridge: Cambridge UP, 1971.
Lucretius. The Way Things Are: The *De Rerum Natura* of Titus Lucretius Carus. Rolfe Humphries, trans. Bloomington: Indiana UP, 1968.
Lüthi, Max. The Fairytale as Art Form and Portrait of Man. Bloomington: Indiana U P, 1984.
___. Once Upon a Time (On the Nature of Fairytales). New York: Frederick Ungar Publishing Company, 1970.
Madden, Marie R. Political Theory and Law in Medieval Spain. New York: Fordham UP, 1930.
Manrique, Gómez. Regimento de Príncipes. Madrid: El Crotalón, 1984.
Maravall, José Antonio. El concepto de España en la edad media. Madrid: Instituto de estudios políticos, 1954.
___. Estudios de historia del pensamiento español. Madrid: Ediciones cultura hispánica, 1967.
Martín, José Luis. La Península en la Edad Media. Barcelona: Editorial Teide, 1988.
Maurer, Armand A. Medieval Philosophy. Toronto: Pontifical Institute of Mediaeval Studies, 1982.
Minnis, A.J. and A.B. Scott, eds. Medieval Literary Theory and Criticism c.1100-1375. the Commentary Tradition. Oxford: Clarendon Press, 1988.
___. "'Moral Gower' and Medieval Literary Theory" in Gower's *Confessio amantis*. A.J. Minnis, ed. Suffolk: D.S. Brewer, 1983. 50-78.
Morse, Charlotte Cook, Penelope Reed Doob, and Marjorie Curry Woods, eds. Uses of Manuscripts in Literary Studies: Essays in Memory of Judson Boyce Allen. Kalamazoo: Medieval Institute Publications, 1992.
Murphy, James J. Medieval Rhetoric: A Select Bibliography. Toronto: U of Toronto P, 1989.
___. Medieval Eloquence. Berkeley: U of California P, 1978.
___. Rhetoric in the Middle Ages. Berkeley: U of California P, 1974.
___. Medieval Rhetorical Arts, The. Berkeley: U of California P, 1971.
Nepaulsingh, Colbert I. Towards a History of Literary Composition in Medieval Spain. Toronto: U of Toronto P, 1986.
Nilsen, Thomas R., ed. Essays of Rhetorical Criticism. New York: Random House, 1968.
Norrick, Neal R. How Proverbs Mean. New York: Mouton Publishers, 1985.
O'Kane, Eleanor S. Refranes y frases proverbiales españolas de la edad media. Madrid: S. Aguirre Torre, 1959.
Olson, Glending. Literature as Recreation in the Later Middle Ages. Ithaca: Cornell U P, 1982.
Oring, Elliott, ed. Folk Groups and Folklore Genres: A Reader. Logan, Utah: Utah State U P, 1989.
Porqueras Mayo, A. El prólogo como género literario: su estudio en el siglo de oro español. Madrid: Consejo Superior de Investigaciones Científicas, 1957.

Post, Chandler Rathfon. Mediaeval Spanish Allegory. Cambridge: Harvard U P, 1915.
Propp, Vladimir. Theory and History of Folklore. Anatoly Liberman, ed. Minneapolis: U of Minnesota P, 1984.
Renoir, Alain. "Oral-Formulaic Rhetoric: An Approach to Image and Message in Medieval Poetry" in Medieval Texts and Contemporary Readers. Laurie A. Finke and Martin B. Shichtman, eds. Ithaca: Cornell University Press, 1987. 234-254.
Riffaterre, Michael. "The Mind's Eye: Memory and Textuality" in The New Medievalism. Marina S. Brownlee, Kevin Brownlee and Stephen G. Nichols, eds. Baltimore: Johns Hopkins UP, 1991. 29-45.
Robertson, D. W., Jr. Essays in Medieval Culture. Princeton: Princeton U P, 1980.
Rouse, Richard A. and Mary Rouse. Preachers, Florilegia and Sermons: Studies on the Manipulus florum of Thomas of Ireland. Toronto: Pontifical Institute of Medieval Studies, 1979.
Rovira, Luis Iscla. Spanish Proverbs: A Survey of Spanish Culture and Civilization. Lanham: U P of America, 1984.
Runacres, Charles. "Art and Ethics in the 'Exempla' of 'Confessio amantis'" in Gower's *Confessio amantis*. A.J. Minnis, ed. Suffolk: D.S. Brewer, 1983. 106-134.
Said, Edward W. "Foucault and the Imagination of Power." pp. 149-155 in Hoy, David Couzens, ed. Foucault: A Critical Reader. Oxford: Blackwell, 1986.
Scanlon, Larry. Narrative, Authority, and Power. Cambridge: Cambridge U P, 1994.
Schenck, Mary Jane Stearns. The Fabliaux: Tales of Wit and Deception. Philadelphia: John Benjamin Publishing Company, 1987.
Sem Tob. Proverbios Morales. Sanford Shepard, ed. Madrid: clásicos castalia, 1985.
Stahl, Sandra Dolby. Literary Fokloristics and the Personal Narrative. Indiana University Press: Bloomington, 1989.
Sweeny, James Ross and Stanley Chodorow, eds. Popes, Teachers, and Canon Law in the Middle Ages. Ithaca: Cornell U P, 1989.
Szittya, Penn R. The Antifraternal Tradition in Medieval Literature. Princeton: Princeton UP, 1986.
Thompson, Stith. The Folktale. Berkeley: U of California P, 1977.
Tolan, John. Petrus Alfonsi and His Medieval Readers. Gainesville: UP of Florida, 1993.
Travis, Peter W. "Affective Criticism, the Pilgrimage of Reading, and Medieval English Literature" in Medieval Texts and Contemporary Readers. Laurie A. Finke and Martin B. Shichtman, eds. Ithaca: Cornell U P, 1987. 210-215.
Ullman, B.L. Classical Authors in Mediaeval Florilegia. Reprinted from Classical Philology, 23 (1928).

Ullmann, Walter. Principles of Government and Politics in the Middle Ages. New York: Barnes and Noble Books, 1961.

Vaquero, Mercedes. Tradiciones Orales en la Historiografía de Fines de la Edad Media. Madison: Seminary of Hispanic Medieval Studies, 1990.

Vendôme, Matthew of. The Art of Versification. Aubrey E. Galyon, ed. Ames: Iowa State UP, 1980.

Vinsauf, Geoffrey of. Poetria Nova. Margaret F. Nims, trans. Toronto: Pontifical Institute of Mediaeval Studies, 1967.

Von Moos, Peter. "The use of exempla in the *Policraticus* of John of Salisbury" in The World of John of Salisbury, Michael Wilks, ed. Oxford: Basil Blackwell, 1984. 207-261.

Wagner, David L., ed. Seven Liberal Arts in the Middle Ages, The. Bloomington: Indiana U P, 1983.

Walsh, John K., ed. El libro de los doze sabios o tractado de la nobleza y lealtad. Madrid: Anejos del boletín de la real academia española, 1975.

Wasserman, Julian N. and Lois Roney, eds. Sign, Sentence, Discourse: Language in Medieval Thought and Literature. Syracuse: Syracuse U P, 1989.

Wilks, Michael, ed. World of John of Salisbury, The. Oxford: Basil Blackwell, 1984.

Yates, Frances A. The Art of Memory. Chicago: U of Chicago P, 1966.

Zahareas, Anthony N. The Art of Juan Ruiz. Madrid: Estudios de Literatura Española, 1965.

# Index

*accessus* 63
*adelantado (mayor)* 24, 43, 64
allegoresis 18
Alfonso X 18-20, 39, 43, 51-52
Alfonso XI 21, 24, 43, 51, 57 n8, 101 n35
*Alphabetum Narrationum* 24
*apostrophe* 149
Aquinas 7, 70, 179 n2
*argumentatio* 48
Aristotle 59 n21, 67-68, 99 n19, n23, n24, 157 n5, 163, 179 n4, 180 n8, Aristóteles 104, *Ethics* 59 n21, 67-68, 99 n19, 179 n4, *Eticas* 41-42, 114
Arnulf of Orleans 5
*assertor* 44
*assimilantur* 164, 166
*assimilatio* 164-166
*auctores* 29, 47, 59 n20, 66, 140, 157 n5, 183, 187
*auctoritas* 14, 43, 44, 66, 69, 146, 187
Augustine 7, 165-166, Agostin 81
Averroes 163-166
baptism 168-170
*Barlaam y Josafat* 25
*bienandanza* 60 n29, 81, 83, 85, 130 n4
*Bocados de oro* 25, 141, 181
body politic 19, 21, 22, 109
Boethius 31, 34
Brunetto Latini 7, 47-48, 62-63, 100 n27, 130 n4, *Libro del tesoro* 47, 59 n26, 62-63
*Caballero Zifar* 181, 188

*Calila e Dimna* 25, 181, 188
*causae* 62-63, 188, material 66-67, formal 69-70, efficient 63-65, 188, final 67-69, duplex 64, 68
charity 165-166, 170
*cobdiçia* 37, 108, 130 n3
*collectio* 70
comparison 47, 96, 163-164, 166, 175-176
compiler 44, 66
*componer* 66
*conocerse* (self-knowledge) 92, 98-99 n17, 101 n31, 116, 121, 123-129
Conrad of Hirsau 61
*consejar* 82-90, 99 n19, 142, 153
consonance 134
*contentio* 148
contraries, the function of 162-166,
*cortes* 23
counselors 99 n24, 116-121, 130 n1
*Crónica abreuiada* 4, 133
deception 106-112
*defensores* 6, 22
*definitio* 70
*Dialogus Creaturarum* 24
*Disciplina clericalis* 25, 140-141, 181, 188
Dominicans 24, 72, 101-102 n35, 108-110, 112, 123
Don Iohan 14, 44, 54, 75-77, 78-79, 94-96, 121, 142-146, 161
Don Jayme de Xérica 64-65, 85, 136-137, 146, 157 n3
*ejemplares* 188
*El libro de los buenos proverbios* 25
*enxiemplos* 3, 14, 48

*envidia* 108, 130 n3, envy 108
*epithet* 149
ethics 5, 40, 71, 98 n10, 162-163, 179 n4
estate 2, 23, 31, 33, 36-37, 43, 45, 50, 54, 84, 91, 93-96, 101-102 n35, 106, 113,115,122-124,131 n15, 133,137, 155, 162, 174, 176, 177, 183-184, 190 *estado* 35, 36-37, 41, 45, 58 n19, 71, 91, 94, 97 n1, 98 n11, 101 n33
*exclamatio* 148
exempla 5,10,13,16 n1, 24, 46-49, 52-55, 57 n1, 59 n22, 69, 73-75, 77-78, 98 n13,100 n26,101-102 n35, 102 n36, 140-141, 158 n12
*Exempla Communia* 24
*Exempla Deodati* 24
exemplarity 3, 6, 9, 13, 15, 25-26, 28, 55, 195
*Exemplos muy notables* 25
exemplum 21, 41, 74, 79, 95, 98 n14, 101-102 n35, 106, sermon 24, 39, 80, public 39
*favorito* 106-111
*fechos* 41, 68-69, 82-83, 85, 87, 90-92, 95, 99-100 n24, 105, 179 n3, n6, *fazer* 33-34, 36-37, 45, 51, 53-54, 59 n26, 62, 73-75, 82, 90-92,110,127, 131 n13, 134, 137, 144-145, 147 n4, 170, 177, 179 n3
*florilegia* 74, 79
*forma tractandi* 69
*forma tractatus* 69
frame 8, 15, 45, 48-50, 55, 66, 69, 74-77, 83-84, 104-106, 107-108, 114-116,127,141-143, 145, 154, 172 181
Franciscans 24, 109, 111, 123
*franqueza* 19, 170

Fray Juan García de Castrojeriz 22, 40-41, 99 n22, 99-100 n24, 104, 105, 130 n5, 179 n7
friendship 106, 113-114, 116-117, 120-121,
Geoffrey of Vinsauf 7
*Gesta Romanorum* 24
Giles of Rome 14, 22, 28, 40-41, 80-81, 82 Aegidius Romanus 29
good works 2, 6, 27, 33-34, 42, 50, 79, 81, 84-85, 91, 92-94, 121, 124-127, 131 n13, 172, 176, versus bad works 161-166, 167-174, 176-178
*hermandades* 23
*hidalgos* 19, *fijos de algo* 19
*hombres ricos* 46, *homes ricos* 115, 123
*homoeoteleuton* 148
Hugh of St. Victor 7, 32
honor 2, 10, 30, 33, 36, 45, 50, 52, 54, 91-92, 95, 105-106, 108, 113, 115, 120, 123, 127, 130 n4, 131-132 n15, 133, 138, 154-155, 162,169, 173-174, 176-177, 178, *onra* 35-36, 41, 45, 91, 100 n30, 101 n32, 159-160, 169
Horace 67, (*Ars poetica*)
*hyperbaton* 151
intention 31, 53, 63, 73, 89, 97 n7, 98 n14, 136, 161-162, 173-174, literary 63 bad intention 173-174
*labradores* 6, 21-22
*Lego* 36, 38
*Liber Exemplorum Ad Usum Praedicantium* 24
*libro* (concept of) 8-11, 27-28, 33, 64-65, 68-69, 71, 98 n11,134, 137, 144
*Libro de buen amor* 181, 188
*Libro de las armas* 21, 51

*Libro del caballero et del escudero* 39, 91-92, 95, 170
*Libro de los doze sabios* 99 n24, 101 n33, 131 n13, 158 n11, 179 n3, n6, 187-188
*Libro de los engaños* 25
*Libro de los estados* 36, 44, 51, 57 n8, 71, 98 n11,135,160-161,178
*Libro de los exenplos por A.B.C.* 25
*Libro Enfenido* 29, 33, 71, 73, 80-81
*Libro de los gatos* 25, 181
Lobera 21
Lucretius 34
ludic 33
magnanimity 170-172
Matthew of Vendôme 7, 147
*membrum orationis* 148
memory 16 n1, 29, 61-62, 71-80, 97 n4, 98 n9, 142, 182, & reading 76, architectural mnemonic 72, hermeneutic dialogue 73-74, *memoria ad res* 76-77, 142, & illumination 77-78, & *brevitas* 78-79, 150 & moral virtues 80, 98 n10, *Divisio* 70-72
Prognostication 86-87 Foresight 86-87, 95
*Metalogicon* 74
*modus parabolicus* 69
morality 5, 13, 50, 103
*mundo*, 39, 82, 99 n18, 100 n30, 109, 123, 131 n12, 131-132 n15, 169, etimology of 176
nakedness 114-116
nobility, the sacramental nature of 167-178, 182, 187
*obrar* 80, 82-83, 85, 99 n19, 153-154
*oradores* 6, 21-22
*ordinatio* 25
*paronomasia* 148

*paranomeon* 148
poetics 5, 58 n14
*polysyndeton* 148
*poridat* 99 n24, 130 n1
*Poridat de las poridades* 98 n11, 99 n18, n23, n24, 100 n28
power, 1-11, 13, 15-20,23-24, 30-31, 36, 38, 42-44, 46, 48-52, 56, 61-64, 66, 69, 81-83, 93, 98 n14, 99 n17, 101 n35, 103, 105, 117-118, 120-122,125, 128-129, 130 n1, n4, 133, 147-148, 150, 154, 159, 161, 162, 168, 170-171, 174, 182, 185, pastoral & royal power 30, 58 n13
*poder* 39, 45, 57 n7, 81, 101 n33, 103,119, 147
praxis 71, 90
primogeniture 20, 56
privilege 2, 5, 20, 30, 147
Prologue (general to *CL*) 2, 6, 13-14, 28, 31-32, 53, 61, 63-70, 71-72, 83, 185 *Libro Enfenido* 71, 73 *Crónica abreviada* 133-134 *Razonamiento* 41, 64, 71, 85, 136-137, 153, 157 n3,161
proverbs 1-11, 13, 14, 16 n1, 27-28, 33, 48-49, 55, 69-70, 78-79, 85, 133, 138-140, 144-146, 157 n3, 158 n9, n12, 185 texture 147-151, 157 n7, text 151-152, 157 n7 context 152-156, 157 n7, *proverbios* 133, 138, 154
*Proverbios morales* 158 n14
Prudence 15, 29, 62, 71, 81-86, 90, 98 n16, 99 n19, n20, n22, 130-131 n6,153, 166, 174, 176, 182-183
Quintilian 140, 153, 157 n5
*Qur'an* 27, 58 n11
*Razonamiento* 71, 136-137, 161
Regiment of princes 14, 41, 181, 184

rhetoric: epideictic, 8, 10, 62,
  demonstrative 8, 10, ornamental
  42, persuasive 42 obscurity 133-
  136, 137-139, 174 rewards 11,
  161-162, 168, tropes 34, 53, 136-
  137, 148 figures 4, 22,147-148,
  *sententiae* 1, 3, 133-156 experience
  54, 86, 93, 139-140, 141-146,
  reception 53, 69, 143
*ricos homes* 115, 123
*romance* 134, *romançe* 38
salvation 2, 30, 33, 36-37, 50, 69, 84,
  93, 111, 121, 138, 159-161, *salvar
  las almas* 35-36, 161
Sancho IV 20, 43, 51-52, 57 n5, n7,
  59 n27, 60 n29, 63, 88, 97 n1, 98-
  99 n17, 99 n19, 100 n28, n30, 101
  n31, 101 n32, 115, 159-160
Scholasticism 25
script 2, 52-55
secret 58 n13, 105, 113-114, 116
  130 n1, 136, 144
*seglar* 38, (secular, secular
  authority)
semiotics 55
Sem Tob 158 n14
*Sendebar* 25
*señoríos* 20
*seso* 78, 85, 91-92, 99 n18, 99-100
  n24, 101 n34, 124, 131 n12, 147,
  149,151, 157 n8,170
shame 88, 91-93, 95, 101 n33, n34,
  121, 126-129, 131 n15, *vergüença*
  126-129
*sic et non* 149, 163
similitude 47, 69, 81, 91, 134, 164
social advancement 108-109
subtlety 32,134-135,137, *sotil* 32,
  41, 64, 101 n32,134-135
transubstantiation 167-170
*tristeza* 108

tyrant 80-81, 93, 115-116, 130 n5,
  152, 160, 172, 190, tyranny 117,
  130-131 n6
understanding 25, 32, 35, 37, 40, 53,
  58 n15, 65, 71-73, 75, 81-84 131
  n12,134-138, 142, 145, 175, 178,
  *entendimiento* 35, 41, 65, 78, 97
  n3, 98-99 n17, 99-100 n24, 101
  n31, n32, 123-124, 130 n3, 134-
  135, 137-138
*vademecum* 43
wealth 2, 19-21, 23, 30, 45,100 n27,
  113,115,124,127-128,130 n6,148,
  160,171,173-175, *fazienda* 35-36,
  122,124-125, 154
zeugma 147